PROSPERITY FOR ALL?

PROSPERITY FOR ALL?

The Economic Boom and African Americans

Robert Cherry and William M. Rodgers III
Editors

RUSSELL SAGE FOUNDATION / NEW YORK

The Russell Sage Foundation

The Russell Sage Foundation, one of the oldest of America's general purpose foundations, was established in 1907 by Mrs. Margaret Olivia Sage for "the improvement of social and living conditions in the United States." The Foundation seeks to fulfill this mandate by fostering the development and dissemination of knowledge about the country's political, social, and economic problems. While the Foundation endeavors to assure the accuracy and objectivity of each book it publishes, the conclusions and interpretations in Russell Sage Foundation publications are those of the authors and not of the Foundation, its Trustees, or its staff. Publication by Russell Sage, therefore, does not imply Foundation endorsement.

Library of Congress Cataloging-in-Publication Data

Prosperity for all? : the economic boom and African Americans / Robert Cherry and William M. Rodgers III, editors.
    p. cm.
    Includes bibliographical references and index.
    ISBN 0-87154-197-1
    1. Afro-Americans—Economic conditions—Congresses. 2. United States—Economic conditions—1981—Congresses. 3. Afro-Americans—Employment—Congresses. I. Cherry, Robert D., 1944- II. Rodgers, William M. III. Russell Sage Foundation.

E185.8.P68 2000
331.6'396073—dc21
          00-027656

RUSSELL SAGE FOUNDATION
112 East 64th Street, New York, New York 10021
10 9 8 7 6 5 4 3 2 1

To our wives, Rochelle and Yana, and our children, Sara, Joshua, Eliana, William, and Charles

CONTENTS

CONTRIBUTORS

ROBERT CHERRY is professor of economics at Brooklyn College and the Graduate Center of the City University of New York.

WILLIAM M. RODGERS III is chief economist of the U.S. Department of Labor. He is on leave from the College of William and Mary where he is the Frances L. and Edwin L. Cummings Associate Professor of Economics.

HEATHER BOUSHEY is postdoctoral research fellow at the New York City Housing Authority.

CECILIA CONRAD is associate professor of economics at Pomona College.

MARY CORCORAN is professor of political science, public policy, and social work and director of the Women's Studies Program at the University of Michigan.

SANDRA DANZIGER is associate professor of social work and director of the Michigan Program on Poverty and Social Welfare Policy at the University of Michigan.

SHELDON DANZIGER is Henry J. Meyer Collegiate Professor of Social Work and Public Policy and director of the Center on Poverty, Risk and Mental Health at the University of Michigan.

WILLIAM DARITY JR. is Cary C. Boshamer Professor of Economics and Sociology at the University of North Carolina at Chapel Hill. He is also research professor of public policy, African American studies, and economics at Duke University.

GREGORY E. DEFREITAS is professor of economics at Hofstra University. He is also director of the Center for the Study of Labor and Democracy and the editor of *Regional Labor Review*.

RICHARD B. FREEMAN is Herbert Ascherman Professor of Economics at Harvard University. He is also director of labor studies at the National Bureau of Economic Research and codirector of the Centre for Economic Performance at the London School of Economics.

COLLEEN HEFLIN is senior research associate at the School of Social Work, Poverty Research and Training Center at the University of Michigan.

JOYCE P. JACOBSEN is professor of economics at Wesleyan University.

CHINHUI JUHN is professor of economics at the University of Houston and faculty research fellow at the National Bureau of Economic Research.

ARIEL KALIL is assistant professor at the Harris Graduate School of Public Policy at the University of Chicago.

SANDERS KORENMAN is professor at the School of Public Affairs, Baruch College, City University of New York, and research associate at the National Bureau of Economic Research.

LAURENCE M. LEVIN is a senior statistician at Providian Financial Corporation.

JUDITH LEVINE is assistant professor at the School of Service Administration at the University of Chicago.

PHILIP MOSS is professor of regional economics and social development at the University of Massachusetts, Lowell.

SAMUEL L. MYERS JR. is Roy Wilkins Professor of Social Justice at the Hubert H. Humphrey Institute of Public Affairs at the University of Minnesota.

CORDELIA W. REIMERS is professor of economics at Hunter College and the Graduate School of the City University of New York.

DANIEL ROSEN is postdoctoral research fellow at the School of Social Work at the University of Michigan.

KRISTIN SEEFELDT is senior research associate at the School of Social Work, Poverty Research and Training Center at the University of Michigan.

KRISTINE SIEFERT is professor at the School of Social Work and associate director of the center on Poverty, Risk and Mental Health at the University of Michigan.

WILLIAM E. SPRIGGS is director of research and public policy for the National Urban League.

CHRIS TILLY is professor of regional economics and social development at the University of Massachusetts, Lowell.

RICHARD TOLMAN is associate professor at the School of Social Work at the University of Michigan.

RHONDA M. WILLIAMS is acting director of the Afro-American Studies Program at the University of Maryland, College Park.

ACKNOWLEDGMENTS

The chapters in this volume are based on a conference held at the Russell Sage Foundation in 1998. We are grateful to Eric Wanner and the Russell Sage Foundation for funding this conference. We are also indebted to Cheryl Seleski for her extremely able work in organizing the conference. Finally, we owe an extreme debt of gratitude to Suzanne Nichols for her editorial assistance in the preparation of this volume.

ROBERT CHERRY
WILLIAM M. RODGERS III

INTRODUCTION

Robert Cherry and William M. Rodgers III

Between 1982 and 1989, the United States unemployment rate fell from 10.8 percent to 5.5 percent, with over 21 million new jobs created. Despite structural changes—the shift away from government and manufacturing employment, for example—major metropolitan areas, disproportionately home to African Americans, fared reasonably well. Unemployment rates in large cities fell just as much as they did in smaller cities and nonurban areas.

There were, however, limitations to the 1980s expansion. Official unemployment rates for men aged twenty to sixty-four years old did not, for instance, reach the low levels that they had at the previous business cycle's peak in 1979. Moreover, the African American unemployment rate remained more than double the white rate. By contrast, however, unemployment rates for both white and African American women in this same age group declined to a level lower than that of 1979. For African American women, the decline was from 10.8 percent to 9.8 percent, while for white women the drop was from 5.0 percent to 4.0 percent (Browne 1999).

Although African American employment rates improved over the 1980s business cycle, the ratio of black-to-white female earnings among full-time year-round workers fell from 0.98 to 0.91. This deterioration remains after adjusting for potential experience and education (Bound and Dresser 1999). African American female earnings did increase, however, with respect to those of both African American and white men. Movement in the wages of African American and white men over the business cycle was more complicated. Among full-time year-round workers, the unadjusted racial annual-earnings ratio improved, but the black-to-white hourly-earnings ratio for all male workers with positive income declined. This suggests that among African American men, earnings and employment varied depending upon strength of attachment to the labor market. Moreover, a number of studies including William M. Rodgers III (1997) and John Bound and Richard B. Freeman (1992), found that after controlling for levels of education, the unexplained racial earnings gap among men increased substantially during the 1980s in the Midwest and among workers with college degrees.

The economic expansion of the 1990s provides analysts and policy makers with another opportunity to assess the ability of economic booms to solve a variety of social concerns. The current economic expansion, which began in March 1991, is the longest peacetime economic boom on record. By many measures, the current boom might even be more beneficial than the 1980s boom, for unlike in the 1980s expansion, African American–male unemployment rates have in this cycle declined to levels substantially below where they were in the previous economic expansion—from 10.3 percent in 1988 to 8.5 percent by 1997. This current expansion's lower unemployment rates and extremely long period of continuously low unemployment rates distinguishes it from the 1980s boom.

Understanding the impact of tight labor markets on the economic and social experiences of African Americans is particularly important today. Given the movement away from targeted programs to aid low-wage workers, the weakening of affirmative action to aid minorities and women during the 1980s, and a toughening of sanctions for participation in criminal activity, it is of paramount importance to know how much the boom of the 1990s has benefited African Americans. Has the prosperity disproportionately benefited the most vulnerable Americans, benefited all Americans equally, or left some groups behind? To answer these questions, a conference was held at the Russell Sage Foundation in October 1998, just over ninety months into the boom. *Prosperity for All?* contains revised versions of the papers presented at that conference.

Contributors to this volume note that assessments of the 1990s boom's effect on minorities depend much upon the measures used and the time frame observed. While overall unemployment rates declined substantially, labor-force participation rates for twenty- to sixty-four-year-old African American men declined from 82.7 percent to 79.4 percent between 1988 and 1997. This reinforced a growing concern that there exists a significant share of African American men who have decreasing attachment to the labor market. To address this issue, Chinhui Juhn analyzed the nonemployment rate of young men.

Another concern is the degree to which African American workers face employment problems as a result of employers favoring newer groups of disadvantaged workers, such as immigrants from Asia or Latin America. In a widely quoted 1991 paper, Joleen Kirschenman and Kathryn Neckerman found that employers favor

Hispanic over African American workers in the low-wage-labor sector, which further suggests that young black men with low educational attainment might have employment difficulties relative to similarly educated Hispanic workers. Cordelia W. Reimers explores this issue. In addition, Richard B. Freeman and William M. Rodgers III focus on young, noncollege-educated African American men, the group most likely to be detached from the labor market.

The Freeman and Rodgers paper is also valuable because in it the authors extend their analysis through the first half of 1999, enabling them to judge the particular importance of very tight labor markets, or those in which the national unemployment rate remained below 5 percent. From 1992 to 1996, real hourly wages remained constant, but in the tight market of 1999, they had increased by 4 percent. Freeman and Rodgers assess the extent to which young, noncollege-educated black men benefited during each of these subperiods of the expansion.

At the beginning of this decade, employment audit studies, together with some of the other evidence discussed in the preceding paragraphs, led many policy analysts to fear that discriminatory labor-market practices, including exclusion from high occupations as well as other forms of racial queuing, were ineradicably rooted in American business. With this in mind, William Spriggs and Rhonda Williams explore the inability of the current expansion to reduce the black-to-white unemployment-rate ratio. Philip Moss and Chris Tilly, meanwhile, assess to what degree the tightening of labor markets weakens the racial profiling that so adversely affects the employment possibilities of African American job applicants.

Earnings data from the current expansion seem to support those who believe that significant discriminatory labor-market practices remain. Between 1991 and 1998, for instance, there was only a slight decrease in the racial earnings gap among full-time year-round workers. Through 1996, however, there is some evidence that the earnings of African American workers fell behind those of white workers, which suggests that only when labor markets are extremely tight and remain so for an extended period of time is it possible to substantially undermine the aversion of employers to hire African Americans.

A further concern has been the declining economic base of many Midwestern urban areas and expanding economic base of many Southern urban areas. Both continue to be populated by disproportionately large numbers of African Americans. Heather Boushey and Robert Cherry assess the expansion's effect the Midwest and South Atlantic regions, focusing on how occupational changes have influenced regional racial earnings ratios. Boushey and Cherry also evaluate the expansion's impact on occupational barriers and the glass-ceiling effect. Under certain conditions, economic expansions make it costlier for employers to discriminate, resulting in the opening of occupations and providing opportunities for promotion that had previously not been available to minorities and women. In another paper, Joyce Jacobsen and Laurence Levin detail the glass-ceiling effect as experienced by black, Hispanic, and white women through the early 1990s.

At the same time that the Midwestern and Southern urban economic bases have been shifting, the current economic expansion has also come at a time of dramatic change in national welfare policies. During the 1980s expansion, welfare caseloads did not fall, but starting in 1994, the number of caseloads fell from over 5 million to below 4 million by the middle of 1997. Sandra Danziger and her colleagues at the University of Michigan assess the factors that help predict the employability of former welfare recipients during this period of economic expansion.

In addition to changing workforce dynamics, welfare reform may also have had a systematic impact on racial earnings ratios. The Personal Responsibility and Work Opportunity Reconciliation Act (PRWORA) of 1996 led to the mandatory participation of welfare recipients in the labor market. Because former welfare recipients often serve as substitutes for noncollege-educated and low-skilled men, their increased numbers in the workforce put downward pressure on wages and employment. As a result, wages and employment levels during the current boom may actually be lower than they would have been in the absence of the PRWORA. The fact that PRWORA disproportionately affected African American welfare recipients might explain why racial earnings ratios did not rise substantially throughout the expansion. Boushey and Cherry explore this possibility.

Yet another factor related to employment levels and the economy is crime. The current expansion spanning 1992 to 1997 has seen a dramatic 13.9 percent drop in crime rates, whereas from 1983 to 1989 crime rates increased by 11.2 percent. Over both periods, incarceration rates increased, with a marked acceleration during the 1990s. Blacks of both sexes are about twice as likely as Hispanics and nearly eight times more likely than whites to be in state or federal prison. At the end of 1996, there were 1,571 African Americans serving time per 100,000 African Americans in the general population, compared with 688 Hispanic inmates per 100,000 Hispanics and 193 white inmates per 100,000 whites. Young African American men have the highest rates of incarceration of any American demographic group. Changes in federal, state, and local policies toward criminal activity contribute to the pattern of change. William Darity Jr. and Samuel L. Myers Jr. look more closely at the linkages among unemployment rates, crime rates, and incarceration rates.

OVERVIEW OF THE VOLUME

The papers in this volume are organized around four broad topics. The first describes the boom's impact on employment, unemployment, and wages, using the beginning of the boom as the point of reference. The second places the boom into an historical context by comparing it to earlier expansions, and the third offers explanations of why race continues to play a major role even in today's tight labor market. The fourth uses the 1990s expansion as a laboratory to examine the effects of recent changes in U.S. social policy, the success of which depends heavily on the availability of jobs. Collectively, these studies provide a comprehensive description and analysis of the economic and social benefits of the 1990s boom for African Americans.

The chapters in part I by Richard B. Freeman and William M. Rodgers III, Cordelia W. Reimers, and Chinhui Juhn set the stage for the others by using the March Annual Demographic and Outgoing Rotation Groups of the Current Population Survey to measure the boom's impact on the employment, unemployment, and earnings of African Americans. Freeman and Rodgers and Reimers present relatively optimistic assessments. Freeman and Rodgers find that as a response to the boom, the employment of young men experienced a larger boost than the employment of older men. Within the young-male labor market, blacks' gains exceeded the gains of young whites. Meanwhile, the boom increased the hourly wages of young men but not the hourly wages of older men. From 1991 to 1996, the hourly-wage increase was substantially greater for young white men than it was for young black men, but since 1996, the reverse is true.

Freeman and Rodgers's findings reflect the fact that young African American men are disproportionately located in higher unemployment areas. In these areas, wage gains came only after 1996 when the boom finally lowered unemployment rates sufficiently for wage pressures to materialize. Since the wages of older men appear to be much less sensitive to economic conditions unique to the 1990s boom, very tight labor markets might improve the earnings of young noncollege-educated workers without creating overall wage inflation. Finally, young African American men living in areas that did not have a deep 1990 to 1991 recession experienced stronger employment gains.

Cordelia W. Reimers describes the boom's impact on an individual's probability of unemployment. Reimers shows that African Americans have benefited disproportionately from the expansion, even within industry, occupation, education, and age-level cohorts. During the boom, black unemployment rates fell more than those of any other group, while Hispanic men and women also experienced greater benefits than whites. Hispanic unemployment rates fell, but the drop was not as large as the decline for African American workers. This should not be surprising, as at the beginning of the boom Hispanic unemployment rates stood at lower levels than the rates of African Americans.

Reimers then assesses whether racial differences in local labor-market unemployment rates can explain the overall black-white unemployment gap. She finds that the local labor markets in which African Americans and whites live have similar unemployment rates. Consequently, she reasons, almost none of the gap in individual unemployment rates can be explained by differences in labor-market tightness. However, just over one-third of the male Hispanic–white unemployment gap and one-fifth of the female gap are attributable to differences in the unemployment rates of areas where Hispanics and whites reside.

Chinhui Juhn's contribution to *Prosperity for All?* tells us that the work of analysts and policy-makers is not finished. Even though black employment and unemployment rates are at historically low levels, African American nonemployment rates (the percentage of the civilian population that is either out of the labor force or unemployed) and the duration of nonemployment are both at higher levels than during the peaks of earlier booms. This sobering finding suggests the continued existence and growth of a "core" group of African Americans who appear to be permanently unattached to the labor market. Juhn asks whether relative decline in attachment can be attributed to a larger erosion in the inflation-adjusted wages of African Americans, and she finds little support for this explanation.

A common theme running through the Freeman and Rodgers, Reimers, and Juhn papers states that dramatic gains have been achieved in African American employment. Yet even during the 1990s boom, race remains a key factor in determining labor-market outcomes. So, why does race and ethnicity continue to matter even in tight labor markets? Aren't competitive forces supposed to raise the costs of discrimination to employers, leading to its erosion? William E. Spriggs and Rhonda M. Williams, Joyce P. Jacobsen and

Laurence M. Levin, and Heather Boushey and Robert Cherry's papers offer answers to these questions in part II and part III of the volume. They argue that racial queuing, in the form of continued exclusion of blacks from higher-wage occupations and the glass-ceiling effect within occupations, explains the persistence of race as a key factor in labor-market dynamics.

In developing their argument, Spriggs and Williams shift the focus from the relationship between tight labor markets and the level of African American joblessness to why even in the presence of tight labor markets the ratio of black to white unemployment rates remains two to one. Historically, this ratio has not been sensitive to economic booms, and Spriggs and Williams show that the experience of the 1990s is no different. Yes, unemployment levels are lower, but the two-to-one ratio holds steady.

Spriggs and Williams suggest a dynamic model of racial queuing to explain the endurance of the two-to-one ratio. At all times, firms must weigh the benefits and costs of having a diverse workforce, keeping the morale of white workers high, and the efficiency losses from not hiring the "best-qualified" applicants. Spriggs and Williams contend that coming out of a recession and having many qualified white applicants, firms see little risk in showing preference to this group and anticipate substantial benefit by responding "positively" to the anxieties of their white workforce. This results in a more-rapid lowering of white unemployment rates than the African American unemployment rates, thereby explaining the rise in the observed black-white unemployment ratio over the economic expansion.

Two additional explanations for the continuance of discrimination as an important contributor to racial wage inequality during the current boom are exclusionary practices and the glass-ceiling effect. If the competitive forces of the tight labor market are not strong enough, exclusion from high-wage occupations and glass-ceiling effects within occupations could serve as potential sources of the drag on female and African American earnings. These barriers make it difficult for minorities to advance in their careers.

Using the Bureau of the Census's Surveys of Income and Program Participation, Joyce P. Jacobsen and Laurence M. Levin contrast the wage-tenure and wage-experience profiles of college-educated and noncollege-educated women and minorities to the same profiles of white men. The different profiles observed by race and gender are consistent with the existence of exclusionary practices and discrimination. Jacobsen and Levin observe that the relative wage disadvantages that minority college graduates experience can be attributed to lower economic returns to tenure and experience, and these disadvantages accumulate over time. For noncollege-educated minorities, the wage disadvantage starts earlier in their careers and is caused by a glass-ceiling effect.

Heather Boushey and Robert Cherry explore the extent to which the tight labor market of the 1990s eroded exclusionary and glass-ceiling practices. Motivated by the facts that the majority of African Americans live in the South Atlantic and Midwest regions of the United States and that both regions have tremendous historical importance for African Americans, Boushey and Cherry focus on these regions to measure the boom's ability to erode the disadvantages that exclusionary practices and the glass-ceiling effect create for African Americans. They find that racial earnings ratios for both men and women in each region were adversely affected by growing racial wage gaps in occupations requiring college educations and skilled occupations that do not require postsecondary education. Analyzing these racial wage gaps, Boushey and Cherry find that for males, the glass-ceiling effect remains more important in occupations requiring college, while exclusionary practices are more important in noncollege occupations. Their data for women indicate that the glass-ceiling effect is small and did not change during the current boom. However, it does appear that white women have been able to move into higher-paying college-requiring occupations at a faster rate than African American women have, and this is at least somewhat consistent with competitive pressures making it more costly for employers to discriminate. The question is, then, why white women have been able to move into these positions at higher rates.

A cautionary note to Boushey and Cherry's work must be made. Due to the aggregate nature of their data, they were not able to factor out the role that skill differences play in creating the occupational outcomes. Still, they do comment that skill differences have not changed significantly during the boom, implying that their results would not be affected were skill differences taken into account. The economy is quite tight in the regions that Boushey and Cherry examine, but not tight enough to significantly erode exclusionary practices or the glass ceiling.

We now must move to the question of why race remains important in tight labor markets, or, why do hiring queues based on race exist? To answer this question, Philip Moss and Chris Tilly examine both quantitative and qualitative data collected from employer-based surveys and in-depth one-on-one employer interviews in the Multi-City Study of Urban Inequality. The interviews were conducted in Atlanta, Boston, Detroit, and Los Angeles during the first two years of the boom (1992 and 1994). An advantage of these surveys over Current Population Survey–based surveys is that they allow the analyst to document the attitudes of employers toward minority workers. Given the timing of the interviews, Moss and Tilly can assess the impact that the beginning of the boom had on the attitudes of employers and how that affected minorities' employment prospects.

Moss and Tilly present evidence that employers harbor negative stereotypes with respect to African American workers, and these stereotypes place blacks further back in the hiring queue. Labor market tightness appears not to change employer attitudes about African Americans. Moss and Tilly hypothesize that because employers must go deeper into the hiring queue when labor markets tighten, tight labor markets should raise the probability that a firm will hire African American workers. In such a case, labor-market tightness influences employment decisions without changing the attitudes of employers.

These findings indicate that the probability of an African American applicant being hired increases when the local unemployment rate declines or when the length of the most recent job vacancy lengthens. In contrast, a firm's probability of hiring an African American applicant is inversely related to the length of time taken to complete its most recent hiring. Moss and Tilly suggest that this variable may be a measure of skill requirements desired rather than labor market tightness: if African American applicants are deemed less skilled, then employers may be less apt to hire them for those openings that are considered more skilled. Moss and Tilly's data on the impact that a tightening of the labor market has on employer attitudes suggest no consistent influence on hiring decisions. However, labor-market tightness does influence an employer's willingness to hire individuals with criminal records and those with deficient qualifications.

Our final pair of papers examines several specific social dimensions of the current boom. The first, by Sandra Danziger, Mary Corcoran, Sheldon Danziger, Colleen Heflin, Ariel Kalil, Judith Levine, Daniel Rosen, Kristin Seefeldt, Kristine Siefert, and Richard Tolman, evaluates the impact of welfare-reform policies in an economy where jobs are plentiful. During the first two years after the enactment of 1996 federal welfare-reform bill, welfare caseloads fell by 32 percent nationally. This was accomplished through adoption of government "work first" policies, which focused on immediate employment regardless of the work-related characteristics of welfare recipients. Yet although this strategy might have been appropriate at the time of enactment, it is likely that with declining caseloads, remaining recipients are more likely to possess traits that substantially affect their employability. Danziger and her colleagues identify these traits and examine the links between them and welfare recipients' employability.

In the latter part of 1997, Danziger and her colleagues surveyed over seven hundred individuals who had been on welfare six months earlier. The key to this survey was that the urban Michigan county in which the respondents resided had an unemployment rate at the time of the survey of 4.8 percent. Survey respondents were almost equally divided between black and white mothers, and at the time of the survey, 57 percent were working at least twenty hours per week, and about one-half of the surveyed group no longer was receiving any cash payments. The unique feature of this survey was the construction of fourteen barriers to employment, including skills, work norms, transportation, mental health, and physical-health deficits. Virtually all (85 percent) of those in the survey had at least one deficit; 45 percent had at least three deficits, and 15 percent had at least five deficits.

The Danziger team found that nine of the fourteen barriers have adverse effects on employment, and, in addition, that as the number of barriers increases, the probability of employment falls. These findings imply that government investment in raising educational attainment should be accompanied by counseling and health services. Each could possibly enhance the other's potential to improve employment prospects.

William Darity Jr. and Samuel L. Myers Jr. tackle the perplexing and worrisome issue of crime and incarceration, in the process testing the Rusche and Kirchheimer hypothesis (1939) that prisons serve as labor-market equilibrating devices. When labor surpluses grow, posit Rusche and Kirchheimer, incarceration rates rise to siphon off unwanted workers. Darity and Myers find that a long-term correspondence between higher incarceration rates and higher unemployment rates exists; however, for the current expansion, a marked departure from this long-term pattern occurs. During the 1990s, despite the boom, African American incarceration rates across states have increased measurably over rates observed in the 1970s.

Darity and Myers conclude that changing labor-market conditions cannot be the sole cause of the surge in incarceration, and cite as another cause public policies of the 1990s. Darity and Myers speculate that the privatization of prisons, 1980s drug-enforcement policies that created long sentences, the "three strikes and you're out" legislation of the 1990s, and a "hardening of the social status of black males as a permanent surplus population" are the keys to understanding the surge in incarceration.

From a public policy standpoint, it is incumbent that policy-makers take advantage of the current period of extended prosperity and address the structural barriers that prevent or hinder participating in the labor market, such as weak skills, racism, and spatial mismatch. In particular, we must develop strategies to re-integrate into the labor market not only African Americans, but all Americans that have come into contact with the criminal justice system. Above all, the positive impact that very tight labor markets have on reducing racial labor market disparities should receive greater weight in the development of macroeconomic policies.

REFERENCES

Browne, Irene. 1999. "Latinas and African American Women in the U.S. Labor Market." In *Latinas and African American Women at Work,* edited by Irene Browne. New York: Russell Sage.

Bound, John, and Laura Dresser. 1999. "Losing Ground: The Erosion of the Relative Earnings of African American Women During the 1980s." In *Latinas and African American Women at Work,* edited by Irene Browne. New York: Russell Sage.

Bound, John, and Richard Freeman. 1992. "What Went Wrong? Erosion of Relative Earnings and Employment among Young Black Men in the 1980s." *Quarterly Journal of Economics* 107(February): 201–32.

Kirschenman, Joleen, and Kathryn Neckerman. 1991. "'We'd Love to Hire Them, But . . .': The Meaning of Race for Employers." In *The Urban Underclass,* edited by Christopher Jencks and Paul E. Peterson. Washington, D.C.: Brookings Institution.

Rodgers, William M. 1997. "Male Sub-Metropolitan Black-White Wage Gaps." *Urban Studies* 34(8): 1201–13.

Rusche, George, and Otto Kirchheimer. 1939. *Punishment and Social Structure.* New York: Columbia University Press.

United States House of Representatives. Committee on Ways and Means. 1988. "Welfare Decline." In *1988 Green Book.* Washington: U.S. Government Printing Office.

PART I

Employment and the Boom

Chapter 1

THE EFFECT OF TIGHTER LABOR MARKETS ON UNEMPLOYMENT OF HISPANICS AND AFRICAN AMERICANS: THE 1990S EXPERIENCE

CORDELIA W. REIMERS

This chapter examines the unemployment rates of Hispanics, African Americans, and non-Hispanic whites during the recession of 1990 to 1992 and the expansion of 1992 to 1996 in order to investigate and compare the effect of tighter labor markets on these groups.[1] Differences in time worked during an average week significantly affect the racial and ethnic disparities in earnings in the United States, and cyclical variation in time worked during an average week is driven primarily by variation in unemployment rates. Unemployment rates are not only higher for African Americans and Hispanics than for non-Hispanic whites, but they also have varied more over past business cycles for these minority groups. Thus, in order to understand the effect of tighter labor markets on earnings for blacks and Hispanics vis-à-vis whites, it is important to gain a better understanding of the effect of tight labor markets on the unemployment rates of these three groups.

Using a probit model, this chapter assesses the effect of a tighter local labor market, as measured by the area unemployment rate, on the probability of being unemployed during 1990 to 1996 for each of these groups. The effects of labor market conditions are allowed to vary with education, age, occupation, and industry, as well as with race or ethnicity and gender. The results are used to determine whether black and Hispanic unemployment still exhibits greater sensitivity to local labor market conditions than unemployment of similarly situated whites. We also evaluate the extent to which differences in location contribute to cross-sectional differences in unemployment rates among the groups, and the extent to which

3

changes in local labor market tightness contributed to the changes in minority and white unemployment rates over the 1990s business cycle.

We find that black men and women still benefit much more from tighter labor markets than do whites, even those in similar industries and occupations, and of similar education and age levels. Overall, Hispanic men and women benefit slightly more than whites (but less than blacks) because Hispanics, on average, have less education than their white counterparts. But when industry, occupation, education, and age level are identical, Hispanic men's unemployment rates are *less* sensitive to local unemployment rates than are those of white men.

Depending on the occupation, the comparison between Hispanic and white women within industry, occupation, education, and age group can go either way. Further, we find that because the local-area unemployment rates are so similar where blacks and whites live, virtually none of the difference between their unemployment rates can be explained by cross-sectional differences in labor market tightness. However, over one-third of the Hispanic-white unemployment rate gap for men, and one-fifth of the gap for women, can be attributed to differences in area unemployment rates. Over the business cycle spanning 1990 to 1996, changes in local labor market tightness can explain at least two-thirds of the actual changes in unemployment rates for black and white men, for black women in the recession, and for Hispanic women in the expansion. Changes in area unemployment rates in the 1990s, though, can explain only about half of the actual changes in unemployment rates for Hispanic men, black women in the expansion, and Latinas in the recession, and only one-third of the actual change for white women. During the expansion of 1992 to 1996, minority as well as white unemployment rates fell more than would be predicted based on the increased average tightness of local labor markets alone.

Previous studies of the cyclical sensitivity of black and Hispanic unemployment rates are discussed in the next section. Because the changing patterns of job displacement in the 1980s and 1990s may have implications for minority unemployment in the 1990s, studies that address white-nonwhite differences in job loss and reemployment are also discussed. The following section describes the data and methods used in the analysis of unemployment rates, after which the results are presented and conclusions are offered.

BUSINESS CYCLES, JOB DISPLACEMENT, AND MINORITY UNEMPLOYMENT

In the business cycles of past decades, black unemployment has been more volatile than that of whites. Curtis Gilroy (1974) introduced the black-white incremental ratio of percentage-point changes in unemployment rates, which indicates that black unemployment rose proportionately more than that of whites during recessions and decreased proportionately more than white unemployment when the economy expanded.[2] Kim Clark and Lawrence Summers (1981) found that over the period from 1954 to 1976, a one-point decline in the prime-age-male unemployment rate elicited a more significant response in the proportion of nonwhite teenagers and adults who were employed than of whites. They showed that procyclical surges in labor-force participation of teenagers (the "encouraged worker" effect) partially offset the impact of economic expansions on unemployment rates and that if participation remained constant, expansion of aggregate demand would reduce teenage unemployment rates by much more than it actually does. The benefits of aggregate demand expansion are understated by focusing exclusively on unemployment rates.

Hispanic unemployment has received less attention from researchers than that of African Americans, but it has been analyzed in a few studies, such as Morris Newman (1978), John Abowd and Mark Killingsworth (1984), and, in particular, Gregory DeFreitas (1986, 1991). DeFreitas's analysis of Hispanic unemployment is the most thorough to date, and he has established that from 1973 to 1984, Hispanic unemployment rates, though never as high as blacks', averaged 1.64 times those of whites. Overall Hispanic unemployment rates were significantly more sensitive to changes in aggregate demand than those of whites, but unemployment among Hispanic teenage girls and adult men was not much more affected than that of white teenage girls and adult men. When participation as well as changes in unemployment levels is taken into account, the Hispanic employment-to-population ratio was nearly twice as elastic with respect to aggregate demand as the white ratio was. During the expansions of 1975 to 1980 and 1980 to 1981, the unemployment situation (as measured by Gilroy's [1974] incremental ratio of percentage-point changes in unemployment rates) improved for Hispanic teenagers and adult men relative to whites, but deteriorated for blacks relative to whites. During the 1980 to 1981 upturn, unemployment actually increased among black teenagers and black and Hispanic women.

It has long been observed that tight labor markets especially benefit groups that are subject to discrimination, for discrimination places them at the proverbial head of the queue for layoffs and at the end of the queue when equally qualified job applicants are considered by employers (Thurow 1969). Another reason why minority unemployment rates vary more over the business cycle than white rates is that minorities are more likely to be blue-collar workers in cyclically sensitive industries such as construction, mining, and durable manufacturing. In addition, the same educational disadvantage that makes the minorities more likely to be unemployed at any point in time also contributes to their greater cyclical variation in unemployment. Wayne Howe (1988) showed that high school graduates experienced much larger fluctuations in their unemployment rate during recessions and recoveries than did college graduates. College graduates have been less vulnerable to downturns in the business cycle partly because they tend to work in less cyclically sensitive industries (for example, professional services rather than the goods-producing sector).

Walter Oi (1962) provided the classic explanation of why less-educated workers have higher levels of unemployment and greater variation in unemployment over the business cycle, even within the same firm. As he put it, firm-specific human capital complements general human capital, so firms tend to invest more in training highly educated workers. This results in a higher fixed cost to replace skilled employees, thus giving employers a greater incentive to keep them on the payroll through temporary downturns in demand. Less-educated workers are more interchangeable and hence easier to replace; consequently they are the first to be laid off in a downturn. This explains why their unemployment rates are both higher and more variable than those of more-educated workers.

In addition to the greater volatility of minority unemployment rates observed in past business cycles, shifting patterns of permanent layoffs in the 1980s and 1990s also have important implications for the unemployment rates of minorities and whites in the 1990s. Lori Kletzer (1991) found that blacks faced a higher risk of job displacement during 1979 to 1986 because of their concentration in production-related occupations; that the black-white differences in likelihood of reemployment were large, but narrowed as the economy recovered from the recession of 1981 to 1982; and that blacks remained jobless for considerably longer periods than whites. Steven Hipple (1997) traced displacement rates of workers with more than three years' job tenure from 1981 to 1994 and found that while in most years black men and Hispanic men and women were displaced at higher rates than whites of the same gender, after 1985, black and white women had very similar displacement rates. Overall, however, blacks had more trouble finding another job after being displaced: of those displaced between 1993 and 1994, 13.5 percent of black men and 9.4 percent of black women remained unemployed in February 1996, compared with 7.7 percent of white men, 7.2 percent of Hispanic men, and 5.3 percent of white women.

Recent changes in the U.S. economy, especially the increasing instability of white-collar, managerial, and professional jobs, have led to rising job displacement of better-educated workers. Robert Fairlie and Lori Kletzer (1996, 1997) found that although black men were nearly 30 percent more likely than white men to experience job displacement during 1982 to 1991, the black disadvantage narrowed over time and had vanished by 1993. Differences in education levels and occupations explain a sizable share of the gap. More than two-thirds of the decline in the gap was due to a narrowing of the black-white displacement difference *within* education levels, occupations, industries, and regions. In addition, the increased displacement of higher-skilled white-collar workers in the 1990s helped to narrow the black-white gap. Blacks and Hispanics had higher displacement and quit rates than whites, but temporary layoff rates were quite similar for all three groups.

Henry Farber (1998) found that, controlling for age, education, gender, and year, nonwhites had slightly higher rates of job loss from 1981 through 1995, both overall and due to slack work and "other" reasons. There were no racial differences due to plant closings, and nonwhites were *less* likely than whites to have their positions abolished. This is surprising, for, during the period studied, workers in blue-collar occupations, manufacturing, and nonprofessional services were the most likely to have their positions abolished. Likewise, among college graduates, nonwhites were somewhat less likely to lose their jobs than whites. This was because the small positive nonwhite-white difference in job loss due to slack work was balanced by an equally small negative difference in job loss due to "other" reasons.

Farber's (1998) study also discovered that nonwhites who had lost jobs were much less likely than whites to be reemployed at the follow-up survey date, even after controlling for age, education, gender, year, and reason for job loss. The difference ranged from 17 percentage points for high school graduates to 4 points for college graduates. In addition, less-educated workers and those who lost their jobs due to slack work or other reasons (besides plant closing and position abolished) were less likely to be reemployed. Considering that nonwhites had higher rates of job loss for these reasons and were less educated, their chances of reemployment were much worse than those of whites. As a result, some nonwhite job losers withdrew from the labor force, but 34 percent remained unemployed, compared with 23 percent of whites.

Over time, the average educational level of younger blacks has been approaching that of whites, and blacks have been entering management and the professions in greater numbers. And while discrimination has not disappeared, many of the barriers that blocked blacks from stable jobs in the past have disappeared, and the black occupational distribution has become more akin to that of whites. These developments—greater similarity in skills and occupations among blacks and whites, less discrimination against blacks, as well as increasing job displacement affecting blacks and whites alike— might have affected African Americans' and whites' relative unemployment rates during the 1990s business cycle. One might predict that the sensitivity of black unemployment rates to labor-market conditions would be converging with that of whites, particularly within education-level, occupation, and industry groupings.

The dramatic changes in the American Hispanic population in the past couple of decades, particularly the increased immigration of poorly educated workers, could mean that Hispanic unemployment rates are less sensitive to labor market conditions in the 1990s than in the past. Such changes could also mean that Hispanic unemployment rates today are less sensitive to market conditions than those of blacks. If many recent immigrants, particularly undocumented ones, have lower reservation wages than natives of the same low skill level, they are likely to find work more quickly and therefore to have lower unemployment rates than other low-skilled groups in a slack labor market. On the other hand, the recent Hispanic immigrants are not likely to benefit disproportionately from tight labor markets in the 1990s, as demand expansion since 1992 has been skewed toward highly skilled workers. Only since 1996 or 1997 has expansion begun to reach those lacking skills.

To assess the sensitivity of black and Hispanic unemployment to labor market conditions, this study examines the effect of a tighter labor market (that is, a lower metropolitan-area or state unemployment rate) on Hispanic, black, and white male and female unemployment rates in the 1990s. Of particular interest is whether black and Hispanic unemployment still exhibits greater sensitivity to local labor market conditions than unemployment of similarly situated whites; that is, whether the effect of the local unemployment rate on the likelihood of unemployment is greater for the minorities, after controlling for education, age, industry, and occupation. Given the estimates of this effect, a second question is how much a tighter labor market, either between cities or over time, contributes to cross-sectional differences in unemployment rates among groups and to changes in minority and white unemployment rates over the business cycle.

ANALYSIS OF UNEMPLOYMENT RATES: DATA AND METHODS

To answer these questions, a probit model of the likelihood of being unemployed is estimated for each of six separate samples comprising Hispanic, African American, and white men and women. The data are a pooled time series of cross sections from the Current Population Survey Monthly Outgoing Rotation Group (CPS-MORG) files for 1990 through 1996, as provided by the National Bureau of Economic Research (NBER) in its CPS Labor Extracts file. Thus, both cross-sectional and cyclical variations in local unemployment rates are used to identify the effect of a tighter labor market. The samples are restricted to persons who were in the labor force in the current month, so that the probit estimates (translated into partial derivatives) can be interpreted as effects on the group's unemployment rate. Population weights are used. No adjustment is made for the partial overlap between the samples for adjacent years, which would affect standard errors but not means or point estimates.

In the first model estimated, the only predictor is the local-area unemployment rate in the current month. Its effect is allowed to differ between the recession of 1990 to 1992 and the expansion of 1993 to 1996. The area unemployment rates are the rates reported by the Bureau of Labor Statistics (on its Web site: http://www.bls.gov) for the same metropolitan area and month as the observation. Where the metropolitan area could not be matched, the state unemployment rate is used.

This model summarizes the overall responsiveness of the groups' unemployment rates to local labor market conditions during the recession of 1990 to 1992 and the expansion that followed. Because these responses may differ due to differences in age, education, industry, and occupation rather than due to race or ethnicity per se, two additional models are estimated for each race- or ethnic-gender group. Model 2, then, includes dummy variables for three education levels (high school dropout, twelve to fifteen years, college graduate) and five age brackets (sixteen to twenty-four, twenty-five to thirty-four, thirty-five to forty-four, forty-five to fifty-four, fifty-five to sixty-four), and these age and education variables interact with the current local-area unemployment rate. The estimates delivered by this model reveal differences in the sensitivity of unemployment to local labor-market conditions between younger and older workers and between more- and less-educated workers in the same racial- or ethnic-gender group.

Model 3 includes the same variables as model 2 and adds additional dummy variables for nine occupations and eleven industries, plus interactions of these variables with the current local-area unemployment rate. One of the reasons why age and education affect the cyclical sensitivity of unemployment rates is that better-educated and older workers have greater access to the less cyclically-sensitive skilled occupations and service industries. Discrimination and job-search networks have also affected the occupational and industrial distributions of minority workers. Therefore, disproportionate numbers of blacks and Hispanics work in more cyclically-sensitive blue-collar occupations and goods-producing industries. The estimates of model 3 sort out the roles of industry, occupation, age, and education in the change in a group's unemployment rates during times of area labor-market tightness.

In alternative specifications of models 2 and 3, the effects of the area unemployment rate on unemployment for the various combinations of race, gender, age, education, industry, and occupation groups were allowed to vary between the recession of 1990 to 1992 and the 1993 to 1996 expansion. So few of the differences between the recession and expansion were statistically significant (even at the 10 percent level), however, that only the results of models 2 and 3, which restrict the effects of the area unemployment rates to be identical for both the recession and expansion, are included here.[3]

Finally, we use measures of the inequality of area unemployment rates among groups in a given year, together with the estimated effects of local unemployment rates, to assess the degree to which differences in geographic location may contribute to cross-sectional differences in unemployment rates between the surveyed groups. Furthermore, we use the estimated effects of area unemployment rates, together with the magnitudes of the changes in mean area unemployment rates between 1990 and 1992 and between 1992 and 1996, to determine how much these changes in local labor-market tightness contributed to the changes in minority and white unemployment rates over the 1990s business cycle.

ANALYSIS OF UNEMPLOYMENT RATES: RESULTS

The effects of the business cycle, plus the trends in job displacement discussed earlier, resulted in the unemployment rates for 1990 to 1996 listed in table 1.1. Because published unemployment rates do not distinguish between Hispanics and non-Hispanics among whites or blacks, these rates are calculated from the same data that are used in the rest of this study (that is, the NBER's Labor Extracts from the CPS-MORG files for 1990 through 1996). To produce the rates for a given year, each monthly sample is restricted to those in the labor

Table 1.1 Average Annual Unemployment Rates, by Sex and Ethnicity (Percentages)

	Males			Females		
Year	Whites[a]	Blacks[b]	Hispanics	Whites[a]	Blacks[b]	Hispanics
1990	4.6	12.1	7.7	3.2	11.0	8.3
1991	6.1	12.6	10.2	3.6	12.1	9.7
1992	6.5	15.0	11.4	4.0	13.3	11.2
1993	6.0	13.6	10.7	3.9	12.1	11.6
1994	4.9	12.0	9.5	3.6	11.1	11.0
1995	4.4	10.5	8.8	3.2	10.1	9.6
1996	4.2	10.7	7.6	2.9	9.6	10.3
Average, 1990 to 1996	5.2	12.3	9.4	3.5	11.3	10.3

Source: Author's tabulations of Current Population Survey Monthly Outgoing Rotation Group files (weighted).
[a] This category refers to non-Hispanic whites
[b] This category refers to non-Hispanic blacks

force that month, all twelve months are pooled, and population weights are used. Table 1.1 lists the annual average unemployment rates for men and women between the ages of sixteen and sixty-four in each broad ethnic group—Hispanics, non-Hispanic blacks, and non-Hispanic whites. The relative changes in unemployment for these groups are shown in figure 1.1, which plots the gaps between blacks and whites and between Hispanics and whites by gender.

Figure 1.1 and table 1.1 show that the unemployment rates for Hispanic and black males have been more volatile, as well as considerably higher, than that of whites over this business cycle. The Hispanic-male unemployment rate rose from 7.7 percent to 11.4 percent and then fell back to 7.6 percent. Meanwhile, black men, who generally have an even higher unemployment rate than Hispanics, saw their unemployment rate rise less in the recession and decline more in the expansion, going from 12.1 percent in 1990 to 15.0 percent in 1992, a climb of 2.9 percentage points, and then declining by 4.3 points to 10.7 percent in 1996. White male unemployment rose from 4.6 percent in 1990 to 6.5 percent in 1992 before falling to 4.2 percent in 1996.

Hispanic women are the only group whose unemployment rate in 1996 was higher than it had been in 1990. In that year, their un-

Figure 1.1 Differences in Unemployment Rates

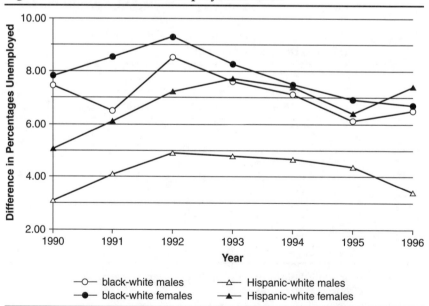

Source: Author's tabulations.

employment rate was 2.7 points lower than black women's, but by 1996 it was 0.7 point higher. From 8.3 percent in 1990 unemployment among Hispanic women had risen to 11.6 percent in 1993, and then declined by 1996—but only to 10.3 percent. Black women's unemployment rate rose by less between 1990 and 1992 (from 11.0 percent to 13.3 percent), and began declining a year earlier, falling to 9.6 percent in 1996. During the same 1990 to 1996 period, white women had a lower and more stable unemployment rate than did minority women. White-female unemployment rose from 3.2 percent to 4.0 percent from 1990 to 1992, and then declined to 2.9 percent in 1996. Thus, as measured by unemployment rates, Hispanics suffered more from the recession of 1990 to 1992 and by 1996 did not recover as much of their 1990 position as did blacks, much less whites.

Table 1.2 shows the results of estimating model 1, in which the only predictor is the local-area unemployment rate in the current month. The probit results (reported in table 1.10) have been translated into the partial derivatives shown in table 1.2, and they reveal, for example, that for black males, a one-percentage-point-lower area unemployment rate in the current month reduced the probability of unemployment by 1.4 percentage points during the recession and 1.3 points during the expansion.[4] Although the differences between the effects in the recession and expansion are statistically significant for black and white men and black and Hispanic women, they are in fact quite small—on the order of 0.1 percentage point. Therefore, adopting the restrictions in models 2 and 3 that the effects of area unemployment rates are symmetrical over the business cycle does not appear to do violence to the data.

Black unemployment was more sensitive to local labor-market conditions than was Hispanic or white unemployment. Table 1.2, for example, indicates that during the recession of 1990 through 1992, a one percentage point increment in the area unemployment rate corresponded with a 1.4-percentage-point-greater probability of being unemployed for black men, 1.0 for black women, 0.8 for Hispanic men, 0.7 for white men, 0.6 for Hispanic women, and 0.3 for white women. During the subsequent expansion these responses were slightly smaller for black males (1.3), black females (0.8), and white males (0.6) and slightly higher for Hispanic females (0.7). Within gender, the differences between African Americans and the other groups are statistically significant, as is the difference between Hispanic and white women. The difference between Hispanic men and white men is not significant.

Table 1.2 Effects of Area Unemployment Rate on Percentage Unemployed (Percentage-Point Change)

	Males		
	Whites[a]	Blacks[b]	Hispanics
Effect, in percentage-point change, of a one-percentage-point-higher area unemployment rate in			
1990 to 1992	0.67	1.43	0.75
1993 to 1996	0.62*	1.34**	0.73
Predicted percentage unemployed at mean area unemployment rate	5.11	12.15	9.18
Observed percentage unemployed	5.25	12.33	9.37
Mean area unemployment rate	5.93	5.99	7.37
	Females		
	Whites[a]	Blacks[b]	Hispanics
Effect, in percentage-point change, of a one-percentage-point-higher area unemployment rate in			
1990 to 1992	0.26	0.98	0.59
1993 to 1996	0.27	0.85*	0.74*
Predicted percentage unemployed at mean area unemployment rate	3.43	11.20	10.12
Observed percentage unemployed	3.47	11.29	10.27
Mean area unemployment rate	5.89	5.96	7.37

Source: Table 1.10
* Difference between recession and expansion significant at 5 percent level.
** Difference between recession and expansion significant at 10 percent level.
[a] This category refers to non-Hispanic whites.
[b] This category refers to non-Hispanic blacks.

The results of model 2, which allows the effect of the area unemployment rate on the likelihood of being unemployed to vary with education and age, are displayed in table 1.3. (The full sets of partial derivatives from the probits appear in tables 1.11 and 1.12, at the end of the chapter.) As a baseline, the first row of table 1.3 shows the predicted unemployment rate for each race-gender grouping in a reference category (in this case, thirty-five- to forty-four-year-old high school graduates without bachelor's degrees), evaluated at the group's mean area unemployment rate for 1990 through 1996.[5] The next two panels in table 1.3 show the incremental effect that raising the area unemployment rate by one percentage point has on various education and age groups.

Table 1.3's three bottom rows show each group's predicted unemployment rate using its own mean area unemployment rate, education, and age; the group's observed unemployment rate; and the group's mean area unemployment rate. The difference between the observed unemployment rate and that predicted at the means of all of the variables is due to the nonlinearity of the probit function. The difference between the predicted unemployment rates at the means and for the reference category indicates the effect of the difference between the group's own education and age distribution and the reference category (age thirty-five to forty-four with twelve to fifteen years of education) on the group's unemployment rate.

With due caution, the predicted unemployment rates may be compared across groups. Still, it should be kept in mind that the difference between any two groups in predicted unemployment rates will vary with the reference category chosen, because the effects of age and education on unemployment vary across groups. Because of this arbitrariness, the intergroup difference in predicted unemployment rates for any reference category is not a useful summary measure of the effect of unexplained factors on the intergroup difference in unemployment rates. For example, the intergroup difference for a reference category cannot be used to divide the difference in predicted unemployment rates at the means into a portion due to difference in mean characteristics and a portion due to unexplained factors. All it can tell us is the difference in predicted unemployment rates for that particular age-education group. Nonetheless, this may be of some interest.

When the response of the unemployment rate to the area unemployment rate is allowed to vary with education and age, the

Table 1.3 Effects of Area Unemployment Rate, Education, and Age on Percentage Unemployed (Percentages)

	Males			Females		
	Whites[a]	Blacks[b]	Hispanics	Whites[a]	Blacks[b]	Hispanics
Predicted percentage unemployed at mean area unemployment rate, for reference category (education = twelve to fifteen, age = thirty-five to forty-four)	4.10	8.60	6.46	3.21	7.60	6.63
Effect, in percentage-point change, of a one-percentage-point-higher area unemployment rate, for age-education group[c]						
education zero to eleven, age thirty-five to forty-four	0.70*	1.31	0.67*	0.17*	0.81	0.72*
education twelve to fifteen, age thirty-five to forty-four (reference category)	0.58	1.36	0.51	0.34	0.94	0.51
education sixteen+, age thirty-five to forty-four	0.40*	1.02	0.20*	0.23**	0.46*	0.20**

age sixteen to twenty-four, education twelve to fifteen	0.57	1.13	0.52	0.22**	0.90	0.28*
age twenty-five to thirty-four, education twelve to fifteen	0.59	1.29	0.52	0.35	0.80	0.40
age thirty-five to forty-four, education twelve to fifteen (reference category)	0.58	1.36	0.51	0.34	0.94	0.51
age forty-five to fifty-four, education twelve to fifteen	0.57	1.05	0.53	0.28	1.01	0.43
age fifty-five to sixty-four, education twelve to fifteen	0.61	1.30	0.23*	0.32	0.96	0.30
Predicted percentage unemployed at mean area unemployment rate, education, age	4.52	10.59	8.65	3.14	9.24	9.30
Observed percentage unemployed	5.25	12.33	9.37	3.47	11.29	10.27
Mean area unemployment rate	5.93	5.99	7.37	5.89	5.98	7.37

Source: Tables 1.11 and 1.12.
* Significantly different from reference category at 5 percent level.
** Significantly different from reference category at 10 percent level.
[a] This category refers to non-Hispanic whites.
[b] This category refers to non-Hispanic blacks.
[c] For the effects of a higher area unemployment rate, the differences among education levels are the same for other age groups, and the differences among age groups are the same for other education levels.

similarity between Hispanic and white men within education and age cohorts is striking. The only appreciable differences are found in college graduates and men aged fifty-five to sixty-four; in each the response is much stronger for the white men than for the Hispanics. Hispanic women, meanwhile, have a stronger response to the area unemployment rate than do white women of the same age or education level, with the exceptions of college graduates and the youngest and oldest age groups. In these three groups, the responses of Hispanic and white women are similar.

Within the particular racial and ethnic groups, the effect of local labor-market conditions on black males' unemployment does not vary significantly with education, but for black women, the response is only about half as large for college graduates (0.5) as for those with less education (0.8-0.9). (See the second group of rows in table 1.3.) For Hispanics of both sexes, the response decreases significantly at each successive level of education. Where local unemployment rates are one percentage point higher, the unemployment rate of Hispanic high school dropouts is 0.7 point higher, that of Hispanic high school graduates is 0.5 point higher, and that of Hispanic college graduates was 0.2 point higher. For white men, the response also decreases significantly as education rises, though the differences are not as large as they are for Hispanics. A one-percentage-point increase in the local unemployment rate is associated with a 0.7-point-higher unemployment rate for white male dropouts, a 0.6-point-higher rate for high school graduates, and a 0.4-point-higher rate for college graduates. For white women, however, the response to local labor-market conditions is significantly *smaller* for high school dropouts (as well as college graduates) than for high school graduates. A one-percentage-point-higher local unemployment rate results in a 0.3-point-higher rate for high school graduates and a 0.2-point-higher rate for both high school dropouts and college graduates.

The only significant differences in the response of the unemployment rate to the area unemployment rate among age cohorts occurs in older (age fifty-five to sixty-four) Hispanic men and young (age sixteen to twenty-four) Hispanic and white women. For Hispanics in these age groups, the response is only about half as large as it is for the middle aged; for the white women, it is about two-thirds as large.

In summary, a tighter local labor market, as measured by a lower area unemployment rate, has a significantly stronger effect on reducing unemployment for blacks than for whites or Hispanics in all age or education categories. This effect is particularly strong for black men, the only group where a one-percentage-point drop in the area unemployment rate reduces the probability of unemployment by more than one percentage point. The effect does not differ much between Hispanic and white men. In general, local labor-market tightness also matters more for the less educated in each race-gender group, although for black men and women there is no difference between high school graduates and dropouts, for black men the difference between college and high school graduates is not significant, and for white women the effect is *weaker* for high school dropouts than for graduates.

The results of model 3, which allows the response of the unemployment rate to the area unemployment rate to vary by industry and occupation as well as by age and education, are shown for men and women in tables 1.4 and 1.5 respectively. (The full sets of partial derivatives from the probits are in tables 1.13 and 1.14.)[6] Like table 1.3, tables 1.4 and 1.5 first show the predicted unemployment rate for a reference category (here, a thirty-five- to forty-four-year old operative or laborer in the trade industry with twelve to fifteen years of education), evaluated at the race-gender group's mean area unemployment rate for 1990 to 1996. The next four groups of rows show the incremental effect that raising the area unemployment rate by one percentage point has on different education, age, occupation, and industry cohorts.

Examination of the occupation and industry rows of tables 1.4 and 1.5 reveals very few significant differences from the reference category in the effect of a tighter local labor market on unemployment probabilities. This is somewhat surprising, as some industries are more cyclical than others. Comparison with a different reference category, however, might reveal more significant differences. Furthermore, it should also be kept in mind that in this analysis the effect of the area unemployment rate is calculated using cross-sectional as well as intertemporal variation, and the cross-sectional variation may dominate the data.

Even within the same industry, occupation, education, and age groups, black-male and -female unemployment rates respond more strongly to the area unemployment rate than do those of whites or Hispanics. The effects of the area unemployment rate on group unemployment rates are greater than 1.0 for blacks in almost all age,

Table 1.4 Effects of Area Unemployment Rate, Education, Age, Occupation, and Industry on Percentage Unemployed of Males (Percentage-Point Change)

	Whites[a]	Blacks[b]	Hispanics
Predicted percentage unemployed at mean area unemployment rate, for reference category (ed = twelve to fifteen; age = thirty-five to forty-four; occ = operator-laborer; ind = trade)	5.03	10.55	7.45
Effect, in percentage-point change, of a one-percentage-point-higher area unemployment rate, for education, age, occupation, and industry group[c]			
Education (age = thirty-five to forty-four; occ = operator-laborer; ind = trade)			
Zero to eleven	1.00*	1.68	0.51
Twelve to fifteen (reference category)	0.68	1.75	0.42
Sixteen+	0.50*	1.11*	0.15
Age (ed = twelve to fifteen; occ = operator-laborer; ind = trade)			
Sixteen to twenty-four	0.57	1.37	0.39
Twenty-five to thirty-four	0.71	1.70	0.42
Thirty-five to forty-four (reference category)	0.68	1.75	0.42
Forty-five to fifty-four	0.70	1.42	0.44
Fifty-five to sixty-four	0.73	1.71	0.08*
Occupation (ind = trade; age = thirty-five to forty-four; ed = twelve to fifteen)			
Management	0.65	1.53	0.20
Professional	0.68	2.01	0.61
Technical	0.44	1.82	0.34
Sales	0.44*	1.90	0.52
Clerical	0.63	2.05	−0.07*
Service	0.46**	1.38	0.62
Farming, forestry, fishing	0.57	0.48**	0.19
Craft	0.57	1.33**	0.48
Operator-laborer (reference category)	0.68	1.75	0.42
Industry (occ = operator-laborer, age = thirty-five to forty-four; ed = twelve to fifteen)			
Agriculture, forestry, fishing	0.53	2.10	0.98*
Construction, mining	0.74	2.16	0.77*

(Table continues on page 21.)

Table 1.4 *Continued*

	Whites[a]	Blacks[b]	Hispanics
Nondurable manufacturing	0.72	2.31**	0.89*
Durable manufacturing	0.94*	1.96	0.61
Utilities	0.58	1.54	0.68
Trade (reference category)	0.68	1.75	0.42
FIRE	0.80	1.27	0.05
Business services	0.65	1.54	0.52
Personal services	1.20*	1.58	0.76
Professional services	0.56	1.61	0.35
Public administration	0.43	1.75	−0.01
Predicted percentage unemployed at mean area unemployment rate, ed, age, occ, ind	4.17	9.35	7.80
Observed percentage unemployed	5.02	11.06	8.59
Mean area unemployment rate	5.93	5.99	7.37

Source: Table 1.13.
Note: ed = years of education; age = age in years; occ = occupation; ind = industry
* Significantly different from reference category at 5 percent level.
** Significantly different from reference category at 10 percent level.
[a] This category refers to non-Hispanic whites.
[b] This category refers to non-Hispanic blacks.
[c] For the effects of a higher area unemployment rate, the differences among industries are the same for other ed-age-occ groups, the differences among occupations are the same for other ed-age-ind groups, the differences among age groups are the same for other ed-occ-ind groups, and the differences among education levels are the same for other age-occ-ind groups.

education, occupation, and industry categories, and less than 1.0 for Hispanics and whites.

Because the magnitudes of the estimated effects of local-area unemployment rates on particular cohorts depend on which occupation or industry group is used as the reference category, it is difficult to make general comparisons between Hispanics and whites in tables 1.4 and 1.5. For example, within the chosen reference occupation—operatives and laborers—Hispanic women show a stronger response than white women of the same education level, age, and industry. But among the Hispanic female cohort itself, the response for operatives and laborers is exceptionally large in comparison with other occupations, whereas among white women, operatives and laborers have the second-smallest response of any occupation. Thus it is seen that the relative sensitivity of Hispanic women's and white women's unemployment rates to local labor-market tightness varies

Table 1.5 Effects of Area Unemployment Rate, Education, Age, Occupation, and Industry on Percentage Unemployed of Females (Percentage-Point Change)

	Whites[a]	Blacks[b]	Hispanics
Predicted percentage unemployed at mean area unemployment rate, for reference category (ed = twelve to fifteen; age = thirty-five to forty-four; occ = operator-laborer; ind = trade)	6.66	14.44	9.51
Effect, in percentage-point change, of a one-percentage-point-higher area unemployment rate, for education, age, occupation, and industry group[c]			
Education (age = thirty-five to forty-four; occ = operator-laborer; ind = trade)			
Zero to eleven	0.34*	1.85	0.89
Twelve to fifteen (reference category)	0.65	2.10	0.92
Sixteen+	0.42**	1.42**	0.68
Age (ed = twelve to fifteen; occ = operator-laborer; ind = trade)			
Sixteen to twenty-four	0.34*	1.72	0.65
Twenty-five to thirty-four	0.69	1.89	0.76
Thirty-five to forty-four (reference category)	0.65	2.10	0.92
Forty-five to fifty-four	0.54	2.31	0.91
Fifty-five to sixty-four	0.68	2.34	0.81
Occupation (ind = trade; age = thirty-five to forty-four; ed = twelve to fifteen)			
Management	0.86	1.91	0.68
Professional	0.68	1.69	0.33**
Technical	0.76	0.96	0.61
Sales	0.59	1.55	0.62
Clerical	0.77	2.11	0.54
Service	0.93	1.43	0.64
Farming, forestry, fishing	1.70**	1.83	0.56
Craft	0.94	4.04*	0.43
Operator-laborer (reference group)	0.65	2.10	0.92
Industry (occ = operator-laborer, age = thirty-five to forty-four; ed = twelve to fifteen)			
Agriculture, forestry, fishing	0.25	-0.12	1.39
Construction, mining	0.39	2.69	1.15

(Table continues on page 23.)

Table 1.5 *Continued*

	Whites[a]	Blacks[b]	Hispanics
Nondurable manufacturing	0.57	2.14	1.19
Durable manufacturing	1.06*	1.77	1.21
Utilities	0.16*	1.96	0.16*
Trade (reference category)	0.65	2.10	0.92
FIRE	0.69	2.27	1.16
Business services	0.55	1.52	0.87
Personal services	0.25*	1.98	0.81
Professional services	0.44**	1.46*	0.72
Public administration	0.46	2.10	1.50
Predicted percentage unemployed at mean area unemployment rate, ed, age, occ, ind	3.52	7.90	7.82
Observed percentage unemployed	3.94	9.93	8.86
Mean area unemployment rate	5.89	5.96	7.37

Source: Table 1.14.
Notes: ed = years of education; age = age in years; occ = occupation; ind = industry
*Significantly different from reference category at 5 percent level.
**Significantly different from reference category at 10 percent level.
[a] This category refers to non-Hispanic whites.
[b] This category refers to non-Hispanic blacks.
[c] For the effects of a higher area unemployment rate, the differences among industries are the same for other ed-age-occ groups, the differences among occupations are the same for other ed-age-ind groups, the differences among age groups are the same for other ed-occ-ind groups, and the differences among education levels are the same for other age-occ-ind groups.

by occupation. For men, on the other hand, within most categories the unemployment rate of Hispanics is even less sensitive to the area unemployment rate than that of whites.

The results in tables 1.4 and 1.5 also reveal differences among industries, occupations, age, and education levels *within* ethnic- or racial-gender groups. For black and Hispanic men, for example, the effect of a tighter labor market on unemployment rates within occupation, age, and education level is strongest in nondurable manufacturing, construction, and agriculture and weakest in financial services as well as, for Hispanics, public administration. For black men in the same industry, age, and education sectors, the effect is strongest in the white-collar occupations other than management and weakest for farmers. The occupational pattern is different for Hispanic men, where the strongest effects are for professionals and service workers and the weakest for clerical workers.

For black women sharing the same occupation, age, and education levels, the strongest effects of a tighter labor market on unemployment rates are found in construction, financial services, nondurable manufacturing, trade, and public administration. The weakest effects are in business services, professional services such as health care, and agriculture. For Hispanic women, the effects are strongest in public administration and agriculture and weakest in utilities. Within industry, age, and education cohorts, the effect for black women is strongest for crafts workers and weakest for technicians. For Hispanic women, the effect is strongest for operatives and weakest for professionals.

Patterns for age and educational groupings are similar to those without the controls for occupation and industry, except that the difference between black male high school and college graduates becomes statistically significant while the differences among Hispanics by education level are statistically insignificant. Apparently, the intra- and interoccupation effects of college graduation work in opposite directions for black men, such that college graduation's significance appears only if occupation remains constant. For Hispanics, the effect of education appears to operate largely between occupations.

Finally, the estimated effects of area unemployment rates from table 1.2 are used to assess the degree to which differences in geographic location contribute to cross-sectional differences in unemployment rates among the groups, and how much changes in local labor-market tightness contributed to the changes in minority and white unemployment rates over the 1990s business cycle.

Means, medians, and a measure of the inequality of area unemployment rates for men and women in each year are contained in tables 1.6 and 1.7 respectively. The distribution of area unemployment rates is similar for blacks and whites, which is somewhat surprising considering their differing geographic distributions: blacks are more likely than whites to live in the South and in large northern cities, and whites are more likely than blacks to live in the West and in smaller urban and rural areas in the North and Midwest. It may be surmised that the distribution of high- and low-unemployment areas across the country compensated for these differences in location, at least in the 1990s. Therefore, location—at least at as aggregate a level as metropolitan area—cannot explain the difference between black and white unemployment rates. (Of course, this does not mean that the particular locations where blacks live *within* metropolitan areas— which include central cities and outer suburbs—do not factor into blacks' higher unemployment.)

Table 1.6 Means, Medians, and Quartiles of Area Unemployment Rate Distributions, by Ethnicity and Year, for Males

	Means			Medians		
	Whites[a]	Blacks[b]	Hispanics	Whites[a]	Blacks[b]	Hispanics
1990	5.3	5.4	6.2	5.2	5.3	5.9
1991	6.5	6.5	7.6	6.4	6.4	7.3
1992	7.2	7.2	8.8	7.0	7.0	8.6
1993	6.6	6.6	8.3	6.4	6.5	8.0
1994	5.7	5.8	7.5	5.5	5.6	7.1
1995	5.3	5.4	6.7	5.1	5.2	6.4
1996	4.9	5.1	6.6	4.7	4.8	6.1
Total	5.9	6.0	7.4	5.7	5.8	7.0

	Whites[a]			Blacks[b]			Hispanics		
	75 Percentile	25 Percentile	75 – 25 Difference	75 Percentile	25 Percentile	75 – 25 Difference	75 Percentile	25 Percentile	75 – 25 Difference
1990	6.0	4.4	1.6	6.1	4.5	1.6	6.5	5.1	1.4
1991	7.4	5.4	2.0	7.3	5.3	2.0	8.4	6.2	2.2
1992	8.1	5.9	2.2	8.2	6.0	2.2	10.0	6.9	3.1
1993	7.5	5.2	2.3	7.6	5.3	2.3	9.7	6.6	3.1
1994	6.5	4.5	2.0	6.7	4.6	2.1	9.0	5.6	3.4
1995	6.0	4.3	1.7	6.1	4.4	1.7	7.7	5.2	2.5
1996	5.6	3.9	1.7	5.7	3.9	1.8	8.0	4.7	3.3
Total	6.9	4.6	2.3	7.0	4.7	2.3	8.5	5.5	3.0

Source: Author's tabulations of Current Population Survey Monthly Outgoing Rotation Group files (weighted).

[a] This category refers to non-Hispanic whites.

[b] This category refers to non-Hispanic blacks.

Table 1.7 Means, Medians, and Quartiles of Area Unemployment Rate Distributions, by Ethnicity and Year, for Females

	Means			Medians		
	Whites[a]	Blacks[b]	Hispanics	Whites[a]	Blacks[b]	Hispanics
1990	5.3	5.4	6.4	5.2	5.2	6.0
1991	6.5	6.5	7.6	6.4	6.4	7.3
1992	7.1	7.2	8.7	6.9	6.9	8.4
1993	6.5	6.6	8.3	6.4	6.4	7.9
1994	5.7	5.8	7.5	5.4	5.6	7.1
1995	5.2	5.4	6.7	5.1	5.2	6.4
1996	4.9	5.1	6.6	4.7	4.9	6.1
Total	5.9	6.0	7.4	5.6	5.7	6.9

	Whites[a]			Blacks[b]			Hispanics		
	75 Percentile	25 Percentile	75 − 25 Difference	75 Percentile	25 Percentile	75 − 25 Difference	75 Percentile	25 Percentile	75 − 25 Difference
1990	6.0	4.4	1.6	6.2	4.5	1.7	6.6	5.1	1.5
1991	7.3	5.3	2.0	7.3	5.3	2.0	8.4	6.2	2.2
1992	8.1	5.8	2.3	8.1	6.0	2.1	10.0	6.8	3.2
1993	7.5	5.2	2.3	7.6	5.3	2.3	9.7	6.5	3.2
1994	6.5	4.5	2.0	6.8	4.6	2.2	9.0	5.6	3.4
1995	6.0	4.3	1.7	6.1	4.4	1.7	7.7	5.2	2.5
1996	5.6	3.9	1.7	5.8	3.9	1.9	8.0	4.7	3.3
Total	6.9	4.6	2.3	7.0	4.7	2.3	8.5	5.5	3.0

Source: Author's tabulations of Current Population Survey Monthly Outgoing Rotation Group files (weighted).
[a] This category refers to non-Hispanic whites.
[b] This category refers to non-Hispanic blacks.

The areas where Hispanics live, however, clearly tend to have higher unemployment rates than those where blacks and whites are concentrated, and this gap has been growing since 1990. In that year, the area unemployment rate of the median Hispanic man was only 0.7 point higher than that of the median white man, but it was 1.6 points higher in 1992 through 1994 and 1.4 points higher in 1996. The areas where Hispanics live also experienced slightly greater swings in unemployment over the cycle than did the areas where blacks and whites live. The local unemployment rate where the median Hispanic man lived in 1996 was 2.5 points lower than the median in 1992 (6.1 percent versus 8.6 percent). For black and white men at the median, the local unemployment rate dropped by 2.2 and 2.3 points respectively over the same four-year period.

Besides varying over time with the business cycle, unemployment rates vary by geographical location. One measure of this variation is the "spread" of the distribution of local unemployment rates for a group, as measured by the difference between the seventy-fifth and twenty-fifth percentiles in a given year. By this measure, the inter-city variation in unemployment is of the same order of magnitude as the aggregate variation over the business cycle. For example, if the blacks at the seventy-fifth percentile could move to where the blacks at the twenty-fifth percentile live, unemployment in their local labor market would be 1.6 to 2.3 percentage points lower, depending on the year. Like the medians, the degree of inequality in area unemployment rates is virtually identical for blacks and whites. However, since 1992, it has been much larger for Hispanics, for whom the seventy-five–twenty-five difference was 3.3 points in 1996, in contrast to a 1.7 point spread for whites. Thus, for Hispanics, the geographic variation in labor-market tightness is even greater than the aggregate cyclical variation. For them, where one lives can be said to matter more than what year it is.

The geographic inequality of labor-market tightness appears to behave countercyclically, at least for blacks and whites, for while it increased for all three groups from 1990 to 1993, it decreased again for blacks and whites from 1993 to 1996. The increase in inequality of local unemployment rates was much more dramatic for Hispanics than the others, and there occurred virtually no reequalization for them by 1996. In that year, an Hispanic at the seventy-fifth percentile of his or her distribution of local unemployment rates faced an unemployment rate that was 2.4 points higher than the rate faced by a white at the seventy-fifth percentile of his or her own distribution, whereas the medians for Hispanics and whites were only 1.4 points apart.

One can measure the extent to which the intergroup differences in unemployment rates in a given year can be explained by differences in mean area unemployment rates (which, in turn, are due to differences in geographic distribution) by multiplying the differences in mean area unemployment rates shown in tables 1.6 and 1.7 by the estimated partial derivatives shown in table 1.2. These estimates for men and women in 1992 and 1996 are reported in tables 1.8 and 1.9 respectively. Because the black and white distributions of area unemployment rates are so similar, virtually none of the black-white difference in unemployment is due to differences in area unemployment rates. However, 37 percent of the Hispanic-white male difference in unemployment rates in 1996 can be attributed to this difference, and 20 percent of the Hispanic-white female difference in 1996 can be so explained. In other words, if Hispanics were distributed across the country in the same locations as whites, over one-third of the Hispanic males' excess unemployment, and one-fifth of the Hispanic females' excess unemployment, would disappear.

Similarly, one can predict how much the various groups' unemployment rates would be expected to change over the 1990 to 1996 business cycle due to the actual changes in labor market tightness from 1990 to 1992 and 1992 to 1996. The results of these calculations are also shown in tables 1.8 and 1.9. For black men, unemployment rates are predicted to rise by 2.6 percentage points from 1990 to 1992, which turns out to be 87 percent of the actual increase. The rates are then predicted to fall by 2.8 points from 1992 to 1996, and that is 65 percent of the actual decline. For black women, unemployment rates are predicted to rise and fall by 1.8 points, which is 78 percent of the actual increase but only 48 percent of the actual decline. For Hispanic men, the predicted rise in unemployment rate is 2.0 percentage points, and the predicted decline is 1.6 points—respectively 54 percent and 43 percent of the actual rise and fall. For Hispanic women, unemployment rates are predicted to rise by 1.4 points (46 percent of the actual rise) and then fall by 1.6 points—a 68 percent *larger* decline than the one that actually took place from 1992 to 1996, though this actual decline is mitigated by the increase in the Hispanic women's unemployment rate in 1996 (see table 1.1). (If the period spanning 1992 to 1995 is used instead, the predicted decline for Hispanic women is 93 percent of the actual

Table 1.8 Predicted Intergroup Differences and Changes in Unemployment Rates, 1990 to 1992 and 1992 to 1996, for Males

	Whites[a]		Blacks[b]		Hispanics	
	Recession (1990 to 1992)	Expansion (1993 to 1996)	Recession (1990 to 1992)	Expansion (1993 to 1996)	Recession (1990 to 1992)	Expansion (1993 to 1996)
Effect of area unemployment rate per percentage point	0.67	0.62	1.43	1.34	0.76	0.73
	1992	1996	1992	1996	1992	1996
Difference in area unemployment rate from whites	—	—	0.0	0.2	1.6	1.7
Difference in group's unemployment rate from whites						
Predicted	—	—	0.00	0.27	1.22	1.25
Actual	—	—	8.50	6.48	4.89	3.40
Share explained	—	—	0.00	0.04	0.25	0.37
	1990 to 1992	1992 to 1996	1990 to 1992	1992 to 1996	1990 to 1992	1992 to 1996
Change in mean area unemployment rate	1.9	−2.3	1.8	−2.1	2.6	−2.2
Change in group's unemployment rate						
Predicted	1.28	−1.44	2.57	−2.81	1.97	−1.62
Actual	1.89	−2.28	2.95	−4.30	3.69	−3.77
Share explained	0.68	0.63	0.87	0.65	0.54	0.43

Source: Tables 1.1, 1.2, and 1.6.
[a] This category refers to non-Hispanic whites.
[b] This category refers to non-Hispanic blacks.

Table 1.9 Predicted Intergroup Differences and Changes in Unemployment Rates, 1990 to 1992 and 1992 to 1996, for Females

	Whites[a]		Blacks[b]		Hispanics	
	Recession (1990 to 1992)	Expansion (1993 to 1996)	Recession (1990 to 1992)	Expansion (1993 to 1996)	Recession (1990 to 1992)	Expansion (1993 to 1996)
Effect of area unemployment rate per percentage point	0.26	0.27	0.98	0.85	0.59	0.74
	1992	1996	1992	1996	1992	1996
Difference in area unemployment rate from whites	—	—	0.1	0.2	1.6	1.7
Difference in group's unemployment rate from whites						
Predicted	—	—	0.10	0.17	0.94	1.26
Actual	—	—	7.61	5.49	5.54	6.21
Share explained	—	—	0.01	0.03	0.17	0.20
	1990 to 1992	1992 to 1996	1990 to 1992	1992 to 1996	1990 to 1992	1992 to 1996
Change in mean area unemployment rate	1.8	−2.2	1.8	−2.1	2.3	−2.1
Change in group's unemployment rate						
Predicted	0.48	−0.59	1.77	−1.79	1.36	−1.56
Actual	1.27	−1.59	2.28	−3.72	2.96	−0.93
Share explained	0.37	0.37	0.78	0.48	0.46	1.68

Source: Tables 1.1, 1.2, and 1.7.

[a] This category refers to non-Hispanic whites.

[b] This category refers to non-Hispanic blacks.

decline.)[7] For white men, the unemployment rate is predicted to increase by 1.3 points and then decline by 1.4 points—68 percent and 63 percent of the actual rise and fall respectively. For white women, the predicted rise is only 0.5 point and the predicted decline is 0.6 point, just 37 percent of the actual change in each case.

Thus, the changing tightness of the local labor market explains more than three-fourths of the actual changes in unemployment rates for black men and women during the recession and Hispanic women during the expansion. It explains two-thirds of the actual change for black men in the expansion and two-thirds of the actual change for white men in both the recession and expansion, but only about half of the actual changes for Hispanic men in the recession and expansion, Hispanic women in the recession, and black women in the expansion, and only about one-third of the actual changes for white women. Some of the "unexplained" changes result from the nonlinearity of the probit function and consequent approximation error, and the rest are due to changes in the shape of the distribution of local-area unemployment rates and variation in the effects of those rates among more discrete subgroups of the population. Consequently, during the expansion of the 1990s, minority as well as white unemployment rates fell more than would be expected based on the increased average tightness of local labor markets alone.

SUMMARY AND CONCLUSIONS

This chapter has used probit models to summarize and compare fluctuations in the unemployment rates of Hispanics, blacks, and whites between 1990 and 1996, and especially to investigate and compare the effect of tighter labor markets on these groups. To this end, the effect of a tighter local labor market, as measured by the area unemployment rate, was estimated directly. We investigated whether the effects of labor market conditions varied with education, age, occupation, and industry by interacting the area unemployment rate with these variables. Finally, we used the estimated effects of area unemployment rates to assess how much inequality in local labor market conditions due to differences in geographic location contributed to cross-sectional differences in unemployment rates among the groups, and the degree to which changes in local labor-market tightness contributed to the changes in minority and white unemployment rates over the 1990s business cycle.

The results of the study indicate that in the 1990s, as in the past, black men and women benefited more from tighter labor markets than did whites, both overall and when broken down by age and education level, industry, and occupation. Hispanic men benefited slightly more than white men overall, but this was because they were disproportionately at lower education levels. When compared within age groups, Hispanic male high school dropouts' and graduates' unemployment rates were no more sensitive to local labor-market tightness than those of white men, and Hispanic male college graduates' unemployment rates were less sensitive than white men's. Within industry, occupation, education, and age level, moreover, Hispanic men's unemployment rates were less sensitive to labor-market tightness than white men's. Among women, Hispanics also benefited more than whites—though less than blacks—from lower area unemployment rates. This held true across age groups for high school dropouts and graduates, but among college graduates, Hispanic women benefited no more than white women. Within industry, education, and age-level groupings, the relative responsiveness of Hispanic and white women's unemployment rates to labor market tightness varied by occupation.

Because the distributions of black and white local-area unemployment rates are so similar, virtually none of the difference between their unemployment rates can be explained by inter-city differences in labor-market tightness. However, over one-third of the Hispanic-white unemployment-rate gap for men, and one-fifth of the gap for women, can be attributed to differences in area unemployment rates. Over the business cycle of 1990 to 1996, changes in local labor-market tightness explain at least two-thirds of the actual changes in unemployment rates for black and white men in the recession and expansion, black women in the recession, and Hispanic women in the expansion. But changes in area unemployment rates in the 1990s can explain only half of the actual changes in unemployment rates for Hispanic men in the recession and expansion, black women in the expansion, and Hispanic women in the recession, and only one-third of the actual change for white women. During the expansion of 1992 to 1996, minority as well as white unemployment rates fell more than would be expected based on the increased average tightness of local labor markets alone.

(*Text continues on page 47.*)

Table 1.10 Slopes of Probit Model of Percentage Unemployed with Area Unemployment Rate Interacted with Recession Dummy (Percentage-Point Change)

			Males			
	Whites[a]		Blacks[b]		Hispanics	
X	dProb(U)/dX	std. err.	dProb(U)/dX	std. err.	dProb(U)/dX	std. err.
Area unemployment rate	0.62*	0.02	1.34*	0.09	0.73*	0.05
Area unemployment rate × 1990 to 1992	0.05*	0.01	0.09**	0.05	0.02	0.03
Mean area unemployment rate	5.93		5.99		7.37	
Sample size	608,052		59,074		58,154	
Log likelihood	–123936.63		–21885.39		–17903.88	
Observed percentage unemployed	5.25		12.33		9.37	
Predicted percentage unemployed at mean X	5.11		12.15		9.18	

(Table continues on page 34.)

Table 1.10 *Continued*

	Females					
	Whites[a]		Blacks[b]		Hispanics	
X	dProb(U)/dX	std. err.	dProb(U)/dX	std. err.	dProb(U)/dX	std. err.
Area unemployment rate	0.27*	0.03	0.85*	0.08	0.74*	0.06
Area unemployment rate × 1990 to 1992	−0.01	0.01	0.13*	0.04	−0.15*	0.04
Mean area unemployment rate	5.89		5.96		7.37	
Sample size	184,881		70,861		42,540	
Log likelihood	−27755.16		−24871.58		−13969.81	
Observed percentage unemployed	3.47		11.29		10.27	
Predicted percentage unemployed at mean X	3.43		11.20		10.12	

Source: Current Population Survey Monthly Outgoing Rotation Group files (weighted).
* Statistically significant at 5 percent level.
** Statistically significant at 10 percent level.
[a] This category refers to non-Hispanic whites.
[b] This category refers to non-Hispanic blacks.

Table 1.11 Slopes of Probit Model of Percentage Unemployed with Age and Education Dummies Interacted with Area Unemployment Rate, for Males (Percentage-Point Change)

X	Whites[a] dProb(U)/dX	std. err.	Blacks[b] dProb(U)/dX	std. err.	Hispanics dProb(U)/dX	std. err.
Predicted percentage unemployed at mean area unemployment rate, X = 0 (ed = twelve to fifteen, age = thirty-five to forty-four)	4.10		8.60		6.46	
ed = zero to eleven	3.29*	0.36	8.76*	1.71	1.46*	0.66
ed = sixteen+	-1.16*	0.17	-3.33*	1.04	-1.31	0.96
area unemployment rate	0.58*	0.03	1.36*	0.14	0.51*	0.08
× ed = zero to eleven area unemployment rate	0.12*	0.03	-0.05	0.16	0.16*	0.07
× ed = sixteen+ area unemployment rate	-0.17*	0.03	-0.35	0.23	-0.31*	0.14
age = sixteen to twenty-four	4.92*	0.45	16.39*	2.36	6.07*	1.25
age = twenty-five to thirty-four	0.91*	0.26	2.70*	1.42	0.45	0.81
age = forty-five to fifty-four	-0.27	0.25	-0.94	1.29	-0.59	0.91
age = fifty-five to sixty-four	-0.71*	0.27	-4.13*	1.19	2.41**	1.53
× age = sixteen to twenty-four area unemployment rate	0.00	0.04	-0.24	0.18	0.01	0.10
× age = twenty-five to thirty-four area unemployment rate	0.01	0.03	-0.07	0.18	0.01	0.09

(Table continues on page 36.)

Table 1.11 Continued

X	Whites[a]		Blacks[b]		Hispanics	
	dProb(U)/dX	std. err.	dProb(U)/dX	std. err.	dProb(U)/dX	std. err.
area unemployment rate × age = forty-five to fifty-four	−0.01	0.04	−0.32	0.21	0.02	0.12
area unemployment rate × age = fifty-five to sixty-four	0.04	0.05	−0.07	0.29	−0.28*	0.14
Mean area unemployment rate	5.93		5.99		7.37	
Sample size	608,052		59,074		58,154	
Log likelihood	−118348.54		−20270.00		−17423.99	
Observed percentage unemployed	5.25		12.33		9.37	
Predicted percentage unemployed at mean X	4.52		10.59		8.65	

Data source: Current Population Survey Monthly Outgoing Rotation Group files (weighted).
* Statistically significant at 5 percent level.
** Statistically significant at 10 percent level.
[a] This category refers to non-Hispanic whites.
[b] This category refers to non-Hispanic blacks.

Table 1.12 Slopes of Probit Model of Percentage Unemployed with Age and Education Dummies Interacted with Area Unemployment Rate, for Females (Percentage-Point Change)

X	Whites[a] dProb(U)/dX	std. err.	Blacks[b] dProb(U)/dX	std. err.	Hispanics dProb(U)/dX	std. err.
Predicted percentage unemployed at mean unemployment rate, X = 0 (ed = twelve to fifteen, age = thirty-five to forty-four)	3.21		7.60		6.63	
ed = zero to eleven	2.94*	0.68	10.62*	0.02	4.11*	0.96
ed = sixteen+	−0.59	0.34	−3.50*	0.01	−0.91	1.17
area unemployment rate	0.34*	0.05	0.94*	0.00	0.51*	0.10
area unemployment rate × ed = zero to eleven	−0.17*	0.06	−0.12	0.00	0.21*	0.08
× ed = sixteen+	−0.11**	0.06	−0.47*	0.00	−0.31**	0.17
age = sixteen to twenty-four	3.74*	0.75	14.15*	0.02	9.42*	1.72
age = twenty-five to thirty-four	0.45	0.44	5.97*	0.01	2.26*	1.10
age = forty-five to fifty-four	−0.45	0.40	−3.41*	0.01	−0.52	1.01
age = fifty-five to sixty-four	−1.54*	0.33	−4.59*	0.01	−1.25	1.22
area unemployment rate × age = sixteen to twenty-four	−0.12**	0.06	−0.04	0.00	−0.23*	0.12

(Table continues on page 38.)

Table 1.12 *Continued*

X	Whites[a] dProb(U)/dX	std. err.	Blacks[b] dProb(U)/dX	std. err.	Hispanics dProb(U)/dX	std. err.
area unemployment rate × age = twenty-five to thirty-four	0.01	0.06	−0.14	0.00	−0.11	0.11
area unemployment rate × age = forty-five to fifty-four	−0.06	0.07	0.08	0.00	−0.08	0.13
area unemployment rate × age = fifty-five to sixty-four	−0.02	0.08	0.02	0.00	−0.21	0.17
Mean area unemployment rate	5.89		5.96		7.37	
Sample size	184,881		70,861		42,540	
Log likelihood	−27042.45		−22667.67		−13410.41	
Observed percentage unemployed	3.47		11.29		10.27	
Predicted percentage unemployed at mean X	3.14		9.24		9.30	

Source: Current Population Survey Monthly Outgoing Rotation Group files (weighted).
* Statistically significant at 5 percent level.
** Statistically significant at 10 percent level.
[a] This category refers to non-Hispanic whites.
[b] This category refers to non-Hispanic blacks.

Table 1.13 Slopes of Probit Model of Percentage Unemployed with Age, Education, Industry, and Occupation Dummies Interacted with Area Unemployment Rate, for Males (Decimals)

X	Whites[a] dProb(U)/dX	Whites[a] std. err.	Blacks[b] dProb(U)/dX	Blacks[b] std. err.	Hispanics dProb(U)/dX	Hispanics std. err.
Predicted percentage unemployed at mean unemployment rate, X = 0 (ed = twelve to fifteen, age = thirty-five to forty-four, occ = op-lab, ind = trade)	0.0503		0.1055		0.0745	
age = sixteen to twenty-four	0.0523*	0.0104	0.1394*	0.0260	0.0441*	0.0129
age = twenty-five to thirty-four	0.0079	0.0061	0.0247	0.0162	0.0029	0.0089
age = forty-five to fifty-four	−0.0025	0.0059	−0.0086	0.0156	−0.0047	0.0106
age = fifty-five to sixty-four	−0.0036	0.0072	−0.0451*	0.0154	0.0349*	0.0180
area unemployment rate	0.0068*	0.0011	0.0175*	0.0028	0.0042*	0.0014
area unemployment rate × age = sixteen to twenty-four	−0.0011	0.0009	−0.0037	0.0024	−0.0003	0.0011
area unemployment rate × age = twenty-five to thirty-four	0.0003	0.0008	−0.0004	0.0021	0.0001	0.0011
area unemployment rate × age = forty-five to fifty-four	0.0002	0.0009	−0.0033	0.0025	0.0003	0.0013
area unemployment rate × age = fifty-five to sixty-four	0.0004	0.0011	−0.0004	0.0034	−0.0034*	0.0016
ed = zero to eleven	0.0049	0.0061	0.0523*	0.0178	0.0075	0.0076
ed = sixteen+	0.0054	0.0068	0.0026	0.0203	−0.0053	0.0141

(Table continues on page 40.)

Table 1.13 *Continued*

X	Whites[a] dProb(U)/dX	std. err.	Blacks[b] dProb(U)/dX	std. err.	Hispanics dProb(U)/dX	std. err.
area unemployment rate × ed = zero to eleven	0.0032*	0.0009	−0.0007	0.0021	0.0009	0.0009
area unemployment rate × ed = sixteen+ or more	−0.0018*	0.0009	−0.0063*	0.0030	−0.0026	0.0019
agriculture, forestry, fishing	0.0009	0.0207	−0.0163	0.0478	−0.0214	0.0189
construction, mining	0.0436*	0.0112	0.0487**	0.0280	0.0259**	0.0148
nondurable manufacturing	−0.0106	0.0083	−0.0432*	0.0150	−0.0324*	0.0094
durable manufacturing	−0.0113	0.0065	−0.0203	0.0178	−0.0124	0.0114
utilities	−0.0023	0.0089	−0.0265	0.0174	−0.0355*	0.0105
FIRE	−0.0116	0.0099	−0.0073	0.0321	0.0152	0.0255
business services	0.0147	0.0111	0.0620*	0.0272	0.0127	0.0151
personal services	−0.0249**	0.0098	0.0069	0.0326	−0.0160	0.0191
professional services	0.0088	0.0095	−0.0074	0.0195	−0.0009	0.0128
public administration	−0.0045	0.0104	−0.0267	0.0213	0.0075	0.0245
area unemployment rate × agriculture, forestry, fishing	−0.0015	0.0030	0.0036	0.0085	0.0057*	0.0029
area unemployment rate × construction, mining	0.0005	0.0011	0.0041	0.0033	0.0035*	0.0015
area unemployment rate × nondurable manufacturing	0.0004	0.0015	0.0056**	0.0034	0.0047*	0.0017
area unemployment rate × durable manufacturing	0.0025*	0.0012	0.0021	0.0031	0.0020	0.0016

area unemployment rate × utilities	−0.0011	0.0014	−0.0020	0.0032	0.0026	0.0020
area unemployment rate × FIRE	0.0012	0.0018	−0.0047	0.0050	−0.0037	0.0028
area unemployment rate × business services	−0.0004	0.0014	−0.0021	0.0031	0.0010	0.0017
area unemployment rate × personal services	0.0052*	0.0025	−0.0016	0.0048	0.0034	0.0029
area unemployment rate × professional services	−0.0012	0.0012	−0.0014	0.0031	−0.0007	0.0015
area unemployment rate × public administration	−0.0025	0.0017	0.0000	0.0040	−0.0042	0.0028
management	−0.0292*	0.0044	−0.0541*	0.0154	−0.0269**	0.0136
professional	−0.0315*	0.0049	−0.0553*	0.0172	−0.0339*	0.0120
technical	−0.0097	0.0104	−0.0608**	0.0219	−0.0302	0.0189
sales	−0.0083	0.0071	−0.0382**	0.0181	−0.0277*	0.0101
clerical	−0.0150**	0.0078	−0.0414*	0.0148	0.0410*	0.0220
service	0.0112	0.0097	0.0223	0.0187	−0.0263*	0.0087
farming, forestry, fishing	0.0037	0.0209	0.1307*	0.0751	0.0048	0.0244
craft	−0.0109*	0.0050	−0.0085	0.0154	−0.0199*	0.0075
area unemployment rate × management	−0.0004	0.0012	−0.0022	0.0038	−0.0021	0.0024
area unemployment rate × professional	0.0000	0.0015	0.0026	0.0044	0.0020	0.0023
area unemployment rate × technical	−0.0024	0.0018	0.0008	0.0064	−0.0008	0.0036

(Table continues on page 42.)

Table 1.13 *Continued*

X	Whites[a]		Blacks[b]		Hispanics	
	dProb(U)/dX	std. err.	dProb(U)/dX	std. err.	dProb(U)/dX	std. err.
area unemployment rate × sales	−0.0024*	0.0012	0.0015	0.0038	0.0010	0.0016
area unemployment rate × clerical	−0.0005	0.0015	0.0031	0.0032	−0.0049*	0.0020
area unemployment rate × service	−0.0022**	0.0013	−0.0036	0.0025	0.0020	0.0015
area unemployment rate × farming, forestry, fishing	−0.0011	0.0029	−0.0127**	0.0071	−0.0022	0.0027
area unemployment rate × craft	−0.0011	0.0009	−0.0042**	0.0025	0.0006	0.0012
Mean area unemployment rate	5.93		5.99		7.37	
Sample size	151,513		58,190		57,610	
Log likelihood	−28280.96		−18700.44		−16184.28	
Observed probability of unemployment	0.0502		0.1106		0.0859	
Predicted probability of unemployment at mean X	0.0417		0.0935		0.0780	

Source: Current Population Survey Monthly Outgoing Rotation Group files (weighted).
* Statistically significant at 5 percent level.
** Statistically significant at 10 percent level.
[a] This category refers to non-Hispanic whites.
[b] This category refers to non-Hispanic blacks.

Table 1.14 Slopes of Probit Model of Percentage Unemployed with Age, Education, Industry, and Occupation Dummies Interacted with Area Unemployment Rate, for Females (Decimals)

X	Whites[a]		Blacks[b]		Hispanics	
	dProb(U)/dX	std. err.	dProb(U)/dX	std. err.	dProb(U)/dX	std. err.
Predicted percentage unemployed at mean unemployment rate, X = 0 (ed = twelve to fifteen, age = thirty-five to forty-four, ind = trade, occ = op-lab)	0.0666		0.1444		0.0951	
age = sixteen to twenty-four	0.0471*	0.0121	0.1458*	0.0277	0.0725*	0.0195
age = twenty-five to thirty-four	0.0039	0.0078	0.0749*	0.0202	0.0258**	0.0143
age = forty-five to fifty-four	−0.0049	0.0080	−0.0567*	0.0154	−0.0099	0.0134
age = fifty-five to sixty-four	−0.0174**	0.0088	−0.0811*	0.0172	−0.0204	0.0161
area unemployment rate	0.0066*	0.0019	0.0210*	0.0047	0.0092*	0.0028
× age = sixteen to twenty-four area unemployment rate	−0.0031*	0.0013	−0.0039	0.0029	−0.0027	0.0017
× age = twenty-five to thirty-four area unemployment rate	0.0003	0.0011	−0.0021	0.0024	−0.0016	0.0015
× age = forty-five to fifty-four area unemployment rate	−0.0011	0.0013	0.0020	0.0032	−0.0001	0.0018
× age = fifty-five to sixty-four area unemployment rate	0.0002	0.0017	0.0024	0.0045	−0.0011	0.0023
ed = zero to eleven	0.0503*	0.0136	0.0899*	0.0240	0.0304*	0.0130
ed = sixteen+	0.0029	0.0090	−0.0281	0.0200	−0.0030	0.0207

(Table continues on page 44.)

Table 1.14 Continued

X	Whites[a]		Blacks[b]		Hispanics	
	dProb(U)/dX	std. err.	dProb(U)/dX	std. err.	dProb(U)/dX	std. err.
area unemployment rate × ed = zero to eleven	−0.0031*	0.0014	−0.0025	0.0028	−0.0003	0.0013
area unemployment rate × ed = sixteen+	−0.0024**	0.0014	−0.0068**	0.0035	−0.0024	0.0028
agriculture, forestry, fishing	0.0263	0.0379	0.2075	0.2220	−0.0461	0.0263
construction, mining	0.0344**	0.0241	−0.0042	0.0819	0.0187	0.0418
nondurable manufacturing	0.0047	0.0128	−0.0407	0.0261	−0.0001	0.0210
durable manufacturing	−0.0189	0.0106	−0.0129	0.0318	−0.0126	0.0214
utilities	0.0143	0.0176	−0.0651*	0.0246	0.0515	0.0402
FIRE	−0.0170	0.0099	−0.0651*	0.0197	−0.0388*	0.0148
business services	0.0274**	0.0163	0.1140*	0.0379	0.0427	0.0298
personal services	0.0203	0.0160	−0.0059	0.0276	−0.0074	0.0177
professional services	−0.0064	0.0079	−0.0211	0.0192	−0.0168	0.0133
public administration	0.0011	0.0163	−0.0593*	0.0213	−0.0548*	0.0161
area unemployment rate × agriculture, forestry, fishing	−0.0040	0.0042	−0.0222	0.0208	0.0048	0.0042
area unemployment rate × construction, mining	−0.0027	0.0027	0.0059	0.0123	0.0024	0.0047
area unemployment rate × nondurable manufacturing	−0.0008	0.0019	0.0004	0.0050	0.0028	0.0026

area unemployment rate × durable manufacturing	0.0040*	0.0021	−0.0033	0.0052	0.0029	0.0031
area unemployment rate × utilities	−0.0050*	0.0023	−0.0014	0.0055	−0.0076*	0.0039
area unemployment rate × FIRE	0.0004	0.0019	0.0017	0.0045	0.0024	0.0026
area unemployment rate × business services	−0.0010	0.0020	−0.0058	0.0042	−0.0005	0.0030
area unemployment rate × personal services	−0.0041*	0.0020	−0.0012	0.0044	−0.0011	0.0023
area unemployment rate × professional services	0.0022**	0.0013	−0.0065*	0.0033	−0.0020	0.0019
area unemployment rate × public administration	−0.0019	0.0024	0.0000	0.0047	0.0059	0.0037
management	−0.0402*	0.0071	−0.0829*	0.0202	−0.0300	0.0213
professional	−0.0379*	0.0081	−0.0549**	0.0261	−0.0105	0.0252
technical	−0.0415*	0.0101	−0.0247	0.0461	−0.0132	0.0307
sales	−0.0196**	0.0100	0.0052	0.0315	0.0096	0.0230
clerical	−0.0323*	0.0073	−0.0545*	0.0190	−0.0137	0.0179
service	−0.0294*	0.0081	0.0078	0.0274	0.0081	0.0202
farming, forestry, fishing	−0.0523*	0.0113	0.1063	0.1815	0.1814*	0.0846
craft	−0.0300*	0.0121	−0.1073*	0.0174	0.0005	0.0287
area unemployment rate × management	0.0021	0.0020	−0.0019	0.0055	−0.0023	0.0036
area unemployment rate × professional	0.0003	0.0023	−0.0041	0.0054	−0.0058**	0.0034
area unemployment rate × technical	0.0011	0.0033	−0.0114	0.0082	−0.0031	0.0041

(Table continues on page 46.)

Table 1.14 *Continued*

X	Whites[a] dProb(U)/dX	std. err.	Blacks[b] dProb(U)/dX	std. err.	Hispanics dProb(U)/dX	std. err.
area unemployment rate × sales	−0.0006	0.0019	−0.0055	0.0047	−0.0030	0.0028
area unemployment rate × clerical	0.0011	0.0017	0.0001	0.0039	−0.0038	0.0026
area unemployment rate × service	0.0028	0.0019	−0.0067	0.0041	−0.0028	0.0025
area unemployment rate × farming, forestry, fishing	0.0105**	0.0055	−0.0027	0.0191	−0.0036	0.0043
area unemployment rate × craft	0.0028	0.0030	0.0194*	0.0069	−0.0049	0.0038
Mean area unemployment rate	5.89		5.96		7.37	
Sample size	148,915		69,830		41,911	
Log likelihood	−23873.83		−20525.04		−11851.25	
Observed percentage unemployment	0.0394		0.0993		0.0886	
Predicted percentage unemployment at mean X	0.0352		0.0790		0.0782	

Source: Current Population Survey Monthly Outgoing Rotation Group files (weighted).
* Statistically significant at 5 percent level.
** Statistically significant at 10 percent level.
[a] This category refers to non-Hispanic whites.
[b] This category refers to non-Hispanic blacks.

The original version of this paper was prepared for a Russell Sage Foundation conference on the impact of tight labor markets on black employment, held on October 5, 1998, in New York City. The research was supported in part by PSC-CUNY Research Awards. The revision has benefited from comments by Gregory DeFreitas, Robert Cherry, William Rodgers, and an anonymous reviewer.

NOTES

1. Throughout this paper, *Hispanic* and *Latino*; *non-Hispanic black, black,* and *African American*; and *non-Hispanic white* and *white* are used interchangeably. Blacks and whites exclude Hispanics. Hispanics may be of any race.

2. Gilroy's "incremental ratio" is $(U_{b2} - U_{b1}) / (U_{w2} - U_{w1})$, where U is the unemployment rate, b denotes blacks, w denotes whites, and 1 and 2 denote two time periods.

3. The results of the alternative specification, which allows the effect of the area unemployment rate to vary between the periods 1990 to 1992 and 1993 to 1996, are available from the author upon request.

4. The numbers for white females are derived from a random sampling of 25 percent of all white females with nonmissing values because the large number of variables in the model made the X matrix too large to fit into computer memory.

5. This predicted rate ignores the effects of intergroup differences in education and age distribution, but not of geographic location as it affects the mean area unemployment rate. The use of group-specific mean area unemployment rates will not affect black-white comparisons because their mean area unemployment rates are almost identical, as shown in the last row of table 1.3. However, Hispanics' mean area unemployment rate is about 1.5 points higher than that of whites. If desired, a crude adjustment can be made by multiplying this difference (1.44 for men) by the effect of a one-percentage-point higher area unemployment rate for the reference category (0.51), and subtracting the result from the predicted unemployment rate for Hispanics (6.46 for men). This yields an adjusted predicted unemployment rate for Hispanic men of 5.73 at the white men's mean area unemployment rate. Because of the nonlinear nature of the probit function, this differs from the result that would be obtained if the whites' mean area unemployment rate were used in the predicted unemployment rate.

6. The samples for tables 1.13 and 1.14 are somewhat smaller than those used for the other tables due to the lack of industry and occupation values for persons who had not worked recently. The numbers for white males and females in these tables are calculated from a random sampling of 25 percent of those with nonmissing values, because the large number of variables in the model makes the X matrix for the entire white cohort too large to fit into computer memory.

7. This is the product of the change in mean area unemployment from 1992 to 1995 for Hispanic women in table 1.7 ($6.7 - 8.7 = -2.0$) and the partial derivative for 1993 through 1996 in table 1.2 (0.74), divided by the change in actual unemployment rate from table 1.1 ($9.6 - 11.2 = -1.6$). Hence, $(-2.0 \times .74)/-1.6 = .925$, or 92.5 percent.

REFERENCES

Abowd, John M., and Mark R. Killingsworth. 1984. "Do Minority/White Unemployment Differences Really Exist?" *Journal of Business and Economic Statistics* 2(1): 64–72.

Clark, Kim B., and Lawrence H. Summers. 1981. "Demographic Differences in Cyclical Employment Variation." *Journal of Human Resources* 16(1): 61–79.

DeFreitas, Gregory. 1986. "A Time-Series Analysis of Hispanic Unemployment." *Journal of Human Resources* 21(1): 24–43.

———. 1991. *Inequality at Work: Hispanics in the U.S. Labor Force.* New York: Oxford University Press.

Fairlie, Robert W., and Lori G. Kletzer. 1996. "Race and the Shifting Burden of Job Displacement from 1982 to 1993." *Monthly Labor Review* 119(9): 13–23.

———. 1997. "Jobs Lost, Jobs Regained: An Analysis of Black/White Differences in Job Displacement in the 1980s." *Industrial Relations* 37(4): 460–77.

Farber, Henry S. 1998. "The Changing Face of Job Loss in the United States, 1981–1995." In *Brookings Papers on Economic Activity: Microeconomics 1997,* edited by Martin Neil Baily, Peter C. Reiss, and Clifford Winston. Washington, D.C.: Brookings.

Gilroy, Curtis. 1974. "Black and White Unemployment: The Dynamics of the Differential." *Monthly Labor Review* 97(2): 38–47.

Hipple, Steven. 1997. "Worker Displacement in an Expanding Economy." *Monthly Labor Review* 120(12): 26–39.

Howe, Wayne J. 1988. "Do Education and Demographics Affect Unemployment Rates?" *Monthly Labor Review* 111(1): 3–9.

Kletzer, Lori G. 1991. "Job Displacement, 1979-86: How Blacks Fared Relative to Whites." *Monthly Labor Review* 114(7): 17–25.

Newman, Morris J. 1978. "A Profile of Hispanics in the U.S. Work Force." *Monthly Labor Review* 101(12): 3–14.

Oi, Walter. 1962. "Labor as a Quasi-Fixed Factor." *Journal of Political Economy* 70(4): 538–55.

Thurow, Lester C. 1969. *Poverty and Discrimination.* Washington, D.C.: Brookings Institution.

Chapter 2

AREA ECONOMIC CONDITIONS AND THE LABOR-MARKET OUTCOMES OF YOUNG MEN IN THE 1990S EXPANSION

RICHARD B. FREEMAN AND WILLIAM M. RODGERS III

The 1990s economic boom has made the American job market the envy of the world. The proportion of the adult population that is employed has increased to the highest level in history. Unemployment has fallen far below the 6 to 7 percent level that many economists and policy-makers believed was the "NAIRU"—nonaccelerating-inflation rate of unemployment. And while throughout much of the 1980s and 1990s, real wages of workers stagnated, in the late 1990s, real wages began to rise, and at least some workers in the bottom of the distribution saw their first gains in real earnings after years of decline (Mishel, Bernstein, and Schmidt 1998).

To what extent has the 1990s boom improved the labor-market outcomes of young, noncollege-educated men? How much has the boom helped young African American men, who are the most disadvantaged and socially troubled group in the United States?

Previous economic booms have raised employment of young men and often raised their earnings as well.[1] The 1990s, however, comprise a period during which the relationship between unemployment and other economic outcomes has surprised many analysts. Low rates of unemployment have generated smaller increases in wages than in previous economic booms. From the perspective of the aggregate economy, this is good news, because it has convinced monetary authorities to forgo anti-inflationary policies that would end or dampen the boom. But from the perspective of economic disparity and the well-being of young, low-paid, less-skilled workers, it could be bad news. For if the boom of the 1990s proves insufficient to improve substantially the position of young, noncollege-educated workers, it is difficult to imagine that any expansion could do so, and thus would dash any hope that economic growth per se could raise their pay and income.

This chapter examines the effect of the 1990s boom on young, noncollege-educated men. More specifically, we use variation in the level and change in joblessness across metropolitan areas to assess the contribution of local market conditions on the position of young, noncollege-educated men. Unemployment rates differ greatly and have changed differentially among areas, providing considerable variation in local economic conditions from which to assess the effect of market conditions on youth unemployment. Our analysis also allows us to simulate the gains that might occur at the national level should the jobless rate fall below 4 percent.

We find that young men in tight labor markets in the 1990s experienced a noticeable boost in employment and earnings, while older men had no such gains, even in metropolitan areas with unemployment rates below 4 percent. The earnings of youths, including disadvantaged African American youths, improved. Youths do particularly well in areas that started the boom with relatively lower jobless rates, suggesting that they would especially benefit from consistent full employment.

DATA

We utilized three data sources. The first of these sources are the Merged Outgoing Rotation Groups of the Current Population Survey for 1983, 1987, 1989, 1992, 1996, 1998, and the first half of 1999. These years cover the beginning and peak of the 1980s expansion (spanning 1983 to 1989) and six and a half years of the 1990s expansion (1992 through first half of 1999). Our youth sample included sixteen- to twenty-four-year-old men; our adults are defined as twenty-five- to sixty-four-year-old men. We excluded youths in school. In the first four cross sections, our samples are based on responses to the Employment Status Recode (ESR) variable; we dropped every individual whose major activity was in school. The unemployment rate is the ratio of the number of people looking for work to the sum of the number looking for work, the number working, and the number with a job but not working. The statistics for 1996 and 1999 are based on the monthly labor-force recode (MLR) variable. Unlike the ESR variable, which classified those temporarily laid off as employed, this recode classifies those on layoff as unemployed. The change has no impact on the estimates because the share of workers on layoff is typically less than 0.5 percent of the civilian population. The employment-population ratio is the ratio of the number of people working plus the number with a job but not working to the sum of those two numbers and the number of able workers out of the labor force.

We constructed the natural logarithm of real hourly earnings using the respondent's pay status: If the respondent reported that he is paid on an hourly basis, we took the logarithm of his hourly wage. If the respondent was paid on a weekly basis, we took the logarithm of the ratio of his usual weekly earnings and usual hours worked per week. We then adjusted nominal hourly wages for inflation using the using the CPI-UX-1 deflator.

The area unemployment rates come from our second and third sources: various editions of *Employment and Earnings* and *Geographic Profile of Employment and Unemployment*, both published by the Bureau of Labor Statistics. For 1983, "metropolitan" denotes standard metropolitan statistical areas (SMSAs), but for all other years, "metropolitan" encompasses metropolitan statistical areas (MSAs), primary metropolitan statistical areas, and consolidated metropolitan statistical areas. For the data published for 1983, we are able to identify only 44 areas. For the data published for 1987, 1989, and 1992, 212 areas can be identified. For 1996, 1998, and 1999, 332 areas are identifiable. In some calculations we categorize the areas by unemployment rates: below 4 percent, 4 to 5 percent, 5 to 6 percent, 6 to 7 percent, and greater than 7 percent.

AGGREGATE RELATIONS

Before presenting our area analysis, we review briefly the pattern of change in the aggregate national data that represents the phenomenon we want to explain. Figures 2.1, 2.2, and 2.3, as well as table 2.1, present unemployment rates, employment-population ratios, and hourly earnings for the expansions of the 1980s (1983 to 1989) and the 1990s (1992 to 1999). These data show the following:

• Substantial declines in unemployment in both recessions: the unemployment rate fell for African Americans at roughly the same rate as for all other population cohorts.

Figure 2.1 Unemployment Rates: Aggregate National and African Americans

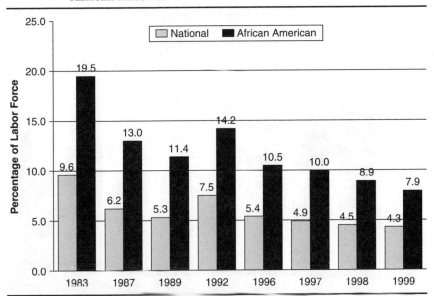

Source: United States Department of Labor, Bureau of Labor Statistics. The 1999 figures are the averages for January through August.

Figure 2.2 Employment Rates: Aggregate National and African Americans

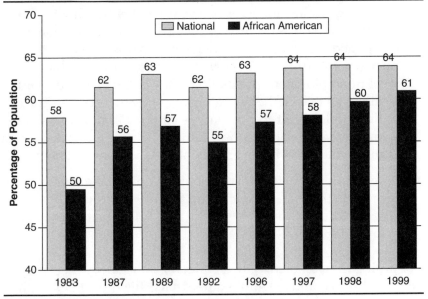

Source: United States Department of Labor, Bureau of Labor Statistics. The 1999 figures are the averages for January through August.

Figure 2.3 Average U.S. Real Hourly Earnings

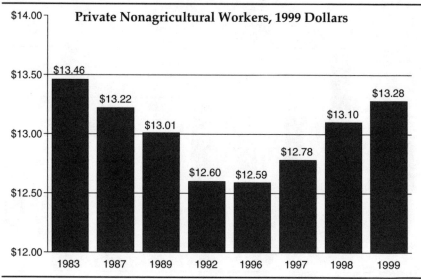

Source: United States Department of Labor, Bureau of Labor Statistics. The 1999 value is the average of the January-through-August values.

- A smaller absolute increase in the employment-population ratio (e-pop) in the 1990s expansion than in previous expansions. The e-pop increased by five percentage points from 1983 to 1989 and by two points from 1992 to 1999. This might be due to the higher level of employment-population rates at the beginning of the 1990s boom than at the beginning of the 1980s recovery. The rise in the employment-to-population ratio for African Americans was larger in absolute terms than for other Americans: seven points in the 1980s boom and six points in the 1990s boom.

- A very different pattern in real hourly earnings: real hourly earnings fell in the 1980s recovery and from 1992 through 1996, then rose in 1997, 1998, and 1999, as the unemployment rate dropped below 5 percent.

Turning from all men to the young, noncollege-educated men of concern to this study, we have used CPS files to calculate their employment and earnings during the periods 1983 to 1989 and 1992 to 1999. Figures 2.4 and 2.5 and table 2.2 show that in the 1980s,

Table 2.1 Selected Aggregate Summary Statistics of the U.S. Economy

All Men and Women

Year	Nominal Hourly Earnings	Real Hourly Earnings (1999 Dollars)
1983	8.02	13.46
1987	8.98	13.22
1989	9.66	13.01
1992	10.57	12.60
1996	11.82	12.59
1997	12.26	12.78
1998	12.77	13.10
1999	13.28	13.28

All Men and Women and All African Americans

	Unemployment Rate		Employment-to-Population Ratio	
Year	National	African American	National	African American
1983	9.6	19.5	57.9	49.5
1987	6.2	13.0	61.5	55.6
1989	5.3	11.4	63.0	56.9
1992	7.5	14.2	61.5	54.9
1996	5.4	10.5	63.2	57.4
1997	4.9	10.0	63.8	58.2
1998	4.5	8.9	64.1	59.7
1999	4.3	7.9	64.2	60.8

Source: Average nominal hourly earnings come from the *Economic Report of the President: February 1998*. To create average real hourly earnings, we deflate nominal hourly earnings using the CPI-U-X1, also from the *Economic Report of the President: February 1998*. The monthly values are seasonally adjusted. The unemployment rates and employment-population ratios for the 1980s, 1992, 1996, and 1997 come from the *Economic Report of the President 1998*. The unemployment rates and employment-population ratios for 1998 come from "Selective Access" (http://www.bls.gov).

employment rates among the noncollege-educated rose, but also that this group's earnings fell. From 1992 to 1996, the pattern is similar, though the increase in employment for the younger men is greater. From 1996 to 1999, however, the picture is different: the employment rate for all noncollege-educated men either ceases to grow or slows in growth, while hourly earnings begin to increase,

**Figure 2.4 Real Earnings of Noncollege-Educated Men,
by Race and Age, 1999 Dollars**

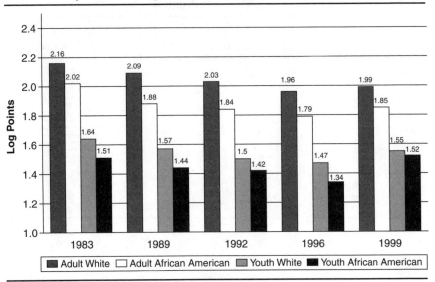

Source: Authors' calculations from Current Population Survey data.

**Figure 2.5 Employment Rates of Noncollege-Educated Men,
by Race and Age**

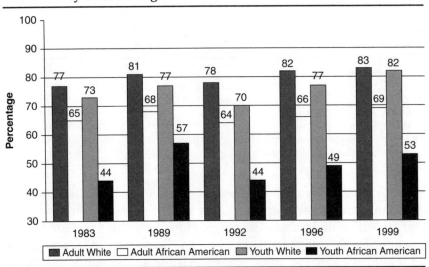

Source: Authors' calculations from Current Population Survey data.

and hourly earnings increase most markedly for young African American men.

The aggregate data thus suggest that the 1990s recovery showed up first in employment and then, as unemployment fell to extremely low levels, in wages. Still, these data do not vary enough to allow us to characterize the effect of the recovery to any greater extent. To determine further the effect of the boom on noncollege-educated young men, we turn to data on labor-market conditions and outcomes across local labor markets. For the 1990s, we have data for 332 local labor markets, reflecting a wide variety of unemployment experiences ranging from continuous low unemployment to slow and rapid reductions in unemployment. These data provide us with market conditions that go beyond the 1990s boom—rates of unemployment below 4 percent in many areas. They allow us to assess what might happen to young workers were the aggregate economy to produce even tighter labor-market conditions, and, in particular, to evaluate the effect of continued low unemployment (below 4 percent for six years of the expansion) on the labor-market outcomes of these workers.

Generalizing from patterns of change among areas to the nation as a whole requires some caution because there are adjustments that occur across geographic areas that do not occur nationally. In particular, migration across areas is a potentially important response to different area economic conditions, for migration is likely to ameliorate the effects of shocks on outcomes, as affected persons move from high- to low-unemployment locales. Still, Robert Topel (1986), David Blanchflower and Andrew Oswald (1999) and others find that local labor markets affect outcomes; in addition, the young noncollege-educated workers on whom we focus are less geographically mobile than others. Another important ameliorative effect is likely to occur through product markets. In industries where prices are set nationally, a booming local market will be unable to raise prices in response to increases in wages, which in turn should mean that low unemployment has a smaller impact on nominal wages than would be observed in a national boom. These and other factors differentiate the local labor-market dynamics during a boom from those in the entire economy, but do not gainsay the insight gained from analyzing local markets' responses to booms. In any case, area data are the only data available with sufficient observations to permit more than a description of events.

Table 2.2 Earnings and Employment Statistics for Less-Educated Men in the Current Population Survey, Selected Years

Logarithm of Real Hourly Earnings (1999 Dollars)

	Adults Twenty-Five to Sixty-Four			Youth Sixteen to Twenty-Four		
Year	Total	White	African American	Total	White	African American
1979	2.22	2.25	2.08	1.79	1.80	1.70
1983	2.14	2.16	2.02	1.62	1.64	1.51
1987	2.07	2.09	1.93	1.56	1.57	1.44
1989	2.06	2.09	1.88	1.55	1.57	1.44
1992	2.01	2.03	1.84	1.49	1.50	1.42
1996	1.94	1.96	1.79	1.46	1.47	1.34
1998	1.97	1.99	1.83	1.53	1.54	1.46
1999	1.98	1.99	1.85	1.55	1.55	1.52

Employment Rates

	Adults Twenty-Five to Sixty-Four			Youth Sixteen to Twenty-Four		
Year	Total	White	African American	Total	White	African American
1979	82	84	74	77	80	57
1983	75	77	65	68	73	44
1987	79	81	70	75	77	60
1989	79	81	68	74	77	57
1992	76	78	64	66	70	44
1996	80	82	66	72	77	49
1998	81	83	68	74	78	55
1999	82	83	69	78	82	53

Note: Figures are calculated from the Current Population Survey (CPS) annual merged files for 1983, 1987, 1989, 1992, 1996, and 1998. The values for 1999 come from outgoing rotation-group interviews from January to June. The statistics for the 1983, 1987, 1989, and 1992 cross sections are based on the Employer Status Recode (ESR) variable in the public-use CPS annual merged file. All respondents whose major activity is in school were dropped. Youths are sixteen to twenty-four-year-old African American and white males only who have completed no more than twelve years of schooling or received no more than a high school diploma or GED. Adults are twenty-five to sixty-four-year-old African American and white men. The unemployment rate is the ratio of the number of people looking for work to the sum of the number looking for work, the number working, and the number with a job but not working. The statistics for 1996, 1998, and 1999 are based on a

AREA VARIATION

Figure 2.6 and table 2.3 show the frequency distributions for the unemployment rates by state and metropolitan area that are the key variables in our analysis. Because the CPS identifies fewer metropolitan areas in 1983 than in later years, we report fewer rates of area unemployment for the 1980s boom. Most areas began the 1980s expansion with unemployment rates that exceeded 7 percent. By 1989, a sizable number had unemployment rates below 5 percent. Most areas began the 1990s boom with unemployment rates in the 6 to 7 percent or over 7 percent range. By 1996, more than ninety-eight metropolitan areas and seven states had unemployment rates below 4 percent. From January to July 1998, these figures jumped to 146 metropolitan areas and 21 states.

The first panel of table 2.4 shows the transition matrix of metropolitan areas for 1983 to 1989 and 1992 to 1999. In both periods, the matrix is nearly-triangular, with zeros in most cells below the diagonal, which reflects the fact that during the 1980s boom no area moved from a grouping with a lower unemployment rate to one with a higher unemployment rate. In the 1990s boom, just two areas had unemployment rates above 1992 levels by 1999. Fifty-three areas had unemployment rates in the same grouping, while the vast majority of areas saw a decline in unemployment. Of the 167 areas that had started with unemployment rates greater than 7 percent, 96 had now moved into either the less than 4 percent or 4 to 5 percent grouping.

The second panel displays the transition probabilities associated with the 1990s boom. The areas that started in the less than 4 percent group in 1992 remain in that group in 1999 with a very high probability. From 1992 to 1996, 65 percent of the areas with 1992 unem-

(*Text continues on page 63.*)

---

new variable called the monthly labor-force recode (MLR) and a school-enrollment variable. The ESR variable classified respondents on layoff as employed and those enrolled in school as being out of the labor force. The enrollment question is given only to sixteen to twenty-four-year-old respondents. The new MLR variable classifies workers on layoff as unemployed and does not factor in school enrollment. To maintain as much continuity as possible with previous surveys, we classified respondents on layoff as employed and used the school-enrollment information to determine whether the respondent's major activity was attending high school or college. If they were, then they were excluded from our sample.

Figure 2.6 Frequency Distributions of Metropolitan Area Unemployment Rates, by Year

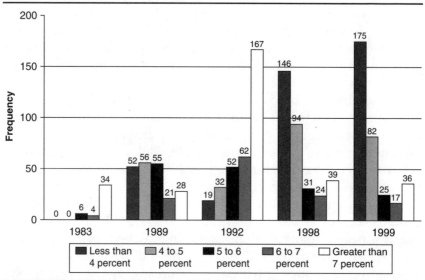

Source: Authors' tabulations from United States Department of Labor, Bureau of Labor Statistics data.

Table 2.3 Metropolitan Frequency Distributions of Unemployment Rates

Metropolitan	1983	1987	1989	1992	1996	1998
Less than 4 percent	0	39	52	19	98	146
4 to 5 percent	0	37	56	32	79	94
5 to 6 percent	6	46	55	52	69	31
6 to 7 percent	4	37	21	62	34	24
Greater than 7 percent	34	53	28	167	54	39

Note: Authors' tabulations from data taken from various editions of the United States Department of Labor, Bureau of Labor Statistics' *Employment and Earnings* and *Geographic Profile of Employment and Unemployment*. For the 1983 published data, "Metropolitan" denotes standard metropolitan statistical areas (SMSAs); we are able to identify only forty-four areas. In all other years, Metropolitan corresponds to metropolitan statistical areas (MSAs), primary metropolitan statistical areas, and consolidated metropolitan statistical areas. For the 1987, 1989, and 1992 published data, 212 areas can be identified. For the 1996, 1998, and 1999 published data, 334 areas are identifiable.

Table 2.4 Metropolitan Frequency Distributions of Unemployment Rates

Movement of Metropolitan-Area Unemployment Rates
During Economic Expansions

| | 1989 Unemployment Rate | | | | | |
1983 Rate	<4 Percent	4 to 5 Percent	5 to 6 Percent	6 to 7 Percent	>7 Percent	Total
Less than 4 percent	0	0	0	0	0	0
4 to 5 percent	0	0	0	0	0	0
5 to 6 percent	2	1	3	0	0	6
6 to 7 percent	2	1	1	0	0	4
Greater than 7 percent	8	14	9	1	2	34
Total	12	16	13	1	2	44

| | 1996 Unemployment Rate | | | | | |
1992 Rate	<4 Percent	4 to 5 Percent	5 to 6 Percent	6 to 7 Percent	>7 Percent	Total
Less than 4 percent	16	0	2	0	1	19
4 to 5 percent	27	4	1	0	0	32
5 to 6 percent	34	14	4	0	0	52
6 to 7 percent	12	37	7	5	1	62
Greater than 7 percent	9	23	54	29	52	167
Total	98	78	68	34	54	332

| | 1998 Unemployment Rate | | | | | |
1992 Rate	<4 Percent	4 to 5 Percent	5 to 6 Percent	6 to 7 Percent	>7 Percent	Total
Less than 4 percent	17	1	0	0	1	19
4 to 5 percent	30	2	0	0	0	32
5 to 6 percent	42	10	0	0	0	52
6 to 7 percent	29	28	5	0	0	62
Greater than 7 percent	28	52	25	24	38	167
Total	146	93	30	24	39	332

| | 1999 Unemployment Rate | | | | | |
1992 Rate	<4 Percent	4 to 5 Percent	5 to 6 Percent	6 to 7 Percent	>7 Percent	Total
Less than 4 percent	17	0	1	1	0	19
4 to 5 percent	32	0	0	0	0	32
5 to 6 percent	47	5	0	0	0	52
6 to 7 percent	40	18	3	1	0	62
Greater than 7 percent	38	58	20	15	36	167
Total	174	81	24	17	36	332

(*Table continues on page 62.*)

Table 2.4 *Continued*

| | Metropolitan-Area Transition Probabilities | | | | | |

| | 1996 Unemployment Rate | | | | | |
1992 Rate	<4 Percent	4 to 5 Percent	5 to 6 Percent	6 to 7 Percent	>7 Percent	Total
<4 percent	0.84	0.00	0.11	0.00	0.05	1.00
4 to 5 percent	0.84	0.13	0.03	0.00	0.00	1.00
5 to 6 percent	0.65	0.27	0.08	0.00	0.00	1.00
6 to 7 percent	0.19	0.60	0.11	0.08	0.02	1.00
>7 percent	0.05	0.14	0.32	0.17	0.31	1.00
Total	0.30	0.23	0.20	0.10	0.16	1.00

| | 1998 Unemployment Rate | | | | | |
1992 Rate	<4 Percent	4 to 5 Percent	5 to 6 Percent	6 to 7 Percent	>7 Percent	Total
<4 percent	0.89	0.05	0.00	0.00	0.05	1.00
4 to 5 percent	0.94	0.06	0.00	0.00	0.00	1.00
5 to 6 percent	0.81	0.19	0.00	0.00	0.00	1.00
6 to 7 percent	0.47	0.45	0.08	0.00	0.00	1.00
>7 percent	0.17	0.31	0.15	0.14	0.23	1.00
Total	0.44	0.28	0.09	0.07	0.12	1.00

| | 1999 Unemployment Rate | | | | | |
1992 Rate	<4 Percent	4 to 5 Percent	5 to 6 Percent	6 to 7 Percent	>7 Percent	Total
<4 percent	0.89	0.00	0.05	0.05	0.00	1.00
4 to 5 percent	1.00	0.00	0.00	0.00	0.00	1.00
5 to 6 percent	0.90	0.10	0.00	0.00	0.00	1.00
6 to 7 percent	0.65	0.29	0.05	0.02	0.00	1.00
>7 percent	0.23	0.35	0.12	0.09	0.22	1.00
Total	0.52	0.24	0.07	0.05	0.11	1.00

Note: Authors' tabulations from data taken from various editions of the United States Department of Labor, Bureau of Labor Statistics' *Employment and Earnings* and *Geographic Profile of Employment and Unemployment*. Each entry represents the probability of unemployment in 1996, 1998, or 1999 conditional on the 1992 unemployment rate.

ployment rates of 5 to 6 percent moved into the less than 4 percent category, 60 percent of the areas with 1992 levels of 6 to 7 percent moved into the 4 to 5 percent grouping, and 63 percent of the areas with unemployment rates over seven percent either moved into the 5 to 6 percent category or remained above 7 percent. By 1999, 90 percent of the areas with 1992 rates of 5 to 6 percent had moved into the less than 4 percent category, and 65 percent of the areas with 6 to 7 percent unemployment in 1992 had moved to the less than 4 percent category. For those areas with unemployment above 7 percent in 1992, almost 58 percent had moved to either the less than 4 percent or 4 to 5 percent category by 1999.

Overall, unemployment fell by about 3 percentage points between 1992 to 1999, but the table shows that the boom affected labor-market areas differently. As a simple way of examining the different experiences of various areas, we divide the areas into three categories: "continuous full employment," "steady high unemployment," and "rapid reductions in joblessness." The first category is characterized by unemployment rates below 4 percent in all years of the recovery, and includes fourteen metro areas. The twenty-eight areas in the second category registered unemployment rates above 7 percent in all years studied. The fifteen areas with "rapid reductions in joblessness" saw unemployment rates fall by more than 5 points. Other approaches exist, but for simplicity we focus on these cases. We created the groups on the basis of metropolitan area experiences from 1992 through 1998, but extending the period to include 1999 changes our grouping only modestly: the number of metropolitan areas with "continuous full employment" is unaffected, while seven areas are added to the "rapid reductions in joblessness," and three areas are dropped from the "steady high unemployment" category.

Figure 2.7 plots the annual average unemployment rate for the three groups. The average for areas with unemployment rates below 4 percent in all years was 3.2 percent in 1992 and fell to 2 percent in 1999. Table 2.5 shows the statistics for the areas that experienced continuous full employment. Concentrated in the middle of the country, these areas ranged from Texas up through midwestern metropolitan areas such as Des Moines and Iowa City, and east into the Research Triangle area of North Carolina. The jobless rates for the areas with continuous high unemployment (rates in excess of 7 percent) also fell, but the group average here remained

Figure 2.7 Area Unemployment by Type of Boom

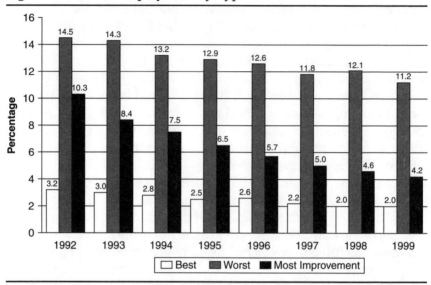

Source: United States Department of Labor, Bureau of Labor Statistics. Values correspond to the group's average unemployment rate in a given year.

**Table 2.5 The Top Metropolitan Areas During the 1990s Expansion
(Unemployment Less than 4 Percent, 1992 Through 1999)**

Area	1992	1993	1994	1995	1996	1997	1998	1999
Bryan, Tex.	2.9	2.7	2.7	3.0	2.5	2.2	1.8	1.8
Columbia, Mo.	2.5	3.2	2.0	1.9	1.7	1.6	1.7	1.2
Des Moines, Ia.	3.7	3.4	2.8	2.6	2.8	2.4	2.1	2.1
Fargo, N.D.-Minn.	3.6	3.1	2.7	2.6	2.5	1.8	1.5	1.8
Fayetteville, Ark.	3.7	2.9	2.5	2.4	2.9	3.1	3.4	2.7
Iowa City, Ia.	3.3	2.7	2.6	2.7	2.9	2.4	2.1	2.2
Lafayette, Ind.	3.8	3.4	3.5	3.1	2.8	2.4	2.3	2.4
Lincoln, Neb.	2.7	2.3	2.4	2.3	2.6	1.8	1.6	2.1
Madison, Wisc.	2.2	2.2	2.3	1.8	1.7	1.7	1.6	1.6
Omaha, Neb.-Ia.	3.6	3.1	3.2	2.8	3.0	2.5	2.1	2.4
Raleigh-Durham-
Chapel Hill, N.C.	3.8	3.1	2.7	2.6	2.4	2.0	1.9	1.5
Rapid City, S.D.	3.2	3.8	3.4	3.0	3.3	2.7	2.7	2.4
Rochester, Minn.	3.0	3.3	3.5	2.9	3.0	2.1	1.8	1.8
Sioux Falls, S.D.	2.4	2.5	2.4	2.0	2.1	1.8	1.7	1.6
Average	3.2	3.0	2.8	2.5	2.6	2.2	2.0	2.0

Source: United States Department of Labor, Bureau of Labor Statistics.

in double digits: it dropped from 14.5 percent to 11.2 percent. Table 2.6 shows that of the twenty-eight areas in this grouping, eleven are in California. Finally, areas with reductions in unemployment rates in excess of five percentage points started at an average of 10.3 percent unemployment in 1992 and fell to 4.2 percent in 1999. Almost half of these metropolitan areas are located in Massachusetts (see table 2.7).

Table 2.6 The Worst Metropolitan Areas During the 1990s Expansion (Unemployment Above 7 Percent, 1992 Through 1999)

Area	1992	1993	1994	1995	1996	1997	1998	1999
Atlantic City– Cape May, N.J.	11.1	10.4	9.9	9.6	9.4	8.6	9.5	8.8
Bakersfield, Calif.	15.5	15.8	14.7	13.8	12.7	11.8	12.6	13.0
Beaumont, Tex.	9.3	11.4	10.1	9.8	9.1	8.0	7.2	8.3
Brownsville, Tex.	14.7	13.5	12.8	12.6	12.6	12.5	12.7	10.9
Chico-Paradise, Calif.	11.7	11.9	10.2	10.0	9.0	8.7	9.2	7.8
Cumberland, Md.-W.V.	12.4	10.6	8.8	8.6	8.0	7.9	8.0	7.9
El Paso, Tex.	11.7	10.8	10.4	10.5	11.6	11.1	10.0	9.8
Fort Pierce, Fla.	13.9	11.9	12.4	10.7	10.2	9.2	8.3	7.0
Fresno, Calif.	15.9	15.5	14.0	14.3	13.2	13.5	14.8	15.4
Jersey City, N.J.	11.2	10.0	9.3	9.3	9.2	8.0	8.0	7.3
Laredo, Tex.	11.0	10.5	9.6	15.4	12.7	10.5	9.5	9.3
Las Cruces, N.M.	7.8	8.5	8.6	8.6	10.2	8.4	9.7	9.0
McAllen, Tex.	22.3	20.6	19.5	19.8	18.9	18.1	17.5	15.8
Merced, Calif.	16.5	17.1	15.6	16.9	16.2	15.2	17.1	15.8
Modesto, Calif.	16.5	16.7	15.7	15.3	14.1	13.1	13.4	12.6
New Bedford, Mass.	12.7	10.6	10.3	9.8	8.5	7.5	7.3	6.2
New York, N.Y.	10.2	9.6	8.1	7.6	8.0	8.4	7.6	6.5
Pine Bluff, Ark.	11.4	9.5	8.8	7.6	7.7	7.5	8.0	7.5
Redding, Calif.	13.2	12.6	11.9	11.3	9.9	9.1	10.0	8.7
Salinas, Calif.	12.4	12.9	12.1	12.5	11.1	10.7	12.2	12.3
Santa Cruz, Calif.	9.8	10.4	9.7	9.2	8.3	7.6	7.9	8.0
Stockton-Lodi, Calif.	14.0	14.0	12.6	12.3	11.2	10.7	11.5	10.3
Texarkana, Tex.-Ark.	9.0	8.6	9.2	7.9	7.4	7.4	7.5	5.6
Vineland, N.J.	12.1	11.3	10.5	9.7	9.9	8.9	10.0	8.9
Visalia, Calif.	16.6	17.9	16.0	16.6	15.9	15.3	16.1	18.7
Yakima, Wash.	13.8	14.6	11.8	12.7	13.6	10.2	10.6	11.4
Yuba City, Calif.	18.2	18.6	16.2	16.3	15.1	14.4	16.7	15.0
Yuma, Ariz.	26.5	27.6	31.5	28.2	30.5	26.7	25.3	23.7
Average	14.5	14.3	13.2	12.9	12.6	11.8	12.1	11.2

Source: United States Department of Labor, Bureau of Labor Statistics.

Table 2.7 The Metropolitan Areas with the Greatest Improvement During 1990s Expansion (Unemployment Decline at Least Five Percentage Points, 1992 Through 1999)

Area	Full Period, 1999 to 1992	Annual Changes						
		1993 to 1992	1994 to 1993	1995 to 1994	1996 to 1995	1997 to 1996	1998 to 1997	1999 to 1998
Brockton, Mass.	−7.53	−2.71	−1.47	−0.79	−0.76	−0.52	−0.60	−0.68
Lowell, Mass.	−7.06	−1.84	−1.49	−1.12	−1.45	−0.22	−0.49	−0.44
Pittsfield, Mass.	−6.61	−2.27	−0.46	−1.51	−1.45	−0.18	−0.32	−0.41
Houma, La.	−4.38	−1.79	−0.33	−1.07	−0.82	−1.16	−0.49	−1.29
Fort Pierce, Fla.	−6.97	−2.03	0.48	−1.68	−0.44	−1.01	−0.95	−1.34
Flint, Mich.	−6.36	−2.38	−1.62	−1.22	−0.50	−0.89	−0.99	−0.74
Jackson, Mich.	−5.62	−2.06	−1.18	−0.92	−0.36	−0.61	−0.49	−0.01
Detroit, Mich.	−5.52	−1.88	−1.54	−0.75	−0.54	−0.68	−0.06	−0.06
Naples, Fla.	−6.56	−1.12	−0.21	−1.19	−1.17	−0.60	−1.09	−1.18
New Bedford, Mass.	−6.46	−2.04	−0.32	−0.52	−1.24	−0.99	−0.24	−1.10
Lakeland, Fla.	−6.34	−1.14	−1.04	−1.50	−0.56	−0.23	−0.88	−0.99
Worcester, Mass.	−5.62	−2.11	−1.47	−0.28	−0.93	−0.37	−0.13	−0.32
Lawrence, Mass.	−5.33	−0.83	−1.45	−1.32	−0.54	−0.63	−0.42	−0.13
Fitchburg, Mass.	−5.30	−2.14	−0.45	−0.44	−0.85	−0.43	−0.86	−0.12
Manchester, N.H.	−5.01	−1.38	−1.54	−0.72	−0.30	−1.09	−0.08	−0.10
Average	−6.04	−1.85	−0.94	−1.00	−0.79	−0.64	−0.41	−0.41

Source: United States Department of Labor, Bureau of Labor Statistics.

THE RELATION OF UNEMPLOYMENT TO
EARNINGS AND EMPLOYMENT

How much do the employment and earnings of noncollege-educated men vary with local labor-market conditions. To answer this question, we compared the economic positions of men across metropolitan areas with different unemployment rates, using the merged Outgoing Rotation Groups of the Current Population Survey (CPS) and applying a logit model for our employment analysis. The dependent variable is a 0-1 dummy variable for whether the male is employed in a given year; the independent variables are the area unemployment rate and measures of demographic characteristics: age, years of schooling, and race. The variable for race is a dummy variable equaling 1 if the respondent is African American and 0 if the respondent is white. To estimate the wage effect, we regress the logarithm (natural log) of hourly earnings on the same variables used in the employment equations.

Tables 2.8 and 2.9 present our main results linking the employment and earnings of noncollege-educated young men to area unemployment rates and measures of crime, and comparative analyses for all men (males twenty-five to sixty-four years old). Although we have wage and employment information for 1998 and 1999, we do not have crime data for both years. Thus, the results in tables 2.8 and 2.9 are based on CPS samples that exclude the 1998 and 1999 data. We estimated models that excluded our measures of crime and included the 1998 and 1999 data, and obtained similar results. The column A regressions give results from cross-section regressions that exploit the differences among areas; the column B regressions give results from regressions that include metropolitan-area dummy variables and show how changes in unemployment in an area affect outcomes. We record both the estimated logit coefficients and their effect on the probabilities. The upper part of the table measures unemployment as a continuous variable, while the lower part divides unemployment rates into groups by unemployment rate (less than 4 percent, 4 to 5 percent, 5 to 6 percent, 6 to 7 percent, and greater than 7 percent), in an effort to find any nonlinearities.

Table 2.8 shows that area unemployment has a sizable effect on the employment of young noncollege-educated men, both in the cross-section and fixed-effects specifications. In all of the calculations, the coefficients on unemployment for young workers exceed

Table 2.8 The Effect of Area Unemployment Rates on the Probability of Employment

Item	All Youths				All Men			
	A		B		A		B	
	Coef.	dP/dX	Coef.	dP/dX	Coef.	dP/dX	Coef.	dP/dX
Unemploy-ment rate	−0.080	−0.016	−0.120	−0.024	−0.058	−0.010	−0.074	−0.012
	(0.007)	(0.001)	(0.015)	(0.003)	(0.004)	(0.001)	(0.008)	(0.001)
African American	−1.073	−0.216	−1.096	−0.220	−0.750	−0.126	−0.787	−0.133
	(0.037)	(0.007)	(0.040)	(0.008)	(0.020)	(0.003)	(0.022)	(0.004)
Crime per youth	0.061	0.012	−0.379	−0.076	−0.049	−0.008	−0.439	−0.074
	(0.070)	(0.014)	(0.180)	(0.036)	(0.035)	(0.006)	(0.090)	(0.015)
Log likelihood	−14875		−14585		−57756		−57179	
< 4 percent	0.545	0.110	0.530	0.107	0.461	0.078	0.419	0.071
	(0.049)	(0.010)	(0.081)	(0.016)	(0.025)	(0.004)	(0.041)	(0.007
4 to 5 percent	0.464	0.093	0.466	0.094	0.300	0.051	0.252	0.043
	(0.048)	(0.010)	(0.067)	(0.014)	(0.025)	(0.004)	(0.033)	(0.006
5 to 6 percent	0.267	0.054	0.298	0.060	0.237	0.040	0.214	0.036
	(0.043)	(0.009)	(0.058)	(0.012)	(0.022)	(0.004)	(0.029)	(0.005
6 to 7 percent	0.202	0.041	0.160	0.032	0.162	0.027	0.110	0.018
	(0.049)	(0.010)	(0.063)	(0.013)	(0.026)	(0.004)	(0.032)	(0.005
African American	−1.062	−0.214	−1.095	−0.220	−0.749	−0.126	−0.787	−0.133
	(0.037)	(0.007)	(0.040)	(0.008)	(0.020)	(0.003)	(0.022)	(0.004)
Crime per youth	0.083	0.017	−0.416	−0.084	−0.028	−0.005	−0.435	−0.073
	(0.070)	(0.014)	(0.181)	(0.036)	(0.036)	(0.006)	(0.091)	(0.015)
Log likelihood	−14,869		−14,589		−57,710		−57,172	

Note: Calculated from the United States Bureau of the Census Current Population Survey's Annual Merged Outgoing Rotation Group files, 1987, 1989, 1992, and 1996. The entries are logit coefficients, followed by the probability effect (logit coefficients multiplied by $p \times [1\text{-}p]$ where p is the share of the sample that is employed). All logit models include year dummy variables, age, age squared, years of schooling dummy variables, and a race dummy variable. Standard errors are in parentheses. Column A excludes Metropolitan Statistical Area (MSA) dummy variables. Column B includes

those for all men. For instance, the estimated effect of area unemployment on the probability of employment in the cross section is −0.016 for young men, versus −0.010 for all men. In the fixed-effects estimates in column B, the estimated coefficients for the effect of unemployment on the employment of youths (persons sixteen to twenty-four years old) are generally larger and diverge more from

African American Youths				African American Men			
A		B		A		B	
Coef.	dP/dX	Coef.	dP/dX	Coef.	dP/dX	Coef.	dP/dX
−0.141	−0.035	−0.130	−0.032	−0.085	−0.019	−0.052	−0.011
(0.020)	(0.005)	(0.038)	(0.010)	(0.010)	(0.002)	(0.019)	(0.004)
0.271	0.067	−0.272	−0.068	0.010	0.002	−0.656	−0.144
(0.138)	(0.034)	(0.315)	(0.078)	(0.066)	(0.014)	(0.152)	(0.033)
−2645		−2467		−10001		−9676	
0.811	0.202	0.148	0.148	0.564	0.123	0.095	0.095
(0.111)	(0.028)	(0.051)	(0.051)	(0.057)	(0.012)	(0.022)	(0.022)
0.625	0.155	0.110	0.110	0.310	0.068	0.030	0.030
(0.114)	(0.028)	(0.041)	(0.041)	(0.060)	(0.013)	(0.018)	(0.018)
0.350	0.087	0.095	0.095	0.282	0.062	0.038	0.038
(0.099)	(0.024)	(0.033)	(0.033)	(0.050)	(0.011)	(0.015)	(0.015)
0.352	0.087	0.054	0.054	0.309	0.068	0.042	0.042
(0.117)	(0.029)	(0.038)	(0.038)	(0.061)	(0.013)	(0.017)	(0.017)
0.242	0.060	−0.088	−0.088	−0.028	−0.006	−0.150	−0.150
(0.139)	(0.035)	(0.078)	(0.078)	(0.067)	(0.015)	(0.033)	(0.033)
−2,642		−2,468		−9,989		−9,669	

MSA dummy variables. Because the 1998 and 1999 crime rates are not available, we also estimated models in which we exclude crimes per youth and include the 1998 and first half of 1999 cross sections. The coefficients from the linear specifications that include the MSA dummy variables are −0.024 (0.002) for all youth, −0.011 (0.001) for all men, −0.016 (0.008) for African American youth, and −0.006 (0.003) for African American men. Standard errors are in parentheses.

those for adults than in the cross-section results. Within discrete local areas, changes in unemployment rates produce gains in employment for younger workers relative to older ones.

The largest logit coefficient is for African American youths (−0.130) and the next-largest is for all youths (−0.120). (Compare to −0.074 for all men and −0.052 for African American men.) Given the different

Table 2.9 Effect of Area Unemployment Rates on the Earnings of Men

Item	All Youths		All Men		African American Youths		African American Men	
	A	B	A	B	A	B	A	B
Unemployment rate	-0.017	-0.021	-0.004	-0.001	-0.018	-0.017	0.006	-0.002
	(0.001)	(0.003)	(0.001)	(0.002)	(0.004)	(0.009)	(0.003)	(0.005)
African American	-0.133	-0.142	-0.187	-0.198	0.000	0.000	0.000	0.000
	(0.008)	(0.009)	(0.005)	(0.005)	(0.000)	(0.000)	(0.000)	(0.000)
Crime per youth	-0.020	-0.128	-0.035	-0.075	0.067	-0.218	0.012	-0.043
	(0.013)	(0.032)	(0.008)	(0.020)	(0.030)	(0.066)	(0.017)	(0.038)
R^2	0.203	0.198	0.147	0.147	0.153	0.117	0.090	0.087
Less than 4 percent	0.115	0.107	0.000	0.022	0.098	0.053	-0.034	0.006
	(0.009)	(0.014)	(0.005)	(0.009)	(0.025)	(0.045)	(0.015)	(0.025)
4 to 5 percent	0.061	0.072	-0.005	0.010	0.067	0.051	-0.021	0.014
	(0.009)	(0.012)	(0.005)	(0.007)	(0.026)	(0.037)	(0.016)	(0.021)

	A	B	A	B	A	B	A	B
5 to 6 percent	0.043	0.063	-0.016	0.010	0.035	0.033	-0.061	-0.005
	(0.008)	(0.011)	(0.005)	(0.006)	(0.024)	(0.031)	(0.013)	(0.017)
6 to 7 percent	0.003	0.027	-0.022	0.009	0.021	0.061	-0.041	0.032
	(0.009)	(0.012)	(0.006)	(0.007)	(0.028)	(0.035)	(0.016)	(0.019)
African American	-0.132	-0.142	-0.185	-0.198	0.000	0.000	0.000	0.000
	(0.008)	(0.009)	(0.005)	(0.005)	(0.000)	(0.000)	(0.000)	(0.000)
Crime per youth	-0.010	-0.129	-0.041	-0.070	0.064	-0.235	0.015	-0.047
	(0.013)	(0.032)	(0.008)	(0.020)	(0.030)	(0.065)	(0.017)	(0.038)
R^2	0.204	0.200	0.147	0.146	0.154	0.112	0.091	0.087
Sample size	18,769		77,065		2,116		9,910	

Notes: Calculated from the United States Bureau of the Census Current Population Survey Annual Merged Outgoing Rotation Group files, 1987, 1989, 1992, and 1996. All regressions include year dummy variables, age, age squared, years of schooling dummy variables, and a race dummy variable. Standard errors are in parentheses. Column A excludes Metropolitan Statistical Area (MSA) dummy variables. Column B includes MSA dummy variables. Because the 1998 crime rates were not available, we also estimated models in which we excluded crimes per youth and included the 1998 cross section. The coefficients from the linear specifications that include the MSA dummy variables are −0.025 (0.002) for all youth, −0.003 (0.002) for all men, −0.031 (0.007) for African American youth, and −0.005 (0.004) for African American men. Standard errors are in parentheses.

levels of employment for the groups, these figures translate into larger gains in the probability of employment for younger African American youths than all youths and similar gains in the probability of employment for older African American men and older white men. In table 2.8's bottom-panel calculations in which we record coefficients on dummy variables for particular levels of unemployment, there is relatively little evidence of any nonlinearities. These results do not change when the crime measures are excluded and the 1998 and 1999 cross sections are added.

Table 2.9 records the estimated effects of unemployment on the natural logarithm of hourly earnings, or the "wage curve" (Blanchflower and Oswald 1999). Here, we find a striking difference between the results for young and older men. In both the cross-section and fixed-effects analysis, unemployment has a strong effect on the hourly pay of young men but has no effect on the hourly earnings of twenty-five- to sixty-four-year-old men. Unemployment has slightly less impact on the earnings of young African American men than it does on those of young white men (in contrast to Freeman [1990], who found a higher effect on young African Americans for the 1983 to 1987 period). However, this result appears to stem from the fact that young African American men tend to live in areas where wages have taken longer to rise. When we add the 1998 and 1999 cross sections, the unemployment coefficient for African American youth jumps from −0.017 to −0.031, while the unemployment coefficient for all youth increases from −0.021 to −0.025. The gains for African American youth occur in the less than 4 percent, 4 to 5 percent, and 5 to 6 percent categories. Indeed, the coefficients shown in table 2.9 all increase by about 0.03 point when the 1998 and 1999 cross sections are added, which implies that the effect of the boom on earnings increased substantially in the 1996 to 1999 period. One reason may be that it takes time for the boom to raise demand and eventually the pay for African American youths.

Turning to the bottom part of the table, we find some evidence of nonlinear effects of unemployment on the log earnings of young workers. In areas with unemployment below 4 percent, the fixed-effects estimates (column B) show that the earnings of young, noncollege-educated men are 0.107 point higher, whereas they are just 0.022 point higher for all noncollege-educated men. The coefficients on areas with 4 to 5 percent unemployment and areas with less than 4 percent unemployment differ by 0.040 point for the young men, but by only 0.012 point for all men. The implication is that very tight labor markets might improve the earnings of young, noncollege-educated workers without creating overall wage inflation.

Finally, in table 2.10 we examine the time pattern of the effect of unemployment on employment and earnings in greater depth by including the unemployment rate at the beginning of the boom—the trough unemployment—to the regressions for earnings and employment. The first panel shows the effect of area unemployment on employment, including the trough unemployment rate. The second panel shows the effect of area unemployment on earnings, including the trough unemployment rate. The trough unemployment rate substantially magnifies the estimated impact of a tight market on youth employment and earnings and increases the differential effect of the labor market on youths as opposed to adults. At the same level of unemployment, a higher trough-unemployment rate implies lower employment and earnings for youths, whereas it has only a modest effect for adults. One interpretation is that this is a kind of hystersis, where the past has an independent effect on young workers, perhaps because it impacts the school-to-work transition. A dynamic adjustment process, with some lags, may determine the wages and employment of youths, so that focusing solely on the current year's area unemployment as the key independent variable in the analysis is incorrect. Perhaps a Phillips curve type of specification is more appropriate than the standard wage curve (Blanchard and Katz 1999).

To examine the pattern of change in employment and wages across areas with different unemployment histories during the boom, we have tabulated in table 2.11 the outcome variables for noncollege-educated men in the three area categories that we specified earlier: continuous-full-employment areas (jobless rates below 4 percent in all years), steady high-unemployment areas (jobless rates exceeding 7 percent in all years), and rapid-improvement areas (jobless rates fell by at least five percentage points). We did not use the first half of 1999 as the end point because disaggregating the data by type of expansion, age, and race generated samples that were not large enough to render reliable estimates.

On the employment side, what is striking is the sizable increase in employment for young workers relative to older workers in the tightest labor markets and labor markets with the biggest declines

Table 2.10 The Effect of Current and Past Unemployment on Earnings and the Probability of Employment

Panel A: Employment

| | Young Adults | | | | All Men | | | |
| | A | | B | | A | | B | |
Item	Coef.	DP/dX	Coef.	dP/dX	Coef.	dP/dX	Coef.	dP/dX
Unemployment rate (1989, 1996)	−0.041	−0.007	−0.047	−0.008	0.007	0.001	−0.092	−0.014
	(0.022)	(0.004)	(0.046)	(0.008)	(0.011)	(0.002)	(0.023)	(0.003)
Trough unemployment rate (1983, 1992)	−0.045	−0.007	−0.096	−0.016	−0.051	−0.008	0.013	0.002
	(0.018)	(0.003)	(0.040)	(0.007)	(0.010)	(0.001)	(0.019)	(0.003)
African American	−0.980	−0.164	−1.008	−0.168	−0.778	−0.116	−0.781	−0.117
	(0.065)	(0.011)	(0.071)	(0.012)	(0.034)	(0.005)	(0.036)	(0.005)
Crime per youth	−0.044	−0.007	−0.437	−0.073	−0.022	−0.003	−0.605	−0.091
	(0.133)	(0.022)	(0.290)	(0.048)	(0.061)	(0.009)	(0.140)	(0.021)
Log likelihood	−4,332		−4,179		−19,119		−18,858	

Panel B: Earnings

| | Young Adults | | All Men | | Young African American Men | | African American Men | |
Item	A	B	A	B	A	B	A	B
Unemployment rate (1989, 1996)	−0.011	−0.021	−0.021	−0.011	−0.012	−0.020	−0.023	−0.016
	(0.004)	(0.007)	(0.002)	(0.005)	(0.011)	(0.020)	(0.007)	(0.013)
Trough unemployment rate (1983, 1992)	−0.011	−0.032	0.011	−0.007	−0.003	−0.017	0.020	0.003
	(0.003)	(0.006)	(0.002)	(0.004)	(0.008)	(0.017)	(0.005)	(0.011)
African American	−0.154	−0.163	−0.162	−0.172				
	(0.013)	(0.014)	(0.008)	(0.008)				
Crime per youth	−0.028	−0.016	−0.055	−0.032	0.055	−0.012	0.037	0.016
	(0.022)	(0.047)	(0.014)	(0.030)	(0.038)	(0.074)	(0.025)	(0.048)
R^2	0.210	0.188	0.173	0.168	0.209	0.189	0.123	0.117
Sample size	5,796	5,796	22,562	22,562	764	764	3,388	3,388

Young African American Men				African American Men			
A		B		A		B	
Coef.	dP/dX	Coef.	dP/dX	Coef.	dP/dX	Coef.	dP/dX
−0.130	−0.029	−0.069	−0.016	−0.004	−0.001	−0.103	−0.021
(0.055)	(0.013)	(0.097)	(0.022)	(0.028)	(0.006)	(0.053)	(0.011)
−0.070	−0.016	−0.154	−0.035	−0.080	−0.016	0.046	0.009
(0.040)	(0.009)	(0.083)	(0.019)	(0.021)	(0.004)	(0.047)	(0.009)
0.123	0.028	−0.621	−0.141	−0.141	−0.029	−0.816	−0.166
(0.234)	(0.053)	(0.462)	(0.105)	(0.097)	(0.020)	(0.195)	(0.040)
−932		−830		−3,827		−3,663	

Note: Panel A calculated from the United States Bureau of the Census Current Population Survey Annual Merged Outgoing Rotation Group files, 1989 and 1996. The entries are logit coefficients, followed by the probability effect (logit coefficients multiplied by $p \times [1-p]$; where p is the share of the sample that are employed). All logit models include variables for age, age squared, years of schooling, and race. Unemployment rate refers to the 1996 and 1989 rates, while trough unemployment rate refers to the 1983 and 1992 rates. Column A excludes MSA dummy variables. Column B includes MSA dummy variables. Standard errors are in parentheses. Panel B calculated from the United States Bureau of the Census Current Population Survey Annual Merged files, 1989 and 1996. All regressions include variables for age, age squared, years of schooling, and race. Unemployment rate refers to the 1996 and 1989 rates, while trough unemployment rate refers to the 1983 and 1992 rates. Column A excludes Metropolitan Statistical Area (MSA) dummy variables. Column B includes MSA dummy variables. Standard errors are in parentheses.

Table 2.11 Mean Employment Rates and Log Hourly Earnings by Type of Expansion

	Continuous Full Employment		Steady High Unemployment		Rapid Declines in Joblessness	
	Employment	LnWage	Employment	LnWage	Employment	LnWage
All youth						
1992	70	1.48	56	1.49	63	1.50
1998	80	1.58	61	1.46	72	1.59
Change	10	0.10	5	-0.03	9	0.09
All men						
1992	81	1.97	70	1.98	75	2.11
1998	85	1.99	76	1.86	80	2.07
Change	4	0.02	6	-0.12	5	-0.04
African American youth						
1992	52	1.42	34	1.58	42	1.38
1998	64	1.53	53	1.53	51	1.53
Change	12	0.11	19	-0.05	9	0.15
All African American men						
1992	70	1.75	65	1.90	61	2.02
1998	72	1.82	64	1.85	61	1.96
Change	2	0.07	-1	-0.05	0	-0.06

Note: LnWage corresponds to the average of the logarithm of hourly earnings.
Continuous Full Employment: Sample of respondents who reside in metropolitan areas in which the unemployment rate was below 4 percent in every year from 1992 to 1998.
Steady High Unemployment: Sample of respondents who reside in metropolitan areas in which the unemployment rate exceeded 7 percent in every year from 1992 to 1998.
Rapid Declines in Joblessness: Sample of respondents who resided in metropolitan areas in which the unemployment rate fell by at least five percentage points from 1992 to 1998.

in unemployment. The data for all youths, when measured in percentages and given their different starting points, show roughly similar gains in employment across the areas. From 1992 to 1998, the gains are ten points in the continuous-full-employment areas, five points in the high-unemployment areas, and nine points in the rapidly improving areas. Across the three types of labor markets, all men experienced roughly similar gains in employment, but relative to the gains of young workers they are quite modest.

By 1998, the young, noncollege-educated in the continuous-full-employment areas have employment rates that actually exceed the employment rates for the older, less-educated men in the continuous-high-unemployment areas. All youths in these areas have roughly 80 percent employment rates! The increases in employment rates for young, noncollege-educated African American men, which are largest in labor markets with continuous full employment, close a substantial portion of the gap between them and similarly educated young white men. The implication is that an extended boom can go a long way toward resolving the African American youth employment problem.

The pattern of change in earnings across areas tells a similar story: larger gains for the young, noncollege-educated men than for older, noncollege-educated men, though here young African Americans do no better than other noncollege-educated men. One possible reason for the absence of any particular wage effect in the continuous-high-employment areas is that initially, in 1992, the wages of young, noncollege-educated African American men were only modestly less than those of young, noncollege-educated men overall in the same areas (see table 2.11). This may be due to the minimum wage, which compresses wages at the bottom of the earnings distribution.

All told, table 2.11 suggests that the economic boom of the 1990s substantially improved the job market for noncollege-educated young men, including young African Americans, and that continuous full employment has the potential to create full employment and rising wages for these workers. By contrast, the benefits of a sustained boom for all noncollege-educated men are less dramatic.

ARE THE WAGE GAINS DUE TO FULL EMPLOYMENT OR HIKES IN THE MINIMUM WAGE?

In 1996, the federal minimum wage increased from $4.25 to $4.75 per hour. In 1997, it rose to $5.15. As these changes undoubtedly affected the wages of noncollege-educated workers, they are a confounding factor in the estimates of the effect of area unemployment on earnings. One possibility is that at any given unemployment rate, earnings in areas where the minimum wage had greater impact will be higher for young, noncollege-educated men than in areas where the minimum wage had a smaller impact. However, employment in areas where the minimum wage had greater impact might be lower for young, noncollege-educated men than in areas where the minimum wage had a smaller impact. Our estimates of area effects will be biased if a correlation exists between the minimum wage and the level or change in area unemployment. However, we shall show that accounting for this omission does not change our previous results.

Table 2.12 presents tests of whether the federal-minimum-wage hikes in 1996 and 1997 biased our estimates of the relationship between area unemployment and the employment and earnings of men. For this analysis we sorted the CPS sample into two groups. The first consists of respondents who live in states where the federal-minimum-wage increases of 1996 and 1997 were binding—that is, areas where the federal minimum exceeded the state's minimum wage or the state did not have its own minimum. The second group is composed of respondents who live in states where the federal-minimum-wage increases were not binding because the state's minimum remained at or above the federal minimum wage. Table 2.13 displays the federal and state minimum wages and the ratios used to create the groups.

To model the impact, we added two variables to our earlier models: a dummy variable equaling 1 if the respondent lived in a state where the increases were binding or 0 if the respondent lived in a state where they were not binding, and interaction between the binding dummy variable and the area unemployment rate. It is the coefficient on the interaction term that is most relevant to our analysis. The results in table 2.12 suggest that the minimum-wage hikes of 1996 and 1997 do not bias our results. The interaction terms are basically zero in both the employment and earnings equations. The coefficient on the binding dummy is nonzero but generally statistically insignificant, with no distinct pattern.[2]

CONCLUSION

The United States economy has experienced nine expansions since World War II.[3] The current expansion, which started in March 1991 and continues as of this writing in late 1999, has surpassed in duration the previous longest peacetime boom that had occurred from November 1982 to July 1990. In the current period, the national unemployment rate started at 6.8 percent and as of October 1999 stood at 4.1 percent. The unemployment rates in many metropolitan areas are well below 4 percent: during the first half of 1999, for example, 52 percent of metropolitan unemployment rates were below 4 percent, indicating that just over half of the United States was enjoying extremely tight labor markets.

What differentiates the 1990s boom from past booms? Why have the least-skilled workers seen real wage gains? The boom's combination of extremely tight labor markets and low inflation is the answer. The NAIRU—the rate of employment that does not accelerate inflation—has seemingly shifted: low rates of unemployment have not generated the same inflationary pressures that they had in previous booms. This downward shift has resulted in the real gains that many Americans have experienced during the 1990s boom.

During the first fifty-six months of the 1980s boom, both the nominal hourly wage and inflation grew at monthly rates of approximately 0.25 percent. During the first fifty-six months of the 1990s boom, the nominal wage and inflation grew monthly at approximately 0.23 percent. After the fifty-sixth month of each boom, when labor markets became their tightest, the nominal hourly wage grew at a rate of 0.31 percent. Meanwhile, inflation during the 1980s boom jumped to 0.38 percent, but fell to 0.18 percent in the 1990s boom. Many economists and policy analysts have speculated about the reason for the lower inflation during the 1990s boom and suggest a variety of reasons ranging from increased foreign competition in product markets and the recessions experienced by many of the United States' trade partners to unmeasured technological improvements to the growth of temporary-help agencies to . . . you name it.

In this chapter, we took the macroeconomic features of the 1990s boom as given and examined how the boom affected the absolute and relative positions of young, noncollege-educated men. We focused exclusively on these men because they are among the most vulnerable to changes in the macroeconomy and have suffered serious economic losses over the preceding two or three decades. If the boom's extremely low, and continuously low, jobless rates were insufficient

(*Text continues on page 84.*)

Table 2.12 Do the Minimum Wage Hikes of the 1990s Contribute to Gains? (Dependent Variables: Probability of Employment and Logarithm of Hourly Earnings)

	Young Adults		Adult Men		African American Young Men		All African American Men	
	A	B	A	B	A	B	A	B
Employment logit coefficients								
Binding	0.191	-0.099	0.217	0.185	0.249	0.435	0.046	0.212
	(0.072)	(0.164)	(0.036)	(0.080)	(0.193)	(0.384)	(0.094)	(0.188)
Binding × unemployment rate	-0.043	0.023	-0.035	-0.014	-0.046	0.017	-0.002	0.013
	(0.011)	(0.020)	(0.006)	(0.010)	(0.033)	(0.047)	(0.016)	(0.023)
Unemployment rate	-0.056	-0.134	-0.038	-0.066	-0.106	-0.121	-0.076	-0.054
	(0.008)	(0.016)	(0.004)	(0.008)	(0.025)	(0.044)	(0.012)	(0.021)
African American	-1.011	-1.047	-0.762	-0.803				
	(0.035)	(0.038)	(0.019)	(0.020)				
Log likelihood	-16,274	-15,995	-66,544	-65,955	-2,997	-2,809	-11,724	-11,377
Sample size	33,110		150,923		4,937		20,415	
DP/dx (partial derivatives)								
Binding	0.035	-0.018	0.034	0.029	0.060	0.104	0.010	0.045
	(0.013)	(0.030)	(0.006)	(0.013)	(0.046)	(0.092)	(0.020)	(0.040)
Binding × unemployment rate	-0.008	0.004	-0.005	-0.002	-0.011	0.004	0.000	0.003
	(0.002)	(0.004)	(0.001)	(0.002)	(0.008)	(0.011)	(0.003)	(0.005)
Unemployment rate	-0.010	-0.024	-0.006	-0.010	-0.025	-0.029	-0.016	-0.011
	(0.001)	(0.003)	(0.001)	(0.001)	(0.006)	(0.011)	(0.002)	(0.004)
African American	-0.184	-0.191	-0.120	-0.127				
	(0.006)	(0.007)	(0.003)	(0.003)				

Dep. var. mean								
Binding	0.75		0.80		0.58		0.70	
Nonbinding	0.77		0.80		0.61		0.70	
Earnings item								
Binding	0.002	-0.013	0.018	0.033	-0.091	-0.215	-0.116	-0.039
	(0.012)	(0.027)	(0.008)	(0.016)	(0.039)	(0.083)	(0.024)	(0.044)
Binding × unemployment rate	-0.005	0.002	0.001	0.001	0.017	0.016	0.028	0.008
	(0.002)	(0.003)	(0.001)	(0.002)	(0.007)	(0.010)	(0.004)	(0.006)
Unemployment rate	-0.015	-0.025	-0.006	-0.002	-0.026	-0.040	-0.011	-0.008
	(0.001)	(0.003)	(0.001)	(0.002)	(0.005)	(0.009)	(0.003)	(0.005)
African American	-0.131	-0.142	-0.184	-0.194				
	(0.007)	(0.008)	(0.004)	(0.005)				
R2	0.196	0.193	0.149	0.148	0.134	0.105	0.092	0.087
Dep. var. mean								
Binding	1.151		2.03		1.43		1.89	
Nonbinding	1.54		1.99		1.43		1.84	
Sample size	21,677		86,813		2,438		11,259	

Note: For detailed descriptions of specifications, see tables 2.8 and 2.9. These models sort the respondents by whether they resided in a state where the increased federal minimum wage exceeds the state's minimum wage. We create a dummy variable (binding) that equals 1 if the ratio of the state's minimum wage to the federal minimum wage is less than 1.0 in 1997 and 1998, or less than 1.0 in either year. The dummy variable equals 0 if the ratio is greater than or equal to 1.0 in 1997 and 1998.

Table 2.13 Federal and State Minimum Wages (Dollars Per Hour)

| | 1996 | | 1997 | | 1998 | | State-to-Federal Ratio | | |
	Federal	State	Federal	State	Federal	State	1996	1997	1998
Alabama	4.25	.	4.75	.	5.15	.	.	.	.
Alaska	4.25	4.75	4.75	5.25	5.15	5.65	1.12	1.11	1.10
Arizona	4.25	.	4.75	.	5.15	.	.	.	.
Arkansas	4.25	4.25	4.75	4.25	5.15	5.15	1.00	0.89	1.00
California	4.25	4.25	4.75	4.75	5.15	5.15	1.00	1.00	1.00
Colorado	4.25	3.00	4.75	4.75	5.15	5.15	0.71	1.00	1.00
Connecticut	4.25	4.27	4.75	4.77	5.15	5.18	1.00	1.00	1.01
Delaware	4.25	4.65	4.75	5.00	5.15	5.15	1.09	1.05	1.00
Florida	4.25		4.75		5.15		.	.	.
Georgia	4.25	3.25	4.75	3.25	5.15	3.25	0.76	0.68	0.63
Hawaii	4.25	5.25	4.75	5.25	5.15	5.25	1.24	1.11	1.02
Idaho	4.25	4.25	4.75	4.25	5.15	5.15	1.00	0.89	1.00
Illinois	4.25	4.25	4.75	4.75	5.15	5.15	1.00	1.00	1.00
Indiana	4.25	3.35	4.75	3.35	5.15	3.35	0.79	0.71	0.65
Iowa	4.25	4.65	4.75	4.75	5.15	5.15	1.09	1.00	1.00
Kansas	4.25	2.65	4.75	2.65	5.15	2.65	0.62	0.56	0.51
Kentucky	4.25	4.25	4.75	4.25	5.15	4.25	1.00	0.89	0.83
Louisiana	4.25	.	4.75	.	5.15	.	.	.	.
Maine	4.25	4.25	4.75	4.75	5.15	5.15	1.00	1.00	1.00
Maryland	4.25	4.25	4.75	4.75	5.15	5.15	1.00	1.00	1.00
Massachusetts	4.25	4.25	4.75	5.25	5.15	5.25	1.00	1.11	1.02
Michigan	4.25	3.35	4.75	3.35	5.15	5.15	0.79	0.71	1.00
Minnesota	4.25	4.25	4.75	4.25	5.15	5.15	1.00	0.89	1.00

State								
Mississippi	.	4.75	.	5.15	.	.	.	.
Missouri	4.25	4.75	4.75	5.15	5.15	1.00	1.00	1.00
Montana	4.25	4.75	4.75	5.15	5.15	1.00	1.00	1.00
Nebraska	4.25	4.75	4.25	5.15	5.15	1.00	0.89	1.00
Nevada	4.25	4.75	4.75	5.15	5.15	1.00	1.00	1.00
New Hampshire	4.25	4.75	4.75	5.15	5.15	1.00	1.00	1.00
New Jersey	5.05	4.75	5.05	5.15	5.05	1.19	1.06	0.98
New Mexico	4.25	4.75	4.25	5.15	4.25	1.00	0.89	0.83
New York	4.25	4.75	4.25	5.15	4.25	1.00	0.89	0.83
North Carolina	4.25	4.75	4.25	5.15	5.15	1.00	0.89	1.00
North Dakota	4.25	4.75	4.75	5.15	5.15	1.00	1.00	1.00
Ohio	4.25	4.75	4.25	5.15	4.25	1.00	0.89	0.83
Oklahoma	4.25	4.75	4.75	5.15	5.15	1.00	1.00	1.00
Oregon	4.75	4.75	5.50	5.15	6.00	1.12	1.16	1.17
Pennsylvania	4.25	4.75	4.75	5.15	5.15	1.00	1.00	1.00
Rhode Island	4.45	4.75	5.15	5.15	5.15	1.05	1.08	1.00
South Carolina	.	4.75	.	5.15	.	.	.	.
South Dakota	4.25	4.75	4.25	5.15	5.15	1.00	0.89	1.00
Tennessee	.	4.75	.	5.15	.	.	.	.
Texas	3.35	4.75	3.35	5.15	3.35	0.79	0.71	0.65
Utah	4.25	4.75	4.75	5.15	5.15	1.00	1.00	1.00
Vermont	4.75	4.75	5.00	5.15	5.25	1.12	1.05	1.02
Virginia	4.25	4.75	4.75	5.15	5.15	1.00	1.00	1.00
Washington	4.90	4.75	4.90	5.15	4.90	1.15	1.03	0.95
West Virginia	4.25	4.75	4.25	5.15	4.75	1.00	0.89	0.92
Wisconsin	4.25	4.75	4.25	5.15	5.15	1.00	0.89	1.00
Wyoming	1.60	4.75	1.60	5.15	1.60	0.38	0.34	0.31

Source: Book of States (1998–1999), table 8.22.

to substantially improve their positions, then it is difficult to imagine that any expansion could do so. A finding of this nature would dash any hope that economic growth per se could raise the pay and income of young, noncollege-educated men. However, our analysis has shown that the 1990s boom has substantially improved the labor market outcomes of young, noncollege-educated men and has helped young African American men. Young men in tight labor markets in the 1990s experienced a noticeable boost in employment and earnings, while adult men saw no such gains. Earnings of adults barely changed, even in metropolitan areas with unemployment rates below 4 percent, but those of youths, including disadvantaged African American youths, improved. Youths have done particularly well in areas that started the boom at lower jobless rates, suggesting that minimizing the impact of recessions allows youths to make real gains instead of making up ground lost during the recession.

On a cautionary note, we observe that in the tightest of local labor markets, one-fifth of young, noncollege-educated men and just over one-third of young, noncollege-educated African American men remained idle in 1998. Further, not all groups had surpassed or even returned to their employment levels of 1989, the peak of the 1980s boom. These more cautionary findings provide fruitful research questions for the future: Who has not benefited from the boom and why have they not benefited? Why have some groups surpassed or made up the lost ground of the 1991 to 1992 recession, while others have not?

The authors wish to thank seminar participants at the Virginia Commonwealth University and the University of Texas, Austin for helpful comments.

NOTES

1. Past studies have found that changes in unemployment rates have greater effects on young adults than on older adults. Kim Clark and Lawrence Summers (1981) found this to be the case in their time-series study of the relationship of youth joblessness and employment to adult unemployment, as did Richard Freeman (1991) in his cross-area study of youth employment and earnings in the 1980s. For a survey on estimates for the 1960s and 1970s, see Gregory DeFreitas (1986); for more recent work see Gregory DeFreitas (1991), Richard Freeman and Harry

Holzer (1986), Samuel Myers (1989), Leslie Stratton (1993), and Henry Farber (1997). Studies that use various waves of the displaced-worker survey also speak to this issue: see, for example, Lori Kletzer (1991) and Steven Hipple (1997).

2. We also estimated models for the largest thirty metropolitan areas. We were concerned that their employment and wage relationships might be different, because few of these areas showed up in our three-group taxonomy. To test for differences, we estimated the equations used to generate the results in Tables 2.8 and 2.9, but added a dummy variable that denoted whether the individual resided in one of these thirty metropolitan areas and an interaction between this variable and the area unemployment rate. The latter is our coefficient of concern, and in none of the regressions was it statistically significant. Further, the coefficient ranges from 0.0002 to 0.0040 for all youth, all men, and African American men. Although it equals 0.0150 for African American youth, the standard error is also 0.0150.

3. The longest expansion, from February 1961 to December 1969, lasted 106 months and included part of the Vietnam War era. If we restrict the analysis to peacetime expansions, then the ninety-two-month expansion from November 1982 to July 1990 is the longest on record. During that expansion, the unemployment rate fell from 10.8 percent to 5.5 percent. At the time, many policy-makers and researchers felt that the 1980s expansion provided the best evidence that macroeconomic growth could vastly improve the labor-market outcomes of noncollege-educated and less-skilled workers, especially African Americans.

REFERENCES

Blanchard, Olivier J., and Lawrence Katz. 1999. "Wage Dynamics: Reconciling Theory and Evidence." National Bureau of Economic Research Working paper 6924. Cambridge, Mass.: National Bureau of Economic Research.

Blanchflower, David, and Andrew Oswald. 1999. "Youth Unemployment, Wages, and Wage Inequality in the U.K. and the U.S." In *Youth Employment and Joblessness in Advanced Countries*, edited by David Blanchflower and Richard B. Freeman. Chicago: University of Chicago Press.

Clark, Kim B., and Lawrence H. Summers. 1981. "Demographic Differences in Cyclical Employment Variation." *Journal of Human Resources* 16(1): 61–79.

DeFreitas, Gregory. 1986. "A Time-Series Analysis of Hispanic Employment." *Journal of Human Resources* 21 (Winter): 24–43.

————. 1991. *Inequality at Work: Hispanics in the U.S. Labor Force.* New York: Oxford University Press.

Farber, Henry S. 1997. "The Changing Face of Job Loss in the United States, 1981–1995." *Brookings Papers on Economic Activity: Microeconomics.* Washington, D.C.: Brookings Institution.

Freeman, Richard B. 1981. "Economic Determinants of Geographic and Individual Variation in the Labor Market Position of Young Persons." In *The Youth Labor Market Problem: Its Nature, Causes, and Consequences,* edited by Richard Freeman and David Wise. Chicago: University of Chicago Press.

————. 1990. "Labor Market Tightness and the Declining Economic Position of Young Less Educated Male Workers in the United States," In *Mismatch and Labour Mobility,* edited by Fiorella Padoa-Schioppa. New York: Cambridge University Press.

————. 1991. "Employment and Earnings of Disadvantaged Young Men in a Labor Shortage Economy." In *The Urban Underclass,* edited by Christopher Jencks and Paul Peterson. Washington, D.C.: Urban Institute.

————. 1999. "The Economics of Crime." In *Handbook of Labor Economics, Vol 3.,* edited by Orley Ashenfelter and David Card. Amsterdam: Elsevier Science B.V. Publishers.

Freeman, Richard B., and Harry Holzer. 1986. *The Black Youth Employment Crisis.* Chicago: University of Chicago Press.

Hipple, Steven. 1997. "Worker Displacement in an Expanding Economy." *Monthly Labor Review* 120(12): 26–39.

Kletzer, Lori G. 1991. "Job Displacement: How Blacks Fared Relative to Whites." *Monthly Labor Review* 114(7): 17–25.

Mishel, Lawrence, Jared Bernstein, and John Schmidt. 1998. *The State of Working America, 1997–1998.* Washington, D.C.: Economic Policy Institute.

Myers, Samuel. 1989. "How Voluntary Is Black Unemployment and Black Labor Force Withdrawal?" In *The Question of Discrimination: Racial Inequality in the U.S. Labor Market,* edited by Steven Shulman and William Darity Jr. Middletown, Conn.: Wesleyan University Press.

Stratton, Leslie S. 1993. "Racial Differences in Men's Unemployment." *Industrial Labor Relations Review* 46(3): 451–63.

Topel, Robert H. 1986. "Local Labor Markets." *Journal of Political Economy* 94 (supp.): 111–43.

United States Department of Commerce, Bureau of the Census. 1983. *Current Population Surveys*. Washington: U.S. Government Printing Office.

―――. 1987. *Current Population Surveys*. Washington: U.S. Government Printing Office.

―――. 1989. *Current Population Surveys*. Washington: U.S. Government Printing Office.

―――. 1992. *Current Population Surveys*. Washington: U.S. Government Printing Office.

―――. 1996. *Current Population Surveys*. Washington: U.S. Government Printing Office.

―――. 1998. *Current Population Surveys*. Washington: U.S. Government Printing Office.

―――. various years. *Statistical Abstract of the United States*. Washington: U.S. Government Printing Office.

United States Department of Justice. Bureau of Justice Statistics. 1996. *Crime in the United States*. Washington: U.S. Government Printing Office.

―――. 1996. *Prisoners in 1996*. Washington: U.S. Government Printing Office.

―――. 1996. *Sourcebook of Criminal Justice Statistics*. 1996. Washington: U.S. Government Printing Office.

―――. 1997. *Lifetime Likelihood of Going to State or Federal Prison*. Washington: U.S. Government Printing Office.

―――. 1997. *Uniform Crime Reports, 1997: Preliminary Annual Release*. Washington: U.S. Government Printing Office.

United States Department of Labor, Bureau of Labor Statistics. Various years. *Employment and Earnings*. Washington: U.S. Government Printing Office.

―――. Various years. *Geographic Profile of Employment and Unemployment*. Washington: U.S. Government Printing Office.

Chapter 3

BLACK-WHITE EMPLOYMENT DIFFERENTIAL IN A TIGHT LABOR MARKET

CHINHUI JUHN

During 1999, the civilian unemployment rate in the United States reached 4.2 percent—the lowest recorded level since the late 1960s. In sharp contrast to the 1970s and 1980s, when economists were asking why the "natural rate" of unemployment seemed to be so high (Hall 1970), economists and policy-makers are now asking why the unemployment rate is so low. While the unemployment rate is low, inflation also appears to be in check, leading many economists to hypothesize that the "natural rate" of unemployment has fallen below 5 percent (Katz and Krueger 1999).

Is the labor market now fundamentally different from the one we observed during the 1970s and the 1980s? During those two decades, the U.S. economy underwent a dramatic increase in income inequality, and saw declining real wages among low-wage workers as well as an apparent downward shift in labor demand for less-skilled workers.[1] In addition, we witnessed a secular decline in the labor-market activity of prime-age males, particularly among the less educated and less skilled (Juhn 1992). These secular trends worked against improving the economic position of the poor and the disadvantaged even as the economy underwent a prolonged cyclical expansion in the 1980s (Cutler and Katz 1991).

Using the March Current Population Surveys for 1967 through 1996, this chapter examines long-term changes in unemployment, nonparticipation, and nonemployment (the sum of unemployed plus nonparticipating) for prime-age males. While the labor market of the 1990s looks different from that of the preceding two decades in terms of unemployment, some of the same trends observed during the 1970s and the 1980s continue in the 1990s. In particular, nonparticipation has continued to increase in the recent period, and the duration of nonemployment has also increased, suggesting that labor-market inactivity has become increasingly concentrated among a core group.

How have African American men fared in this labor market? There is a great deal of evidence to suggest that a robust economy improves the relative economic position of black men (Freeman 1973; Freeman and Rodgers, this volume). In terms of unemployment, the 1980s and the 1990s are no exceptions: the unemployment rate of black men has fallen relative to that of white men since the late 1970s. However, nonparticipation rates have continued to increase, leading to a slight increase in the nonemployment differential between black and white men. The increase in the duration of nonemployment among black men is particularly striking, as is the rising number of black men who experience year-long spells of labor-market inactivity.

BLACK-WHITE EMPLOYMENT DIFFERENTIAL IN A TIGHT LABOR MARKET

Figure 3.1 charts the fraction of twenty- to fifty-four-year-old men who are unemployed, out of the labor force, and nonemployed. As

Figure 3.1 Nonemployment: Males, Age Twenty to Fifty-Four

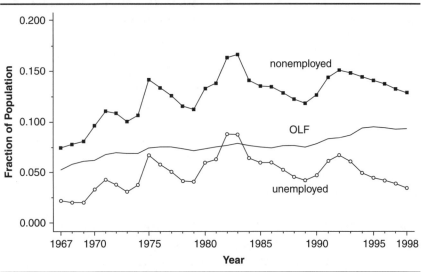

Source: Author's calculations based on numbers published in *Employment and Earnings*, Bureau of Labor Statistics, U.S. Department of Labor.
Note: OLF stands for Out of Labor Force.

the figure illustrates, the unemployment-population ratio is slightly lower than those observed in the late 1970s and the 1980s, other periods of comparable business-cycle activity. However, the portion of nonparticipants (those out of the labor force) has continued to increase through the 1990s. In fact, the diverging long-run trends of unemployment and nonparticipation ratios—or, to put it differently, the continued increase in nonparticipation among prime-age males in the face of a seemingly tight labor market—is one of many interesting questions to be addressed by future research.

Using microdata from the March Current Population Surveys covering the years 1967 through 1996, I calculated unemployment-, nonparticipation-, and nonemployment-population ratios for white and black men in four different periods of strong overall economic activity: 1967 to 1969, 1977 to 1979, 1987 to 1989, and latest years available, 1994 to 1996. These numbers are presented in table 3.1, along with the black-white differential, which is in the table's bottom panel.[2] Figure 3.2 is the corresponding graph of the black-white differential. As figure 3.2 illustrates, the black-white unemployment differential is lower now, in the late 1990s, than during the late 1970s or late 1980s. However, the gap in the nonparticipation rate has steadily increased in the 1990s, going from an average of 6.9 percentage points in 1977 to 1979, 7.9 percentage points in 1987 to 1989, and 9.8 percentage points in 1994 to 1996. The nonemployment differential has increased approximately 1.7 percentage points since the late 1970s.

The increases in nonparticipation and nonemployment differentials are larger when we examine further disaggregated groups. Table 3.1 reports unemployment and nonemployment statistics by experience category, while table 3.2 examines these statistics by education for the group with one to ten years of potential labor-market experience. Table 3.1 shows a pattern of declining unemployment gap and rising nonemployment gap among the younger group. The nonemployment gap for this group has increased by almost three percentage points since the late 1970s. Table 3.2 shows that the nonemployment gap between black and white men among the young and less educated increased by 12.8 percentage points since the late 1970s, 7.8 percentage points since the late 1980s alone. These numbers suggest that while black men have fared well in this tight labor market in terms of unemployment, the beneficial effects of the tight labor market have not extended to nonparticipation and nonemployment rates. For some groups, namely the young and less educated,

Table 3.1 Unemployment and Nonemployment for White and Black Males, by Experience Level

	Unemployed per Population				Nonemployed per Population			
	1967 to 1969	1977 to 1979	1987 to 1989	1994 to 1996	1967 to 1969	1977 to 1979	1987 to 1989	1994 to 1996
White males								
Experience in years								
One to ten	.027	.058	.050	.052	.064	.108	.103	.118
Eleven to twenty	.016	.033	.038	.036	.044	.076	.087	.099
Twenty-one to thirty	.015	.028	.033	.033	.059	.090	.106	.119
Total	.019	.042	.041	.040	.055	.093	.097	.111
Black males								
Experience in years								
One to ten	.061	.124	.097	.101	.139	.240	.232	.278
Eleven to twenty	.029	.066	.071	.063	.088	.167	.192	.209
Twenty-one to thirty	.037	.052	.063	.054	.130	.199	.224	.244
Total	.042	.088	.079	.073	.119	.207	.215	.242
Black-white differential								
Experience in years								
One to ten	.033	.066	.047	.050	.075	.133	.129	.160
Eleven to twenty	.014	.033	.033	.027	.044	.091	.105	.110
Twenty-one to thirty	.021	.024	.030	.021	.071	.109	.118	.125
Total	.023	.045	.038	.033	.064	.114	.117	.131

Source: Author's calculations March Current Population Surveys.

Figure 3.2 Black-White Nonemployment Differential

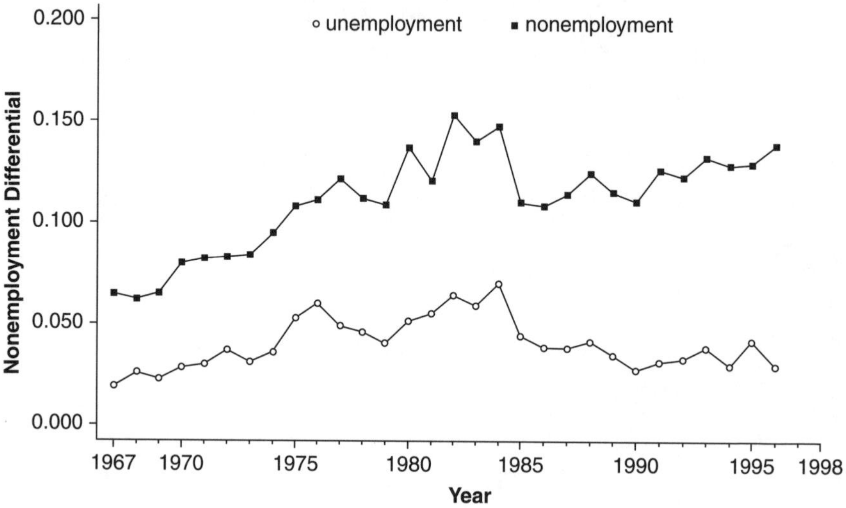

Source: Author's calculations based on numbers published in *Employment and Earnings,* Bureau of Labor Statistics, U.S. Department of Labor.

there is very little evidence of improvement in relative labor-market outcomes.

ENTRY RATES AND DURATIONS OF UNEMPLOYMENT AND NONEMPLOYMENT

While the overall levels of unemployment and nonemployment ratios are of interest, an equally important question is how the unemployed and nonemployed weeks are distributed across individuals. In other words, is there much churning in the labor market so that many individuals are unemployed (nonemployed) for short periods of time or are relatively few individuals unemployed (nonemployed) for long periods? Earlier papers (Juhn 1992; Juhn, Murphy, and Topel 1991) found that there were significant increases in durations leading to a greater concentration of unemployment and nonemployment over time. In this section, I examine whether these trends have continued in the 1990s.

Figure 3.3 examines the distribution of unemployed and nonemployed weeks last year for white males. The three panels represent

Table 3.2 Unemployment and Nonemployment for White and Black Males, by Education Level

	Unemployed per Population				Nonemployed per Population			
	1967 to 1969	1977 to 1979	1987 to 1989	1994 to 1996	1967 to 1969	1977 to 1979	1987 to 1989	1994 to 1996
White males (experience = one to ten years) Education (in years)								
<Twelve	.061	.126	.112	.102	.142	.246	.258	.287
Twelve	.024	.066	.058	.067	.053	.114	.112	.136
Thirteen to fifteen	.016	.043	.030	.038	.039	.082	.061	.079
Sixteen+	.008	.020	.016	.020	.024	.042	.033	.043
Black males (experience = one to ten years) Education (in years)								
<Twelve	.087	.184	.151	.184	.201	.421	.483	.590
Twelve	.049	.118	.113	.108	.106	.202	.232	.287
Thirteen to fifteen	.023	.088	.049	.069	.042	.139	.100	.159
Sixteen+	.008	.054	.035	.036	.031	.087	.067	.078
Black-white differential (experience = one to ten years) Education (in years)								
<Twelve	.025	.058	.038	.082	.060	.175	.186	.221
Twelve	.024	.052	.055	.041	.053	.088	.120	.150
Thirteen to fifteen	.008	.044	.019	.031	.003	.057	.038	.080
Sixteen+	.000	.034	.018	.017	.007	.045	.034	.035

Source: Author's calculations March Current Population Surveys

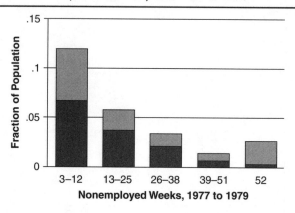

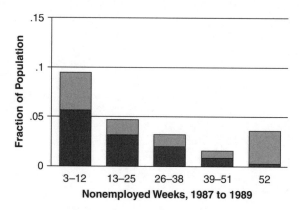

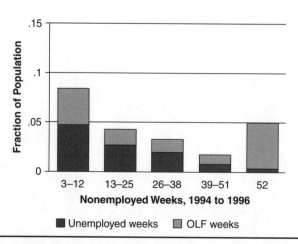

Source: Author's calculations based on numbers published in *Employment and Earnings,* Bureau of Labor Statistics, U.S. Department of Labor.
Note: OLF stands for Out of Labor Force.

1977 to 1979, 1987 to 1989, and 1994 to 1996 respectively. The darkly shaded segments represent unemployed weeks while the lightly shaded segments represent weeks out of the labor force. The largest category (representing those who suffered zero to two weeks of unemployment or nonemployment last year) is omitted. Figure 3.3 shows that there has been a significant decline in the fraction of those who report being nonemployed for three to twelve weeks in the previous twelve months. This fraction declined from approximately 12 percent of the population in the late 1970s to 8.5 percent in the 1994 to 1996 period; the decline most likely reflects the increasing tightness of the labor market. However, there has also been an increase in the number reporting being nonemployed for all fifty-two weeks of the preceding year. This fraction increased from 2.7 percent in the 1977 to 1979 period to 5 percent in 1994 to 1996, an increase due entirely to those who reported being out of the labor force. These trends appear to be more or less continuous throughout the 1980s and the 1990s.

Figure 3.4 presents the same information for black males. The increase in the portion of prime-age black men who report being nonemployed for entire years (fifty-two weeks) is quite striking. The number nonemployed for entire years increased from 8.7 percent in 1977 to 1979 to 14.2 percent in 1994 to 1996. These changes underscore the point that the increases in nonparticipation and nonemployment have been concentrated among relatively few individuals who remain out of the labor market for very long periods.

This notion of increasing concentration can be more specifically defined by examining entry rates and durations of unemployment and nonemployment. Entry rates into unemployment can be calculated using reported number of spells of unemployment during the year as in the following equation

$$S = U_0 + \lambda_{eu} \times E \qquad (3.1)$$

where S represents the average number of reported unemployed or nonemployed spells during the year, U_0 is the percentage of the sample population who report being unemployed at the beginning of the year, λ_{eu} is the entry rate into unemployment, and E is the average employment rate for the year in question. Exit rates from unemployment can be calculated by using this equation in conjunction with the following relationship:

$$U_1 - U_0 = \lambda_{eu} \times E - \lambda_{ue} \times U \qquad (3.2)$$

where U_0 and U_1 are unemployment rates at beginning and end of the year respectively, and λ_{ue} represents the exit rate from unemployment.

Figure 3.4 Distribution of Nonemployed Weeks for Black Males, 1977 to 1979, 1987 to 1989, and 1994 to 1996

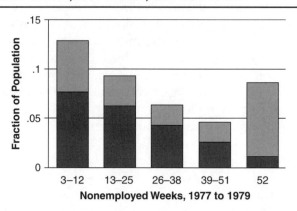

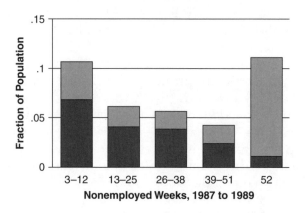

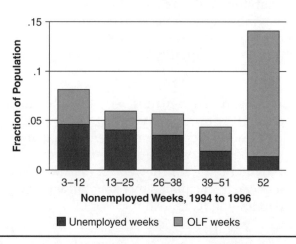

Source: Author's calculations based on numbers published in *Employment and Earnings.* Bureau of Labor Statistics, U.S. Department of Labor.
Note: OLF stands for Out of Labor Force.

This second equation states that the change in the unemployment rate has to be the difference between the flow into and flow out of the unemployed population. Thus, an estimate of λ_{ue} can be backed out from equations 3.1 and 3.2. Unfortunately, the number of nonemployment spells is not reported in the data, so the entry rate into nonemployment has to be calculated using an alternative method. The entry rate into nonemployment is estimated using the following relation:

$$1 - I = (1 - N_0) \times e^{-\lambda en} \tag{3.3}$$

where I represents the fraction who experienced some nonemployment during the year, N_0 is the percentage of the population who are nonemployed at the beginning of the year, and $e^{-\lambda en}$ is the survivor function. Equation 3.3 states that the portion not experiencing any nonemployment during the year is the fraction that started the year employed multiplied by the survival probability. The entry rate into nonemployment, λ_{en}, can be backed out via the following equation:

$$\lambda_{en} = \log(1 - N_0) - \log(1 - I) \tag{3.4}$$

Finally, the exit rate from nonemployment is estimated using a condition similar to equation 3.2, based on inflows and outflows:

$$N_1 - N_0 = \lambda_{en} \times E - \lambda_{ne} \times N \tag{3.5}$$

I report average spell durations, which equal $1/\lambda_{ue}$ and $1/\lambda_{ne}$, when exit rates are constant. Figure 3.5 plots entry rates into and durations of stays in the unemployed and nonemployed populations for prime-age white males during the period spanning 1967 through 1996. Unemployment is presented in the top panel; nonemployment is on the bottom. All entry rates and durations are reported relative to the average for all men over the entire period. Looking first at the top panel of figure 3.5, the entry rate into unemployment has declined substantially during the recent expansion and is now lower than the rate that prevailed in the late 1970s and late 1980s. There is no evidence of a rise in entry rates over this thirty-year span. Duration of unemployment has also fallen in the recent period, although there is evidence of a slight increase in duration over time. When we examine nonemployment as illustrated in the bottom panel of figure 3.5, we observe that the most significant change has been the striking increase in the duration of nonemployment over time. The rise in duration of nonemployment has been particularly sharp during the 1990s.

Figure 3.5 Relative Entry Rates and Durations of Unemployment and Nonemployment, for White Males

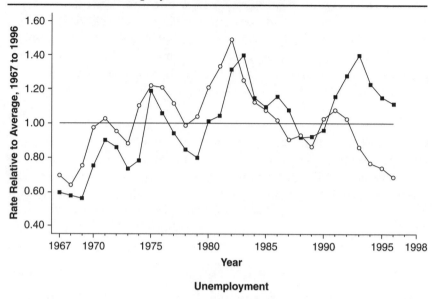

Unemployment

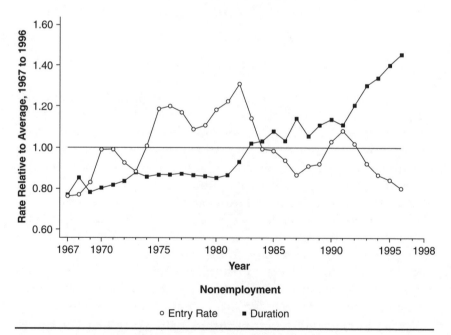

Nonemployment

○ Entry Rate   ■ Duration

Source: Author's calculations based on numbers published in *Employment and Earnings,* Bureau of Labor Statistics, U.S. Department of Labor.

Black entry rates into the ranks of the unemployed and non-employed and the duration of blacks' stays there are presented in figure 3.6. As the top panel of figure 3.6 illustrates, there has been a decline in entry rates over time, and the probability of becoming unemployed is now lower than ever for black men. Unemployment duration, however, has risen at the same time, and similar to the case of white men, the increase in duration of nonemployment for black men (as illustrated in the bottom panel) is particularly striking.

LABOR SUPPLY AND THE ROLE OF WAGES

As illustrated in tables 3.1 and 3.2, unemployment and nonemployment ratios are much higher for less-experienced and less-educated men. The concentration of unemployment and nonemployment among less-skilled men is even more pronounced when we use yet another measure of skill, the individual's relative position in the hourly-wage distribution. Table 3.3 presents unemployment and nonemployment-population ratios for white and black males disaggregated by relative positions in the hourly wage distribution.[3] Figures 3.7, 3.8, and 3.9 graph these ratios for white males: Figure 3.7 shows that the level of unemployment is much higher for low-wage groups and also that unemployment among the low-wage groups exhibits greater cyclical sensitivity than that of higher-paid cohorts. However, there is little evidence that unemployment rates across these groups have diverged since the late 1970s. In contrast, the nonparticipation and nonemployment rates illustrated in figures 3.8 and 3.9 indicate that not only are the levels of nonparticipation and nonemployment much higher for the low-wage groups, but also that the increases in these measures are more pronounced among the low-wage groups than they are among any other groups.

The rising inequality of nonparticipation and nonemployment ratios mirror the well-documented rising inequality in wages. Figure 3.10 charts real hourly wages relative to the 1970 level for prime-age white males. The figure indicates that men in the bottom 10 percent of the wage distribution have lost approximately 40 percent in real wages since 1970. Real wages for men in the top 40 percent, meanwhile, have been essentially flat over this period.

Are less-skilled men dropping out of the labor market in response to declining market wages? To what extent can a stable labor-supply

(*Text continues on page 104.*)

Figure 3.6 Relative Entry Rates and Durations of Unemployment and Nonemployment, for Black Males

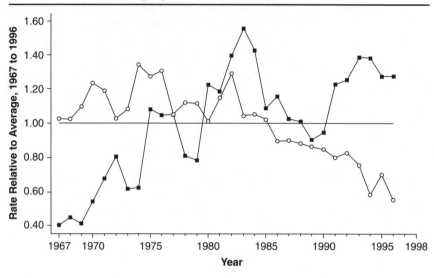

Unemployment

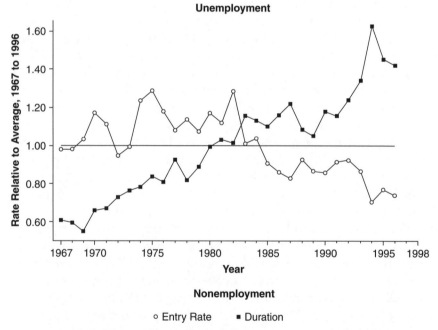

Nonemployment

○ Entry Rate   ■ Duration

Source: Author's calculations based on numbers published in *Employment and Earnings,* Bureau of Labor Statistics, U.S. Department of Labor.

Table 3.3 Unemployment and Nonemployment for White and Black Men, by Wage Percentile

	Unemployed per Population				Nonemployed per Population			
	1967 to 1969	1977 to 1979	1987 to 1989	1994 to 1996	1967 to 1969	1977 to 1979	1987 to 1989	1994 to 1996
White males								
Wage percentile								
1 to 10	.043	.093	.108	.087	.136	.223	.282	.273
11 to 20	.025	.073	.078	.074	.071	.164	.185	.211
21 to 40	.019	.051	.047	.051	.052	.110	.108	.132
41 to 60	.016	.033	.030	.031	.045	.072	.066	.083
61 to 99	.014	.022	.017	.019	.038	.045	.039	.050
Total	.019	.042	.041	.040	.055	.093	.097	.111
Black males								
Wage percentile								
1 to 10	.064	.137	.159	.137	.210	.371	.484	.518
11 to 20	.045	.140	.131	.121	.140	.361	.370	.434
21 to 40	.044	.109	.106	.096	.118	.256	.284	.310
41 to 60	.040	.079	.073	.061	.108	.178	.197	.186
61 to 99	.036	.053	.035	.040	.097	.114	.083	.121
Total	.042	.088	.079	.073	.119	.207	.215	.242

Source: Author's calculations March Current Population Surveys.

Figure 3.7 Unemployment by Wage Percentile, for White Males

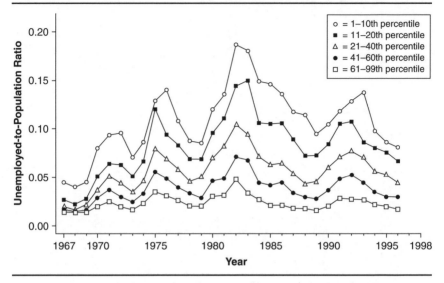

Source: Author's calculations based on numbers published in *Employment and Earnings,* Bureau of Labor Statistics, U.S. Department of Labor.

Figure 3.8 OLF by Wage Percentile, for White Males

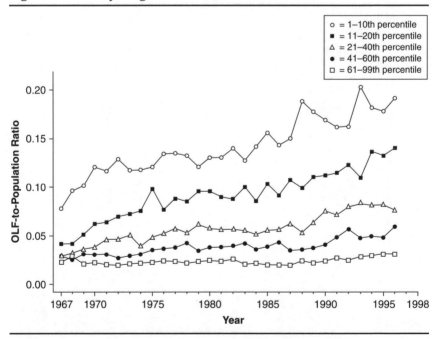

Source: Author's calculations based on numbers published in *Employment and Earnings,* Bureau of Labor Statistics, U.S. Department of Labor.
Note: OLF stands for Out of Labor Force.

Figure 3.9 Nonemployment by Wage Percentile, for White Males

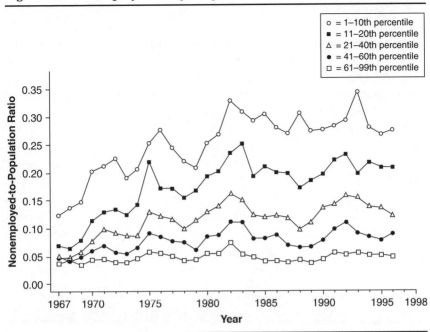

Source: Author's calculations based on numbers published in *Employment and Earnings*, Bureau of Labor Statistics, U.S. Department of Labor.

Figure 3.10 Indexed Wage by Wage Percentile, for White Males

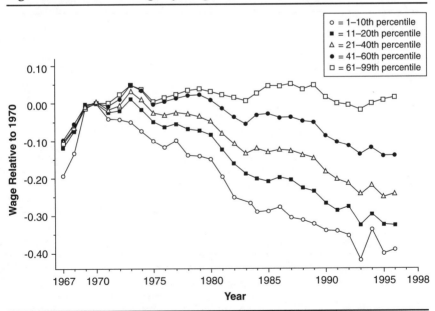

Source: Author's calculations based on numbers published in *Employment and Earnings*, Bureau of Labor Statistics, U.S. Department of Labor.

function and declining wages account for the increases in non-participation and nonemployment? Stable labor supply and declining wages provide a compelling explanation for increased nonparticipation and nonemployment only if low-wage and less-skilled men exhibit relatively large labor-supply responses to changes in real wages—and there is some evidence that this is the case. Figure 3.11 shows the cross-sectional relationship between wages and probability of being employed for white males. The three lines correspond to different periods: the late 1970s, late 1980s, and 1994 to 1996. This empirical relationship has remained remarkably stable since the late 1970s. Figure 3.11 also illustrates that the elasticity of employment with respect to wages is much greater at lower wages and essentially zero at higher wages, which suggests that less-skilled men who command low wages are in a competitive labor market and that their offered market wages may be close to their reservation wages. They may respond to movements in offer wages by dropping in and out of the labor market.

How closely does this labor supply model, together with the observed changes in real wages, predict changes in overall non-

Figure 3.11 Employment-to-Wage Relationship, for White Males

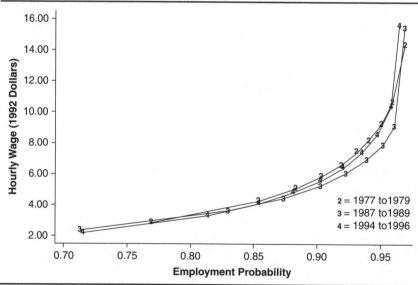

Source: Author's calculations based on numbers published in *Employment and Earnings*. Bureau of Labor Statistics, U.S. Department of Labor.

employment-population ratios? I examine this question in table 3.4. For both black and white males, I use the cross-sectional relationship between employment and wages observed for whites over the 1977 through 1996 period to predict changes in nonemployment-population ratios.[4] Table 3.4 indicates that, consistent with my previously reported findings (Juhn 1992), changes in real wages, together with a stable labor-supply function, closely match the actual changes in nonemployment. Overall, real wages declined approximately 6.3 percent between 1977 to 1979 and 1987 to 1989. Actual nonemployment was essentially flat, rising 0.4 percentage point while the model predicts a small increase of 1.3 percentage points. The model accurately predicts the relatively large increases in nonemployment among the low-wage groups. The increases in nonemployment between 1987 to 1989 and 1994 through 1996 appear to be more neutral across the wage-percentile categories. The model also predicts more neutral nonemployment changes across wage categories, as the wage decline was modest (at 6.2 percent) for the bottom 10 percent and larger (at 9.4 percent and 9.5 percent respectively) for the eleventh-to-twentieth percentile and twenty-first-to-fortieth percentile.

Table 3.4 **Actual and Predicted Change in Nonemployment Rates of White Males**

	Actual	Predicted	Wage Change
1978 to 1988			
Wage percentile			
1 to 10	.059	.048	−.187
11 to 20	.021	.030	−.156
21 to 40	−.001	.017	−.108
41 to 60	−.005	.007	−.065
61 to 99	−.006	.001	.014
1 to 99	.004	.013	−.063
1988 to 1995			
Wage percentile			
1 to 10	−.009	.017	−.062
11 to 20	.026	.020	−.094
21 to 40	.023	.016	−.099
41 to 60	.017	.011	−.088
61 to 99	.011	.003	−.039
1 to 99	.014	.010	−.069

Source: Author's calculations March Current Population Surveys.

Table 3.5 compares actual and predicted nonemployment changes for black men. The model does not work as well for changes in black nonemployment rates. In particular, the model under-predicts the rise in nonemployment rates from 1987 to 1989 through 1994 to 1996. The principal reason is that the observed wage declines for black men in the recent period have been relatively modest. In fact, real wages have increased slightly (by 1.9 percent) for the lowest wage group. While the model predicts that black nonemployment would have stayed essentially constant or increased slightly, we have observed larger increases in nonemployment among low wage black men over this period.

Finally, one can ask to what extent the increase in the nonemployment differential between blacks and whites can be accounted for by a rising wage differential between the two groups. Based on table 3.5, the answer appears to be that wage differentials cannot account for much if any of the increase. In the most recent period (1994 to 1996), black men have gained on white men in terms of real wages, so that we would have predicted, all else being equal, a decline in the nonemployment differential between the two races. The fact that

Table 3.5 Actual and Predicted Change in Nonemployment Rates of Black Males

	Actual	Predicted	Wage Change
1978 to 1988			
Wage percentile			
1 to 10	.113	.052	−.169
11 to 20	.009	.032	−.132
21 to 40	.028	.022	−.110
41 to 60	.019	.013	−.081
61 to 99	−.031	.002	−.017
1 to 99	.009	.016	−.075
1988 to 1995			
Wage percentile			
1 to 10	.035	−.006	.019
11 to 20	.064	.005	−.020
21 to 40	.026	.007	−.034
41 to 60	−.011	.005	−.032
61 to 99	.038	.002	−.009
1 to 99	.028	.003	−.016

Source: Author's calculations March Current Population Surveys.

the nonemployment differential actually rose slightly suggests that factors other than wages have played a role.

CONCLUSION

While the aggregate unemployment rate is approaching the low levels last witnessed during the 1960s, labor-market conditions have not improved for all prime-age males. The tight labor market has improved the relative position of black men in terms of unemployment rates, but as nonparticipation rates have continued to increase, there has been a slight increase in the nonemployment differential between black and white men. A striking finding is that for those black men who are currently employed, the probability of becoming unemployed is now lower than ever, even relative to the late 1960s. The labor market is indeed tight for these men. On the other hand, for those who are not currently employed, average duration of the nonemployed spell has increased through the 1990s. Similar to what we witnessed in the 1970s and the 1980s, labor-market inactivity is increasingly concentrated among a core group who appears to be permanently detached from the labor market. There are signs in the most recent data that real wages have finally begun to increase for low-skilled workers (Mishel, Berenstein, and Schmidt 1998), though it remains to be seen whether this marks the reversal of the secular trends that have for so long worked against less-skilled men.

The original version of this chapter was written while the author was an economist at the Domestic Research Section of the Federal Reserve Bank of New York. Nathaniel Baum Snow provided excellent research assistance. The views expressed are those of the author and do not necessarily reflect those of the Federal Reserve Bank of New York or the Federal Reserve System.

NOTES

1. The literature on the rise in wage and income inequality is much too vast to document here. A sample of this enormous literature includes John Bound and George Johnson (1989), Chinhui Juhn, Kevin Murphy, and Brooks Pierce (1993), Lawrence Katz and Kevin Murphy (1992), and Frank Levy and Richard Murnane (1992).

2. All calculations are based on the 1968 through 1997 March Current Population Surveys (CPS). The sample is limited to prime-age males with one to thirty years of potential labor-market experience whose ages range from eighteen to fifty-three. Potential labor-market experience is calculated by subtracting the sum of years of schooling and six from age. Beginning in 1992, education is reported as a categorical variable based on the highest degree attained. Average years of schooling by degree attained were calculated using the February 1990 CPS and applied to the later years for comparability. Students and noncivilians are excluded from the analysis. The unemployment and nonemployment statistics are based on reported weeks worked and reported unemployed weeks last year. The sample is also restricted to white and black males only.

3. Log hourly wages are calculated by dividing annual earnings last year by the product of weeks worked last year and usual hours per week. Hourly wages are deflated by the personal-consumption expenditure deflator (1992 dollars) established by the National Income and Product Accounts. Wages have to be imputed for men who do not work during the entire year and therefore have no reported annual earnings or hourly wages. The details of this imputation are described in Chinhui Juhn (1992); but the basic empirical strategy behind these imputations is to use the observed wages of marginal workers (those who worked part of the year) as a proxy for those who did not work at all during the year.

4. In order to abstract from lifecycle changes in wages, I first regressed log hourly wages on a quartic function in potential experience and defined percentile categories based on residuals and then averaged employment rates and residuals by percentile category. I fit a simple quadratic to this wage-employment relationship across percentiles and used the parameters estimated from this relation to predict employment changes. Further details of this procedure are in Chinhui Juhn, Kevin Murphy, and Robert Topel (1991).

REFERENCES

Bound, John, and George Johnson. 1989. "Changes in the Structure of Wages During the 1980s: An Evaluation of Alternative Explanations." National Bureau of Economic Research Working paper 2983. Cambridge, Mass.: National Bureau of Economic Research.

Cutler, David, and Lawrence Katz. 1991. "Macroeconomic Performance and the Disadvantaged." *Brookings Papers on Economic Activity* 2. Washington, D.C.: Brookings Institution.

Freeman, Richard. 1973. "Changes in the Labor Market for Black Americans, 1948–72." *Brookings Papers on Economic Activity* 1. Washington, D.C.: Brookings Institution.

Hall, Robert E. 1970. "Why Is the Unemployment Rate So High at Full Employment?" *Brookings Papers on Economic Activity* 3. Washington, D.C.: Brookings Institution.

Juhn, Chinhui. 1992. "Decline of Male Labor Market Opportunities: The Role of Declining Market Opportunities." *Quarterly Journal of Economics* 107(1): 79–122.

Juhn, Chinhui, Kevin M. Murphy, and Brooks Pierce. 1993. "Wage Inequality and the Rise in Returns to Skill." *Journal of Political Economy* 101(3): 410–42.

Juhn, Chinhui, Kevin M. Murphy, and Robert H. Topel. 1991. "Why Has the Natural Rate of Unemployment Increased over Time?" *Brookings Papers on Economic Activity* 2. Washington, D.C.: Brookings Institution.

Katz, Lawrence, and Alan Krueger. 1999. "The High-Pressure U.S. Labor Market of the 1990s." *Brookings Papers on Economic Activity* 1. Washington, D.C.: Brookings Institution.

Katz, Lawrence, and Kevin M. Murphy. 1992. "Changes in the Wage Structure, 1963–1987: Supply and Demand Factors." *Quarterly Journal of Economics* 107: 35–78.

Levy, Frank, and Richard J. Murnane. 1992. "U.S. Earnings Levels and Earnings Inequality: A Review of Recent Trends and Proposed Explanations." *Journal of Economic Literature* 30: 1333–81.

Mishel, Lawrence, Jared Berenstein, and John Schmidt. 1998. *The State of Working America, 1997–1998*. Washington, D.C.: Economic Policy Institute.

Commentary I

URBAN RACIAL UNEMPLOYMENT DIFFERENTIALS: THE NEW YORK CASE

GREGORY E. DEFREITAS

Recent empirical studies have uncovered marked geographic variations in the unemployment experiences of racial and ethnic groups in the United States. In particular, both the levels and cyclical trends of African American joblessness and of the black-white unemployment gap appear to differ greatly by region, metropolitan area, and city. Thus Richard B. Freeman and William M. Rodgers III (this volume) find large differences in these measures among young men (sixteen- to twenty-four-year-old nonstudents) in three metro area groupings: those with continuous low unemployment throughout the 1990s, those with steady high unemployment during the decade, and those areas enjoying rapid drops in jobless rates in the 1990s. The largest employment gains over the decade among non-college-educated African Americans, Freeman and Rodgers find, occurred in areas of continuous low unemployment. In addition, their study suggests that the fewer the number of less-educated residents hindered by prison records, the greater their likelihood of employability.

Such findings are a necessary complement to the broad national results emerging from aggregate empirical studies like that of Chinhui Juhn (this volume). Comparing employment statistics from 1977 through 1979 and 1994 through 1996, she finds a national pattern of widening black-white nonparticipation gaps. The declines in active labor-force participants have been large enough to outweigh the shrinking volume of officially unemployed, leading to a rise in total nonemployment (unemployed plus those out of the labor force). This trend appears to be concentrated among the young and less educated. The differences between Juhn's results and those of Freeman and Rodgers may reflect in part the sensitivity of nonemployment

110

findings to each study's level of geographic aggregation, time span (much longer in the case of Juhn, but omitting the 1997-to-1998 boom years), definition of *youth* (sixteen- to twenty-four-year-olds in Freeman-Rodgers; workers with fewer than ten years of potential work experience in Juhn), and statistical approach (Freeman and Rodgers rely far more on multivariate regression than Juhn).

Cordelia W. Reimers (this volume) expands the set of comparisons by including Hispanics and women, two groups growing at much faster rates than are white or black men. Unlike Freeman and Rodgers and Juhn, she focuses only on the years 1990 through 1996 and looks only at the unemployment rate rather than the broader nonemployment rate. Like earlier studies for the seventies and eighties, Cordelia Reimer's research reveals that black and Hispanic jobless rates have been generally more cyclically volatile than those of whites. Among females as a whole and male high school graduates over thirty-five years of age, African Americans experienced larger drops in unemployment than did either Hispanics or whites. Still, the opposite was the case for young, black male high school dropouts. And despite nationwide reductions in black and Hispanic unemployment rates by 1996, both were still above the white level. After controlling for the influences of age, schooling, occupational, industrial, and locational differences, Reimers concludes that 85 percent or more of the black-white jobless gap and 40 to 50 percent of the Hispanic–non-Hispanic gap is attributable to unobserved characteristics and discrimination.

In an attempt to evaluate how relevant some of the findings from these national studies are for local economies, this essay focuses on minority unemployment in the country's largest urban center, New York City. More blacks—2.1 million—live there than in any other American city. In 1998, after some seven years of a national economic expansion, the city's jobless rate still averaged 8 percent, 3.5 percentage points above the overall U.S. level. Eighteen percent of New York's black labor force is unemployed, nearly twice the national level and five percentage points higher than the average for the largest cities. For comparison, figure C1.1 shows inner-city black unemployment rates for the ten largest metropolitan areas in the United States.

IMPACT OF THE MOST RECENT BUSINESS CYCLE

Historically, New York City's unemployment rate has generally hovered below the national average, but this changed with the most

Figure C1.1 Black Unemployment Rates in Ten Largest Urban Areas, 1998

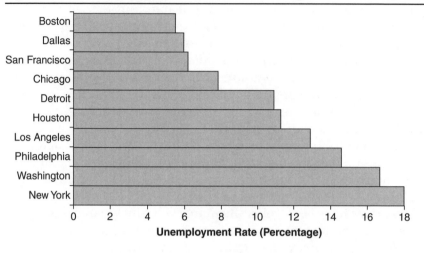

Source: United States Bureau of the Census, Current Population Survey, March 1998. Unemployment rates for blacks ages sixteen and over in center cities of ten largest metropolitan areas. Hispanics, who can be of any race, are excluded.

recent business cycle. In 1988, at the end of the last expansion, for example, the city's unemployment fell to 5 percent, just below the national average of 5.5 percent for that year. However, early in 1989, New York's economy fell into recession well ahead of the rest of the country, and unemployment rose from 6.9 percent in 1989 to a high of 11 percent in 1992—when the national rate peaked at 7.5 percent. The city's recovery has been unusually slow, too: unemployment rates only fell below double digits in 1994, and although they reached 8.2 percent in 1995, they then spiked upward again to 9.4 percent in 1997. In 1988, the black-white unemployment-rate ratio stood at 1.7, below the national average. One of the distinctive aspects of the most recent recession is the substantial rise in New York City's white unemployment rate, which peaked at 10 percent in 1992. With the black rate reaching 14.1 percent that year, the black-white ratio fell to 1.4. Both groups' unemployment levels declined through 1994 and 1995, but the sharp rise in black rates thereafter pushed the black-white ratio up again, to 1.9 by 1998.

These fluctuations in the official unemployment rate appear to have been much affected by changes in labor-force participation. The job growth of the 1980s helped to nudge the city's participation rate up to 57.6 percent by 1989 (when 56.5 percent of whites and 58.9 percent of blacks were economically active), but this figure was still nine percentage points below the national level. In the next few years, as the city lost 230,000 jobs by the end of 1992, the total number active in the labor force barely declined at all.[1] This resulted in the sharp rise in unemployment rates seen during this period. Nevertheless, the length of the recession and the anemic recovery of the mid-1990s eventually took its toll on job seekers: from 1992 to 1995, the labor force shrank by 177,000 and the participation rate fell to 55.1 percent (the white and black rates fell to 53.9 and 55.4 respectively). Because employment crept upward by just 23,000 over these years, the recorded decline in unemployment rates reflected little more than labor-force dropouts.

Why, then, the upward spike in recorded unemployment rates in 1995 to 1997? Optimism about job prospects might have been improving as job growth picked up, but the weakness of the recovery makes this seem a relatively insignificant factor in drawing people back into the job market. From the timing of these changes, it is perhaps more likely that welfare reforms had a strong influence on participation rates. Starting in early 1995, New York City began requiring increasing numbers of public-assistance recipients to actively seek work or be placed in workfare assignments. Over the same 1995 to 1997 span during which the labor force swelled by 181,000, the welfare caseload was cut 151,000. The fact that the sharpest jumps in labor-force participation rates were among black and Hispanic women, the city's largest cohorts among adult aid recipients, underscores the likely importance of welfare restrictions on unemployment rates.[2]

DETAILED CROSS-SECTIONAL ANALYSIS

In order to consider the factors that could possibly explain these patterns, we next examine disaggregated data on unemployment, as well as employment-population ratios and underemployment. Since the BLS time-series statistics cited here include Spanish origin persons in the broad "white" and "black" groupings, it could be that intercity differences in the Hispanic share of each of those groups affect our unemployment comparisons. Likewise, if New York has larger shares of youth or of the elderly, this could bias its employment figures downward.

Table C1.1 presents 1998 unemployment and employment-population rates separately for non-Hispanic whites and blacks, as

Table C1.1 Unemployment and Employment-to-Population Rates in the United States, New York City, and Other Largest Cities, by Age, Race, Spanish Origin, and Educational Attainment, 1998

	Unemployment Rate				Employment-to-Population Rate			
	All	White	Black	Hispanic	All	White	Black	Hispanic
Age sixteen to twenty-four								
Nonstudents								
United States	11.0	8.8	19.4	12.5	73.2	78.4	61.0	66.3
Large cities	13.6	6.0	22.2	15.0	65.8	83.5	53.0	60.5
New York City	14.5	3.1	22.9	15.3	58.7	83.5	44.4	55.1
Students								
United States	10.9	8.6	21.8	17.0	44.4	50.0	28.6	35.5
Large cities	14.9	7.1	32.7	15.1	34.6	47.4	20.7	31.2
New York City	25.0	16.0	50.6	15.5	20.3	24.3	12.1	21.1
Age twenty-five to sixty-four								
Nonstudents								
United States	3.9	3.2	7.4	5.9	77.0	78.6	71.8	71.3
Large cities	5.7	3.7	10.5	6.4	73.7	80.0	67.1	68.0
New York City	8.2	5.4	14.6	9.0	69.1	75.8	65.6	61.7
Noncollege								
United States	5.7	4.5	9.8	7.1	69.8	71.6	64.1	67.2
Large cities	8.9	6.8	14.9	7.4	63.9	67.7	57.9	64.1
New York City	12.8	11.5	20.2	10.7	56.9	58.2	56.1	55.2
College								
United States	2.7	2.3	4.8	3.7	83.5	84.1	82.2	81.0
Large cities	3.3	2.6	5.6	3.5	83.7	86.4	80.2	80.3
New York City	4.6	2.5	9.8	6.1	81.7	86.0	77.7	76.5

Source: United States Bureau of the Census, Current Population Survey, March 1998. White and black samples are here restricted to non-Hispanics. Hispanics may be of any race. "Large cities" are the center cities of the twenty largest metropolitan areas, including New York City. Currently enrolled students are excluded from all tabulations for ages twenty-five to sixty-four. "Noncollege" refers to persons who have completed no more than a high school degree; "college" includes those who completed one or more years of college.

well as Hispanics, all subdivided into two age groups: youth (persons sixteen to twenty-four years old) and adults (persons twenty-five to sixty-four).[3] The calculations also control for whether or not respondents are urban residents or currently enrolled in school. Overall, both black and Hispanic New Yorkers experience higher unemployment rates and lower employment-population rates than their counterparts in other large cities or in the United States as a whole. The same is true for the full sample of white New Yorkers twenty-five to sixty-four years old. Among youth under twenty-five, out-of-school whites in the city do exhibit lower average unemployment rates than youths in other cities, but the majority in this age group were still enrolled students. Among these students, whites in New York had about twice the unemployment rate and half the employment-population ratio of the average big-city white youth. African American students in the city fared still worse: only 12 percent held a job and their unemployment rate stood at about 50 percent.[4]

Among adults twenty-four to sixty-four years of age, 14.6 percent of blacks, 9.0 percent of Hispanics, and 5.4 percent of whites in the New York labor force were unemployed, rates well above those of their counterparts elsewhere. Fewer than two of every three African American adults in the city had a job in this nonrecession year, when nationally 72 percent of blacks and over 78 percent of whites were employed.[5]

To what extent can differences in the educational levels of New Yorkers and workers elsewhere account for these findings? Dramatic increases in high school graduation rates have been achieved by African Americans since the 1960s. Among New Yorkers thirty-five to forty-four years of age no longer in school in 1998, 94 percent of blacks had at least a high school degree, compared with 97 percent of whites. Nevertheless, figure C1.2 shows that whites in this age group were over twice as likely to hold a degree from a four-year college. For all city residents twenty-five to sixty-four years of age, 45.6 percent of non-Hispanic whites in the city had completed college, but only 18.5 percent of African Americans had. Among Hispanics, the fraction of college graduates was just 12.3 percent. Still, all three groupings in New York had higher college-graduation rates than their counterparts in other large cities, where only 15 percent of blacks and 9.3 percent of Hispanics held degrees.

Separate unemployment rates and employment-population ratios for noncollege-educated adults and for those who attended college

Figure C1.2 College Graduation Rates in the United States, New York City, and other Largest Cities, for Adults Ages Twenty-Five to Sixty-Four by Race and Spanish Origin, 1998

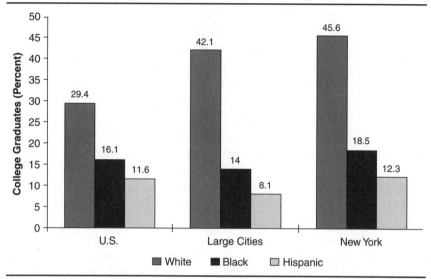

Source: United States Bureau of the Census, Current Population Survey, March 1998. Enrolled students are excluded from these estimates. White and black samples are here restricted to non-Hispanics. Hispanics may be of any race. "Large cities" are the center cities of the twenty largest metropolitan areas, including New York City.

are presented in the bottom six rows of table C1.1. These numbers reveal that regardless of race or Spanish origin, less-educated New Yorkers have higher unemployment rates and lower job-holding rates than the average noncollege-educated adult in a large city or the United States as a whole. The African American unemployment rate is over 20 percent in New York—twice the rate for blacks nationally and five percentage points above the big-city average. Whites and Hispanics in New York have unemployment rates of 11.5 and 10.7 percent respectively, rates that stand well above the national averages for these groups(4.5 percent and 7.1 percent, respectively). The New York-U.S. gaps in employment-population ratios within each racial and ethnic group are smaller than the unemployment gaps. But the job-holding rates of 55 to 58 percent in the city are well below the national average.

Among college-educated adults, black New Yorkers' 1998 unemployment rate of 9.8 percent was twice the U.S. black average and three times higher than the white rate nationally. On the other hand, in contrast to the findings for less-educated whites, white New Yorkers with some college had unemployment and employment-participation rates little different from the white national averages. Although this might be evidence attesting to the importance of racial discrimination in the labor market, more-detailed analysis of larger data sets with additional control variables is needed to better evaluate this issue.

To better gauge the impact of schooling on racial unemployment differentials, I estimated what the black and Hispanic unemployment rates would be were they assigned the same educational distribution as that of whites in the largest twenty American cities. For example, the distributions of urban whites among four educational groupings (less than twelve years of schooling, exactly twelve years, some college, and four-year-college graduate) were applied as weights to the unemployment rates of black New Yorkers at each of these schooling levels. The results suggested that the city's average black unemployment rate would fall by about four percentage points. But even so, it would still be three percentage points above the big-city black average and twice the rate of white New Yorkers. If, instead, blacks in New York kept their current educational distribution but were assigned the urban-white unemployment rate at each educational level, the unemployment reduction for black New Yorkers would be far larger: the New York-big city gap would be eliminated and the black-white unemployment gap in New York would be cut to only 1.5 percentage points.[6]

It is possible that real or perceived deficiencies in the quality of public education in New York factor into these results. In a large-scale survey of New York employers that I directed in 1995 and 1996, employers expressed considerable anxiety about the training of the youngest workers in their applicant pools—but most gave far higher priority to applicants' work attitude and "people skills" than to their educational credentials (DeFreitas, forthcoming). And there is no consistent evidence that New York's public schooling is of significantly lower quality than that of most other large city centers with lower unemployment levels.

IMMIGRATION IMPACTS

One reason some suggest to explain why New York's unemployment levels have exceeded the national average may be its high immigrant concentrations. Long the destination of more new immigrants than any other American city, New York saw the foreign-born portion of its population jump from 18.2 percent in 1970 to 28.4 percent by 1990. Of the 2.1 million immigrants counted in the city by the 1990 census, nearly half had been in the country only since 1980. The fact that the 1990s opened with more immigrants entering an economy mired in recession ignited renewed questioning about whether immigration worsened African Americans' wage and job prospects.

A recent survey of the empirical research literature conducted by a National Academy of Sciences panel concluded that, whether measured by the unemployment rate, employment-population rate, or weeks worked per year, most native-born Americans' employment does not appear to have been harmed substantially by higher immigration rates. Of course, the fact that most national studies have not found strong negative effects on native job holding does not mean that individual native workers are never passed over in hiring or dismissed from jobs in favor of immigrants. And many of the same studies that have found no adverse wage impacts on natives have nevertheless concluded that new immigrants to the United States do tend to depress the earnings of at least one group of workers: earlier immigrants. This impact is likely to be stronger the more clustered different cohorts of immigrants are in the same industrial niches (National Research Council 1997; as well as the empirical surveys in DeFreitas 1991, 1998).

One recent paper has come to quite different conclusions, at least for male workers in the New York metro area in the 1980s: David Howell and Elizabeth Mueller (1998) find an inverse association between the shares of immigrants in industry or occupation sectors and native-born males' employment and wages in both 1979 and 1989. They suggest that this can be explained by a crowding effect, as "recent immigrants are replacing native-born workers in large numbers of jobs in the region." Curiously, Howell and Mueller do not find a negative relationship between immigrant shares and the employment of either native-born Hispanics or recent immigrants in the same secondary sectors. And, in the sixteen African American job "niches" that they identify (half in the downsizing public sector), the number of native-born black jobholders fell by a mere two thousand over the year of the study.

In the most ambitious case study of its kind for New York so far, Roger Waldinger (1996) conducted both statistical and historical analyses of the employment of African Americans and of immigrants in specific industries. Postwar suburbanization of whites, he states, created large numbers of job openings at all skill levels in the city. Vacancies appeared even in shrinking manufacturing industries as whites left at a faster rate than labor demand declined. Despite often weak English-language and educational skills, foreign-born new-comers have won a disproportionate share of these openings. They have not done so, however, by directly displacing native-born blacks from jobs: in fact, the industrial distributions of native-born blacks and nonwhite immigrants have seldom overlapped. Waldinger also finds little evidence to support claims that the availability of immi-grant labor has indirectly displaced natives by enabling employers to keep wages and working conditions at unattractive levels. For example, in hotels, the rapid job and real-wage growth of recent years has not stopped the seepage of native blacks from an industry in which they were overrepresented from the 1940s through 1970s.

Instead of immigration, Waldinger assigns greatest importance to racial discrimination and African Americans' rising job aspirations. Faced with scant prospects of upward mobility out of dead-end, low-skill positions, more and more American-born blacks spurned these industries such as hotels in favor of the greater job security and wage equality offered (at least until recent cutbacks, as will be dis-cussed) in the public sector.

WAGE LEVELS

Have inflated New York wage levels priced less-skilled workers out of jobs more than wage levels have in other cities? To find out, I cal-culated average hourly wages for twenty-five-to-sixty-four-year-old job holders subdivided by years of schooling in the March 1998 CPS. On average, all noncollege-educated workers in the United States earned $10 per hour, well above New York City's average of $8.75 per hour and the $8.88 level for the nation's twenty largest cities. This despite the fact that New York and most other large cities have above-average costs of living.

Despite several months of earnings growth in low-wage retail and service industries in 1997 and 1998, earnings inequality between workers at the top and bottom of the wage scale remains unusually wide in New York and has worsened during the 1990s at a rate much faster than elsewhere. New research has shown that the growing earnings disparities in the New York metro area reflect both above-average raises for the best-paid 10 percent of employees and steep real-wage drops for the lowest paid. Among year-round, full-time male workers in the New York City region, the ratio of average annual earnings at the ninetieth percentile to that at the tenth percentile jumped from 4.6 in 1989 (identical to the national ratio) to 6.8 in 1996—an inequality over one-third greater than that found in the nation as a whole (Federal Reserve Bank of New York 1998).

LABOR DEMAND'S GROWTH AND STRUCTURE

Both the rate of job growth in New York and its industrial composition appear to have contributed to the persistence of joblessness among many minority and noncollege-educated city residents. The city lost over 360,000 jobs from 1989 to 1992, and it lagged far behind its suburban neighbors and the nation as a whole in regaining them. Significant job growth began only in the mid-1990s, and by the end of 1998 the city's 3.6 million jobs still fell nearly 100,000 short of the number of almost a full decade earlier. (Likewise, the late 1980s recovery never recovered all the jobs lost since 1969, when New York City employers provided 3.8 million jobs.)

Manufacturing has long been the single largest employer of non-college-educated workers in the city. New York began the 1970s with over 766,000 jobs in manufacturing, but ended the decade with less than half a million. The industry's decline slowed in the eighties, but still, another 158,000 jobs were lost. An additional roughly 80,000 more manufacturing jobs disappeared in the nineties, and just about 262,000 manufacturing jobs remained by the close of 1998 (New York State Department of Labor, various years).

Meanwhile, job growth has occurred almost exclusively in retail and services, particularly those related to the stock-market boom. The city's economy, in fact, has become increasingly dependent on Wall Street. This disproportionate and growing impact on the city's fortunes was emphasized in a much-discussed August 1999 report by the State Comptroller's Office (New York State Office of the Comptroller 1999). This report found that although the securities industry employs just 5 percent of the local work force, it accounted for 56 percent of the real-earnings growth seen between 1992 and 1997—over twice as large a share of the city's real-earnings gain as Wall Street represented in the 1980s boom. Recognizing recent job growth in tourism, construction, and new media, the report nonetheless predicted sharp losses in average real-earnings growth in the event of a sustained market downturn. Independent forecasters now estimate that without that rebound, the city's job growth would have been cut in half.

New York's worsening economic dependence on Wall Street in a period of skyrocketing real estate prices has also dramatically hiked the price of taxpayer-financed "corporate retention" deals (Bagli 1998). In 1998, for example, the city and the state offered the New York Stock Exchange nearly $500 million in cash and $100 million in tax breaks—a subsidy over twice as large as any ever before offered to a single company to build a new trading complex in lower Manhattan. Meanwhile, garment, printing, and other manufacturing firms threatened with displacement by soaring rents have complained about receiving little or no assistance from City Hall (Center for an Urban Future 1999).

Increasing privatization of government functions has hit black workers especially hard. Throughout the 1970s and 1980s, public-sector jobs in hospitals, the post office, schools, and social services, for instance, provided a major source of secure, unionized employment for the black middle class. Blacks won many of the 90,800 new positions created in this sector during the 1980s. But from a peak of nearly 608,000 in 1990, government jobs had been cut to 521,700 by the end of 1998. And unlike the 1970s, when layoffs in this sector were generally of entry-level workers and largely temporary, privatization in the 1990s has meant the wholesale elimination of many senior positions. Two different studies have estimated the African American share of these job losses to be 40 to 50 percent.[7]

CONCLUDING REMARKS

The national economic boom of the 1990s has had clear, if belated, benefits for high-unemployment cities like New York. The city's unemployment rate dropped from 9.4 percent in 1997 to an annual average of 8 percent that year. Throughout the region, low-wage workers, particularly minorities, finally began to reap significant gains from the tightening labor market, as reflected in their falling unemployment rates and rising wages since 1997.

Despite that, this paper has shown that, even with this recent progress, black and Hispanic New Yorkers experience unemployment at levels far above those of whites or minorities nationally. Differences in workers' educational attainments clearly account for some of their disadvantage relative to whites; whites are still much more likely than blacks or Hispanics to have some college background. Still, the city's black and Hispanic adults are more likely to have some college education than minorities nationally, and yet they nevertheless have higher jobless rates than minorities elsewhere. And, among noncollege-educated adults, not only blacks and Hispanics but also whites in New York exhibit average unemployment rates above the national average for their racial or ethnic and educational cohorts.

To the vast majority of low-income New York youth, the only hope of an affordable college education can be realized at one of the seventeen campuses of the City University of New York (CUNY). But CUNY has been badly battered by well-publicized criticisms of its open-admissions policy and educational standards, which have led to the recent imposition of new admissions-test standards for its four-year colleges. Far too little attention, however, has been paid to the damage inflicted by many years of tuition hikes, funding cuts for facilities and programs, and replacement of tenured faculty positions with underpaid, overworked adjunct teachers. These latter trends clearly need to be reversed if a better balance is ever to be achieved between maximum access to education for low-income high school graduates and improved educational quality.

While CUNY's paramount mission must always be higher education, it has not begun to tap its potential to move graduates from school to careers or to aid the city's job growth. Businesses large and small that leave New York often complain about the difficulties in meeting their skilled-labor needs. A number of other states have successfully integrated their public universities into a coordinated system of skills training and job placement.[8] CUNY took a small step in this direction in 1994 with its Workforce Development Initiative implemented at a handful of campuses. The initiative is the product of a unique arrangement between the city government and a major financial firm considering relocation: in 1992, Bear Stearns won a $12 million tax break in return for funding a ten-year recruitment, training, and hiring initiative. This program, run through CUNY's New York City Technical College, is a small example of how so-called corporate retention deals could be structured to make tax breaks contingent on long-term commitments to the future of CUNY, its graduates, and the city's job growth.

The relatively slow pace of job expansion in New York City suggests that in addition to national policies aimed at full employment, more targeted initiatives might be needed to preserve and increase hiring and training opportunities for less-educated metro-area residents. Manufacturing remains the dominant employer of workers without college educations, but city policy-makers have done little to apply the methods practiced with success elsewhere to cultivate a manufacturing renewal. Too many small business firms in manufacturing and related sectors have been forced out of the city by inadequate supplies of appropriately trained labor, soaring real estate expenses, and little or no access to the sorts of specialized business-assistance programs common in some other cities.[9]

While there is no consistent evidence that immigration to the United States has thus far had sizable effects on natives' wages and employment or on public-sector budget problems, it may have adverse effects on some workers, particularly earlier immigrants. Of perhaps more concern are the 1996 welfare reforms, which continue to drive millions of public-assistance recipients into the job market and thereby fuel worries about the possibility of heightened competition among the low-wage labor force. This alone should motivate efforts to formulate corrective policies today as well as instill caution in advocates of greatly expanded immigration. The federal government both determines immigration policies and, most studies show, reaps the bulk of the fiscal benefits generated by immigrant taxpayers. Hence, a strong case can be made for requiring the federal government to redistribute adequate funds back to high-immigration cities to enable them to better cope with their rising schooling, health, and other public-service needs.[10]

NOTES

1. Labor-force participation rates are from unpublished tabulations by the U.S. Bureau of Labor Statistics, and I am grateful to the New York City Regional Bureau of Labor Statistics for providing them. Jobs figures are from establishment data published by the New York State Department of Labor.

2. For a more detailed analysis of these labor-force trends, see Community Service Society (1998) and New York City Office of the Comptroller (1999).

3. Although the limited sample size used here requires pooling all Hispanic persons, it is important to recognize how heterogeneous the

Hispanic labor force is. For disaggregated analysis of Mexican, Puerto Rican, Cuban, and other Latin American unemployment trends, see DeFreitas (1986; 1991).

4. Given the relatively small sample size in Current Population Survey subsets like these, caution must be exercised in interpreting all such results.

5. In an attempt to go beyond the official government unemployment rate, I tried to estimate broader "underemployment" rates. Unlike official unemployment, underemployment here includes discouraged labor-force dropouts—people who looked for work in the past year and want a job—as well as involuntary part-time employees unable to find full-time work. As seen in table C1.2, nearly 20 percent of black adults in New York were underemployed, compared to fewer than 12 percent of blacks nationwide and 16.2 percent in the top twenty cities. New York's white and Hispanic underemployment levels were below the black level but still above the national averages.

Table C1.2 Underemployment Rates in the United States, New York City, and Other Largest Cities, for Adults Ages Twenty-Five to Sixty-Four, by Ethnicity and Educational Attainment, 1998

	All	White	Black	Hispanic
Age twenty-five to sixty-four				
United States	7.1	5.8	11.9	11.2
Large cities	10.2	6.9	16.2	12.6
New York City	11.9	7.6	19.0	14.5
Noncollege				
United States	10.3	8.4	16.1	13.5
Large cities	15.4	11.7	23.0	14.5
New York City	19.0	16.3	27.7	16.8
College				
United States	4.7	4.3	7.4	6.8
Large cities	6.1	5.1	9.0	7.6
New York City	6.2	3.6	10.5	10.4

Source: United States Bureau of the Census, Current Population Survey, March 1998. The "underemployment rate" is here measured as the total officially counted as "unemployed," plus those "marginally attached" to labor force who want a job now, plus persons employed part-time for economic reasons, expressed as a per-cent of the official labor force plus those counted as marginally attached. White and black samples are here restricted to non-Hispanics. Hispanics may be of any race. Enrolled students are excluded from these estimates.

6. In contrast, the Hispanic unemployment rate would be reduced more by obtaining the white urban educational distribution. This is consistent with Reimers's (this volume) findings and my earlier time-series work in DeFreitas (1986).

7. See studies cited in Kirk Johnson (1997).

8. See the comparative study of CUNY and the Arizona state system in Center for an Urban Future (1999).

9. See the evaluation of alternative urban-industrial strategies in Center for an Urban Future (1999) and New York Industrial Retention Network (1999).

10. For more-detailed immigration-policy analysis, see DeFreitas (1998).

REFERENCES

Bagli, C. 1998. "Wall Street Plays Relocation Card and City Pays." *New York Times*, November 8, p. 39.

Center for an Urban Future. 1999. *The Big Squeeze: How Rising Rents and the Real Estate Crunch Are Forcing Small Businesses out of New York*. New York: Center for an Urban Future.

Community Service Society of New York. 1998. *New York City's Labor Market, 1994–97*. New York: Community Service Society.

———. 1999. *Poverty in New York City: An Update*. New York: Community Service Society.

DeFreitas, Gregory. 1986. "A Time-Series Analysis of Hispanic Unemployment." *Journal of Human Resources* 21(Winter): 24–43.

———. 1991. *Inequality at Work: Hispanics in the U.S. Labor Force*. New York: Oxford University Press.

———. 1998. "Immigration, Inequality, and Policy Alternatives." In *Globalization and Progressive Economic Policy*, edited by Gerald Epstein and Robert Pollin. New York: Cambridge University Press.

———. Forthcoming. *Futures at Risk: Youth in the Urban Economy*.

Federal Reserve Bank of New York, Research and Market Analysis Group. 1998. "Earnings Inequality: NY-NJ Region." *Current Issues in Economics and Finance* (July): 1–4.

Howell, David, and Elizabeth Mueller. 1998. "Immigration and Native-Born Male Earnings: A Jobs-Level Analysis of the New York City

Metropolitan Area Labor Market, 1980–90." Unpublished paper. New York: Milano Graduate School, New School University.

Johnson, Kirk. 1997. "Black Workers bear Big Burden as Jobs in Government Dwindle." *New York Times*, February 2, 1997, p. 1.

National Research Council. 1997. *The New Americans: Economic, Demographic, and Fiscal Effects of Immigration.* Washington, D.C.: National Academy Press.

New York City Office of the Comptroller. 1999 (March). *Economic Notes.* New York: New York City Office of the Comptroller.

New York Industrial Retention Network. 1999. *The Little Manufacturer That Could: Opportunities and Challenges for Manufacturing in New York City.* New York: Industrial Retention Network.

New York State Department of Labor. Various years. *Employment Review.* Albany, N.Y.: New York State Department of Labor.

New York State Office of the Comptroller. 1999. *New York City's Economic and Fiscal Dependence on Wall Street.* Report 5–99. Albany: New York State Office of the Comptroller.

Waldinger, Roger. 1996. *Still the Promised City? African Americans and New Immigrants in Post-Industrial New York.* Cambridge, Mass.: Harvard University Press.

PART II

Racial Discrimination and the Boom

Chapter 4

How Labor-Market Tightness Affects Employer Attitudes and Actions Toward Black Job Applicants: Evidence from Employer Surveys

PHILIP MOSS AND CHRIS TILLY

The labor-market situation for young black and Hispanic male workers was grim throughout the 1980s and 1990s. Following a narrowing of the unemployment gap between black and white workers in the 1970s, things turned worse in the early 1980s and have not improved, in the aggregate, until quite recently (Bound and Freeman 1992; Moss and Tilly 1991, 2000a, 2000b). Based on the idea that employers facing a thinner pool of potential employees as unemployment falls will tend to hire people whom they might have been less likely to hire when there were more potential workers to choose from, one would have expected the labor-market position of black and Hispanic workers to have improved as the economy expanded in the 1980s and then again in the 1990s following the recession that ended in 1991. This, however, did not happen until the late 1990s.

The lack of progress in the years preceding the very recent gains raises a number of questions and possibilities. Shifts in the demand for particular skills, changes in the relative supplies of competing workers, or other changes in employment dynamics might have offset the effect of tightening labor markets. Employers' views of black or Hispanic workers—particularly of young black male workers, whose labor-market outcomes appear to be most unyielding—could prove sufficiently implacable as to put such workers beyond the force of the aggregate labor-market tightness that has marked most of the 1980s and 1990s (though perhaps with some local exceptions). We and others have examined why young black and Hispanic workers might be lower on employer hiring queues (see Bound and Freeman

1992; Kirschenman and Neckerman 1991; Moss and Tilly 1991, 1996, 2000a, 2000b; and the sources cited in those papers). The recent relative gains by blacks, however, may indicate that certain labor markets are achieving a level of activity adequate to force employers further down their hiring queues.

What we know about the effect of tightening labor markets on blacks and Hispanics comes from time-series data, cross sections of labor-market areas, and case studies of particularly tight labor markets. In this paper, we look at the relation of labor-market tightness to the labor-market success of black and Hispanic workers from a fresh standpoint. While we present quantitative cross-sectional analyses, we do so with a new data set that allows a different unit of analysis: the employer. Our main data come from a quantitative survey of employers in four metropolitan areas conducted during the period spanning 1992 through 1995. This survey provides us with several potential perspectives on the tightness of labor-market conditions, including metropolitan-area unemployment rates ("macro-labor-market tightness") as well as the circumstances confronting the individual firms in hiring for particular jobs ("micro-labor-market tightness"). Our results indicate that macro-labor-market tightness significantly reduces the hiring of whites and increases hiring of blacks (because the groups' shares total 100 percent, increased hiring of any group must be offset by a decreased share for another group); it is also associated with increases in the proportions of all other groups, but none of these other effects are significant. Our preferred measure of micro-labor-market tightness, on the other hand, reveals a greater hiring probability for black women, apparently primarily at the expense of Hispanics with inconclusive results for black men. We examine a number of potential mediating variables—including employer attitudes and changes in hiring procedures—but none appears to explain the effects of macro- or micro-labor-market tightness on black and Hispanic unemployment.

We complement our empirical analysis with illustrative data from qualitative in-depth interviews of a subset of the employers who participated in the quantitative survey. These data confirm that employers respond to the size and composition of the labor pool.

LITERATURE REVIEW

Richard Lester's (1954) classic study of hiring practices documented the ways in which employers adjust hiring standards as necessary when faced with changing labor-market conditions. Melvin Reder (1955) formalized Richard Lester's and others' empirical findings into a theory of wage differentials that accounts for how employers move down a skill or quality queue of potential employees as the labor market tightens during business cycles. Since the 1950s, many others have studied the flexibility of hiring practices and standards over the business cycle (see Bills 1988 for a review). Our own research has shown that black and other minority workers are relatively far down in employer hiring queues, whether due to some combination of hard and soft skill deficits, employer stereotypification of minorities, or prejudices of employers, customers, and coworkers toward minorities (Moss and Tilly 2000a). As a result, one would expect these groups' positions in the labor market relative to their white counterparts to be affected by labor-market tightness.

A number of quantitative studies from the 1990s have examined how black workers' (and in some cases, other minority workers') relative labor-market situation has been affected by the tightness of aggregate or local labor markets (see Moss and Tilly 1991 for a more detailed review of the work done before 1991). These studies fall into three categories: time-series analyses of the relative employment and wages of blacks to whites in relation to aggregate unemployment; cross-sectional studies of local labor markets that vary in level of unemployment; and case studies of the Boston-area labor market during the extraordinarily low unemployment rates of the mid- to late 1980s. The cross-sectional studies, as well as the case-study analyses of Boston, show gains for young black workers relative to young white workers in tight labor markets. The time-series evidence, however, does not manifest such relative gains. Other studies based on qualitative data have provided important insight into the nature of employer hiring queues and why blacks in particular appear to be so far back in them.

Quantitative Studies

John Bound and Richard Freeman (1992) have done extensive time series work using Current Population Survey (CPS) data from 1973 through 1988, running yearly earnings and probability of employment regressions for male workers with less than ten potential years of experience. Although the general trend shows a worsening of the relative position of black workers' earnings and employment over the sample period, the fluctuations around the trend do not provide any clear evidence of relative improvement for young blacks as over-all labor demand increases. The relative odds of white versus black employment also fails to show a pattern consistent with the hypothesis that employers increase their hiring of blacks when overall unemployment falls.

Glen Cain and Ross Finnie (1990), Richard Freeman (1989, 1990), and John Bound and Harry Holzer (1996) are cross-sectional studies that use the local labor market as the unit of analysis to study the relation between employment outcomes of, among others, young black workers and a number of measures of labor-market tightness. These studies address several data sets and time periods, including the 1980 census (Cain and Finnie 1990), the CPS for various years (Freeman 1989, 1990; Bound and Holzer 1996), and the National Longitudinal Studies of Youth for 1983 and 1987 (Freeman 1989), and produce consistent results: the relative labor-market position of disadvantaged youth—disadvantaged black youth in particular—is sensitive to local unemployment rates. Other papers in this volume (Freeman and Rodgers, this volume; Reimers, this volume) replicate this finding with updated data.

Richard Freeman (1989) and Paul Osterman (1989) analyzed specialized data sets collected on the experiences of the disadvantaged in the Boston-area boom labor-market conditions in 1988. Osterman designed a survey that focused on poverty rates and found a substantial reduction in poverty during the upswing in demand for labor in Boston, and further, that poverty rates in Boston fell significantly lower than the rates for the nation. Freeman, using a special survey of inner-city youth administered by the National Bureau of Economic Research, found that the tight labor-market conditions drove a 59 percent increase in earnings among young black men over their reported earnings in 1980. Also, black youth in Boston in 1989 had earnings significantly higher than comparable young people in U.S. metropolitan areas as a whole. Still, tight labor market conditions do not eliminate the disadvantage facing young black men: in Boston in 1989, they reported earnings 16 percent lower than comparable white youth—a differential similar to the differential for the country as a whole—and their employment-to-population ratio, at 51 percent, was eleven percentage points below that of white youth.

Qualitative Studies

Joleen Kirschenman and Kathryn Neckerman (1991), Roger Waldinger (1993), as well as Philip Moss and Chris Tilly (1996, 2000a,

2000b), have conducted qualitative in-depth studies in which employers are asked explicitly to evaluate the relative attractiveness of different groups of workers. All of these studies document that many employers are wary of black workers and view their hard and soft skills as deficient relative to other workers. Further, each study has shown that employers tend to believe that the "work ethic" among black workers is not as strong as it is among immigrant workers. For example, in a study that we conducted in Detroit and Los Angeles in 1990 and 1991, a majority of respondents (thirty-eight of fifty-three) reported that they believed or observed that immigrants worked harder than native-born—in some cases, white as well as black—workers did. Black women were frequently cited as better, harder workers than black men; the reason often, but not always, given was that black women are quite often financially responsible for their families, and this makes them more responsible as workers (Moss and Tilly 1996, 2000b).

DATA

Our data are drawn from two of the three coordinated surveys from the Multi-City Study of Urban Inequality: the large-scale, quantitative telephone survey of employers in the Atlanta, Boston, Detroit, and Los Angeles metropolitan areas, and the qualitative face-to-face, in-depth follow-up survey of a selected sample of those employers. The primary source of data is the quantitative survey.

Professor Harry Holzer of Michigan State University administered the telephone survey of employers, in which roughly eight hundred employers in each of the four cities were interviewed between May 1992 and May 1994. The survey questions addressed the characteristics of the business establishment, current job vacancies there, the last person hired by the establishment, and nature of the job that that person filled. Respondents were asked about frequency of performance of certain tasks, recruiting and screening procedures, other hiring requirements, the demographics of their most recently hired worker, the demographics of applicants for the job, and the demographics of their firms' employees and customers. About one thousand of the firms interviewed were identified via participants in the Multi-City Study household surveys who reported their employer. (Kirschenman and the authors administered 297 of these household-linked interviews after Holzer's study was complete.) The balance of the firms in the telephone survey was drawn from lists of firms furnished by Survey Sampling, Inc., which generated them from local telephone directories. The response rate for the telephone survey (including only those firms that passed the screener) was about two-thirds. Holzer (1996) reported many of the major findings from these data. The data oversampled jobs that require no more than a high school degree, and throughout this paper we limit our analysis to jobs that do not require a college degree.

The sample for the in-depth employer survey was drawn from firms identified by Multi-City Study household respondents who held jobs requiring no more than a high school education and had successfully completed a telephone survey. Interviews were conducted between the summers of 1994 and 1996 at 45 firms in both Atlanta and Los Angeles, 46 in Boston, and 39 in Detroit, for a total of 175 firms. The response rate for the in-depth survey was about two-thirds. The in-depth survey involved a series of structured questions and follow-up probes. Interviewers spoke face-to-face with up to three, and in a few cases more, individuals per firm: the chief executive officer or another top manager at the site; a personnel official involved in hiring for the sample job; and a line manager or supervisor who managed employees in the sample job category. In total, 355 interviews were conducted with 365 respondents (some interviews included more than one respondent at a time), averaging just over two interviews and respondents per firm. Questions gathered the details of the recruiting, screening, and hiring procedures used to fill the sample job, and what each procedure was designed to do. Questions were open-ended, and interviewers were trained to encourage respondents to elaborate and thereby tell the story of their business's relationship to the labor market. Finally, the monthly unemployment rates for the four metropolitan areas were obtained from the Bureau of Labor Statistics, Office of Local Area Unemployment Statistics.

VARIABLES AND HYPOTHESES

Our macro variable for labor-market tightness is the metropolitan-area unemployment rate, as measured on a monthly basis. We actually generate two such variables: one based on the unemployment rate at the time that our interview was conducted, and one based on the rate at the time that the last hire was carried out. (Eighty-eight percent of most-recent hires fell within the preceding twelve months, but some reached as far back as early 1982.) Since we have measures of firm behavior at the time of interview and others for the time of hire, both unemployment rates are relevant. And although our sample includes only four metropolitan areas, the variation between the interview date and hire date generates variation in the unemployment rates.

The variation in unemployment rates within our sample falls short of that in typical cross-sectional or time-series studies. However, the employer telephone-survey data include something potentially more useful: information regarding vacancies at each firm surveyed, as well as a measure of the time required to complete the most recent hire. Vacancy rates are well known to vary inversely with unemployment, as characterized in the curve first devised by, and subsequently named for, the British economist William Beveridge (Hamermesh and Rees 1988, 412–15). Beveridge, however, studied the covariation of unemployment and vacancy rates over time at the national level; we, in contrast, have information on vacancies at the firm level. This offers us an index of the labor-market tightness faced by particular firms, hiring for particular jobs, at a particular time—a micro-measure of labor-market tightness or slackness. The time required to conduct the last hire is of interest for the same reason; it represents a completed vacancy.

The telephone survey data yield four vacancy-related indices:

- The number of current vacancies, which can be converted to the number of vacancies as a percentage of the total number of jobs

- The average duration of all current vacancies at the firm

- The duration of the longest current vacancy in a job that does not require a college degree

- The time required to conduct the most recent hire

Note at the outset that while these vacancy-related variables may in part reflect micro–labor-market tightness, they might also reflect other phenomena as well. We will examine this possibility in the discussion that follows.

Table 4.1 shows pairwise correlations among the four vacancy-related indices, along with the two unemployment-rate variables. Reported "longest noncollege vacancies" range as high as ninety months, but jobs left vacant for this long do not fit one's usual concep-

Table 4.1 Pairwise Correlations of Variables Related to Labor-Market Tightness (*p*-Values in Parentheses)

	Vacancies per Job	Average Vacancy Duration	Longest Noncollege Vacancy, up to Twelve Months	Time to Hire Last Person	How Often Hire Less Qualified	Unemployment Rate at Time of Interview	Unemployment Rate at Time of Hire
Vacancies per job (all jobs)	1.000						
Average vacancy duration, all jobs	0.280 (.000)	1.000					
Longest noncollege vacancy, restricted to twelve months or less	0.349 (.000)	0.504 (.000)	1.000				
Time required to hire last person	0.010 (.581)	0.117 (.000)	0.098 (.000)	1.000			
How often hire less-qualified people because needed workers badly	0.096 (.000)	0.052 (.005)	0.113 (.000)	−0.021 (.246)	1.000		
Metro-area unemployment rate at time of last hire	−0.040 (.030)	−0.006 (.747)	−0.046 (.026)	−0.027 (.138)	0.001 (.942)	1.000	
Metro-area unemployment rate at time of interview	−0.029 (.111)	0.013 (.481)	−0.032 (.120)	−0.035 (.054)	0.012 (.499)	0.913 (.000)	1.000

Source: Multi-City Study of Urban Inequality Telephone Employer Survey. Authors' tabulations.

tion of a vacancy (and could reflect data problems), so in our analysis we dropped cases with vacancies greater than twelve months. It is thus this sample-restricted version of the "longest vacancy" measure that is reported in this and other tables. Likewise, we dropped cases in which the time to hire exceeded twelve months. We also incorporate one other variable based on the question "How often do you need unskilled workers so badly that you hire less-qualified workers than you did in the past?"; answers are scaled from 1 (never) to 4 (always).

The vacancy indices display a comforting degree of internal consistency. While the correlations are not large (with the exception of the relation between average vacancy duration and longest noncollege vacancy), they are uniformly positive, and, with the exception of the very weak correlation between vacancies per job (primarily an incidence variable) and the time required to hire the last person (a duration variable), are significant at the 1 percent level or better. As expected, the vacancy-related variables are with one exception negatively associated with the two unemployment-rate variables, though the degree of significance varies widely. All of this suggests that these measures are indeed capturing meaningful, related phenomena.

To the extent that the vacancy variables reflect labor-market tightness, they should also covary with "have hired less-qualified people": when good workers are scarce, firms are likely to both search longer and settle for less. This is indeed true for three out of four of the vacancy variables. But the time spent on the last hire is *negatively* correlated with hiring less-qualified people, and this suggests that variation in hiring time might reflect firm selectiveness rather than labor-market tightness—a possibility that we will explore further later in this paper. In our analyses, we relate a vacancy index to the race and gender of the last hire in a job that does not require a college education. Therefore, we limit our attention to the third and fourth vacancy indices—the longest noncollege vacancy and the time required to complete the most recent noncollege hire—because the other two indices include jobs requiring college educations as well as those that do not. Throughout the paper, we compare these two vacancy indices and the unemployment rate as alternative measures of labor market tightness.

Descriptive statistics for variables employed in the analyses can be found in Table 4.2. The mean duration of the longest vacancy in a job not requiring college is approximately one month. The modal longest

Table 4.2 Descriptive Statistics (Unweighted) for Variables Used in the Analysis

	Mean	Standard Deviation
Labor Market Tightness		
Duration of longest noncollege vacancy, in months	0.99	5.82
Duration of longest vacancy, restricted to twelve months	0.56	1.53
Time required for last noncollege hire, in weeks	2.92	4.96
Unemployment rate (percentage) at time of hire	7.55	1.93
Unemployment rate (percentage) at time of interview	7.32	2.01
Race (And in Some Cases Gender) of Last Hire		
Last hire white	0.55	0.50
Last hire black	0.23	0.42
Last hire black man	0.11	0.31
Last hire black woman	0.12	0.33
Last hire Hispanic	0.17	0.38
Last hire Asian	0.04	0.20
"How Often Would You Hire Someone Who . . . ?"		
Welfare recipient	3.42	0.67
GED or government employment program	3.51	0.60
Criminal record	2.33	0.93
Unemployed one year or more	3.10	0.70
Short-term, part-time experience	2.73	0.83
Less qualified, because need workers badly	1.47	0.62
Report Change in Hiring in Last Five to Ten Years		
More affirmative recruiting	0.12	0.33
Less use of education or criminal record checks	0.24	0.42
Control Variables		
Percentage of applicants white or other	29.94	37.46
Percentage of applicants black	31.46	33.12
Percentage of applicants black men	18.32	23.56
Percentage of applicants black women	14.53	21.29
Percentage of applicants Hispanic	16.67	26.71
Percentage of applicants Asian	6.39	14.02
Natural log of total firm employment	4.09	1.82

(Table continues on page 139.)

Table 4.2 *Continued*

	Mean	Standard Deviation
Uses affirmative recruiting	0.71	0.45
Percent of frontline workers covered by collective bargaining	15.87	33.09
Starting wage, in dollars per hour	$8.32	$3.58
Job requires speaking face-to-face with customers daily	0.60	0.49
Job requires speaking on the telephone daily	0.54	0.50
Job requires reading instructions daily	0.34	0.50
Job requires writing paragraphs daily	0.56	0.47
Job requires doing arithmetic daily	0.64	0.48
Job requires working with computers daily	0.53	0.50
Time required to become competent on the job, in weeks	18.25	20.71

Source: Multi-City Study of Urban Inequality Telephone Employer Survey. Authors' tabulations.

vacancy duration (not shown) is zero, accounting for 72 percent of cases. When we drop vacancy durations over twelve months, the resulting mean longest vacancy is just over one-half month. Henceforth in this paper, references to the longest vacancy refer to the variable restricted to a twelve-month maximum. The mean hiring time for the last noncollege job is about three weeks. The average unemployment rate at the time of that hire is 7.5 percent, whereas unemployment at the time of the interview averages 7.3 percent, reflecting the fact that the nation was emerging from a recession as the survey was conducted.

Our key dependent variables are a set of dummy variables for the race of the last hire in a job not requiring college. Ideally, we would prefer to examine the probability of hire for a full set of race-and-gender combinations (using as dependent variables dummies for white male, white female, black male, black female, and so on), but in estimating the determinants of the probability of hiring someone from a particular demographic group, we wish to control for the proportion of the applicant pool belonging to that group. Because the survey inquired about male and female applicant pools only among black applicants, we only conduct separate hiring analyses by gender for blacks.

We use two sets of variables that might be expected to mediate between labor-market tightness and hiring behavior. One set evaluates willingness to hire stigmatized groups. Employers were asked to report their willingness to hire members of these groups on a scale ranging from "absolutely will not accept" (1) to "definitely will accept" (4). We include "hire less-qualified workers" in this set, despite that scale being defined slightly differently (extending from "never" to "always").

The second set of mediating variables involves changes in hiring position. While discussing the last hire for a noncollege job, employers were asked, "Has your recruiting for such a position changed in the past five to ten years?" and "Have your methods of screening applicants changed in the past five to ten years?" They were then prompted for the recruiting and screening methods that they used more often, and those they used less often, with up to three of each recorded and coded. We built two variables out of these responses: "More affirmative recruiting" categorizes employers who stated that they more often use newspaper advertisements, state employment services, community agencies, school referrals, or union referrals to fill vacancies. (Not included in this category are such recruiting methods as posting signs, accepting walk-ins, current-employee referrals, private employment services or temporary agencies, and referrals from other sources such as acquaintances.) In terms of screening, we constructed a variable for less use of checks on education or criminal record. We singled these screens out because they were the ones most commonly decreased: 11 percent of respondents reported using education checks less often, and 18 percent reported a decrease in criminal-record checks; the next runner-up, tests, was reported by only 7 percent of employers. Moreover, since African Americans and Hispanics continue to lag behind whites in education, and since black and Hispanic men are more likely than any other groups to be entangled with the criminal-justice system, relaxing these screens seemed likely to increase the hiring chances of black and Hispanic applicants.

Finally, table 4.2 shows a set of control variables. The racial composition of the applicant pool is gleaned from asking approximately what percentage of the previous year's applications or job inquiries came from members of the various groups listed. "Uses affirmative recruiting" denotes that for the last hire in a noncollege job, the employer used the recruiting methods that we defined as "affirmative." The remaining control variables are fairly self-explanatory.

Our basic model relates tightness in the labor market for non-college jobs to the race of the most recent noncollege hire:

Probability that the most recent noncollege hire comes
from a given racial group = f(labor market tightness,
racial composition of applicant pool, natural logarithm
of firm size, city effects) (4.1)

We hypothesize that as labor markets tighten (as indicated by falling unemployment rates, longer search times to fill jobs, or increasing vacancy durations), employers will reach further down an employment queue to hire workers including African Americans and Hispanics—whom they view as less preferred. This hypothesis predicts that labor-market tightness will be positively associated with hiring of blacks and Hispanics. We control for the racial composition of the applicant pool by including the percentage of applicants from the each racial group. The firm-size control acts as proxy for widely observed differences between large and small firms, notably greater formality in hiring procedures in large firms. Finally, we use city dummies to control for city-specific differences other than those due to differences in unemployment rates.

This model assumes that the relationship between vacancy duration and race of persons hired is driven by labor-market tightness as encountered by a particular firm. But, as we noted previously, other factors might play roles as well. For example, the relationship between vacancy duration and race of hire can be manifested in:

- How selective the firm is in hiring for the job in question: selective firms, which screen more applicants, are likely to have longer vacancies and to take a longer time to hire their latest last employee than less-particular firms. We would expect the degree of skill and the amount of firm-specific training required to perform a job to be associated with selectiveness. If discriminatory firms tend to be more selective, or if selective firms place greater emphasis on skills that blacks and Hispanics are more likely than whites to lack, selectivity will affect the racial composition of hiring. Unlike any of the other mechanisms we discuss, this predicts a negative association between vacancy duration and hiring of blacks and Hispanics.

- How formal the procedures that the firm uses in hiring for the job are: formal procedures generally take longer than informal ones. We have argued elsewhere that formal hiring procedures, by reducing the ambit for biased attitudes, increase job opportunities for black workers (Moss and Tilly 2000b), so in this case the association between vacancy duration and hiring of workers of color should be positive. In some specifications of our model, we control for two key aspects of formal procedures—affirmative recruiting and union representation.

- How job quality at this firm—as measured by wages and other job characteristics—compares to similar jobs in other firms. There are at least two variants on this account. In the "good job" story, firms paying above-market wages attract large applicant pools that they must sort through, prolonging the search process; these "good" firms, which are often large and visible employers, also practice affirmative action and therefore hire more black workers. In the "lousy job" converse, some firms pay low wages relative to the market as a whole, and therefore have trouble attracting applicants, leading to long vacancies; blacks disproportionately must settle for these jobs. A variant of the lousy-job story points to turnover as a determinant of vacancies. Seventy-two percent of the firms we surveyed had zero vacancies, so the vacancy-related variables (except for the time required to hire) reflect the incidence as well as duration of vacancies; high-turnover firms are more likely to have vacancies. All of these explanations predict a positive association between vacancy duration and hiring of blacks and Hispanics—though, of course, firms offering better jobs might also be among the more selective.

Although we do not incorporate these possible effects directly into model 1, we do use added controls to explore their importance in the analysis.

There is another important disclaimer with respect to the longest noncollege vacancy category: the longest noncollege vacancy and the last noncollege hire do not necessarily fall in the same job category. Nonetheless, the vacancy's duration includes a component due to labor-market tightness in a particular geographic location, based on a given firm's overall level of compensation; the two jobs will hold this component in common. Furthermore, most of the firms in this survey are small—median employment is fifty-two persons (thirty-five in positions not requiring college degrees), with 62 percent of firms employing fewer than a hundred workers (and 72 percent em-

ploying fewer than one hundred in noncollege degree positions)—
and so the noncollege job vacant and the noncollege hire are likely to
be related. However, concern remains that the longest vacancy might
be in a job with particularly stringent requirements and therefore
atypical of jobs at a given firm. If this is the case, the length of this
vacancy will still respond to overall labor-market tightness but will
not accurately capture the tightness of the micro-labor-market affecting the most recent hire. As it turns out, a comparison of the longest
noncollege vacant job to the job of the most recent noncollege hire
reveals that they were indeed fairly similar, but, perhaps not surprisingly, the longest-vacant job was more likely to require a credential—
a high school diploma, general or job-specific experience—than the
job filled by the last hire. However, these differences (measured on a
scale of 1 = absolutely necessary, 2 = strongly preferred, 3 = mildly
preferred, 4 = does not matter for each of the four criteria), while statistically significant, are only about 0.1, or about 10 percent of a standard deviation. The longest vacancy has a starting wage 21 percent
greater than the last hire, but this only represents about one-third of
the standard deviation of the longest vacancy's wage. When we
regress the length of the longest vacancy on the job's starting wage
and credential requirements (including requirements for employer
references and vocational education or training, in addition to the
requirements already listed), this set of variables accounts for less
than 2 percent of the variation in vacancy duration. Thus, the characteristics of the vacant job do affect vacancy length but do not appear
to be a major determinant of it.

How, precisely, would labor-market tightness lead to change in
the racial composition of hires under model 1? We hypothesize that
tight labor markets might affect hiring by altering employers' attitudes about less-preferred groups in the workforce, and/or by leading employers to modify their hiring procedures. Thus:

Employer attitudes about less preferred groups
= g(labor market tightness, natural logarithm of firm size)   (4.2)

Probability that the most recent noncollege hire comes
from a given racial group = g'(employer attitudes about
less preferred groups, racial composition of applicant pool,
natural logarithm of firm size, city effects)   (4.2')

Employer changes in hiring procedures
= h(labor market tightness)   (4.3)

Probability that the most recent noncollege hire comes
from a given racial group = h' (employer changes in
hiring procedures, racial composition of applicant pool,
city effects)   (4.3')

When analyzing variables relating to employer attitude toward
stigmatized groups in the workforce, we do not attempt to distinguish among pure discrimination, statistical discrimination, and
legitimate concern about skill deficits. We believe that all three factor into employers' reluctance to hire certain groups. In the equations 4.2 and 4.2', we once more control for firm size as a proxy for
the many ways in which large and small firms differ, but do not do
so in equations 4.3 and 4.3', as size-of-firm effects on hiring practices
should difference out when looking at changes in these practices.

TESTING THE MODELS

To test our hypotheses, we estimate a set of binary logits, except in
a few cases in which the dependent variables are scale rather than
dummy variables (on these we use ordinary least-squares regression). We set our threshold significance level at 10 percent, and highlight coefficients reaching this significance level in bold in our tables.
The actual number of observations in regressions varied between
1,339 and 2,735, due to missing values for some variables; most
regressions mustered about 2,000 observations.

Table 4.3 begins the examination of the hypotheses. Broken into
three panels, the table reports results using, first, the unemployment
rate as a measure of labor market tightness, second, the time required
to accomplish the most recent hire, and, third, the duration of longest
vacancy of a position not requiring a college education. The first
panel's results conform completely to our hypothesis and the previous findings of others: when and where unemployment rates are
higher, employers are more likely to hire a white person than they
are to hire a person of color. A negative employment effect is statistically significant only among blacks, who experience a negative
impact estimated to be nearly twice as large as that on Hispanics.

The results in table 4.3's second panel provide support for the
hypothesis that the time required to fill the most recent vacancy measures the selectiveness of a firm's hiring strategy more than it measures the micro-labor-market tightness facing the firm. The first row,
with the results from the basic specification, shows that jobs taking a

Table 4.3 Relation Between Three Measures of Labor Market Tightness and Probability of Hiring a Member of a Given Racial Group (Absolute Values of z-Statistics in Parentheses; Bold = Significant at 10 Percent Level)

	Race (and in Some Cases Gender) of Most Recent Hire					
	White	Black	Black man	Black woman	Latino	Asian
Unemployment Rate—Contribution to Hiring Probabilities by Race, Gender						
Coefficient on metro area unemployment rate at time of hire, with controls for firm size, applicants from this racial group, city	**0.226** **(4.22)**	**−0.141** **(1.71)**	−0.148 (1.31)	−0.139 (1.24)	−0.072 (0.87)	−0.093 (0.63)
Time Required for Most Recent Hire—Contribution to Hiring Probabilities						
Coefficient on time required for most recent hire, with controls for firm size, applicants from this racial group, city	**0.023** **(2.39)**	−0.001 (0.08)	0.004 (0.32)	−0.009 (0.60)	**−0.036** **(1.92)**	0.008 (0.34)
Same as above with added controls for formal recruiting, starting wage, tasks required on the job, time required to become competent on the job, unemployment rate	−0.012 (1.13)	0.008 (.56)	0.017 (1.16)	0.015 (0.98)	−0.001 (0.05)	0.0005 (0.02)
Duration of Longest Noncollege Vacancy—Contribution to Hiring Probabilities						
Coefficient on duration of longest noncollege vacancy, with controls for firm size, applicants from this racial group, city	−0.039 (1.18)	**0.113** **(2.54)**	−0.036 (0.73)	**0.153** **(4.27)**	**−0.114** **(1.74)**	−0.09 (0.66)
Same as above with added controls for formal recruiting, starting wage, tasks required on the job, time required to become competent on the job, unemployment rate	−0.037 (0.95)	**0.104** **(2.02)**	−0.051 (0.90)	**0.159** **(3.73)**	−0.113 (1.47)	−0.07 (0.47)

Source: Multi-City Study of Urban Inequality Telephone Employer Survey. Authors' tabulations.

relatively longer time to fill are more likely to be occupied by whites at the expense of Hispanics. Further, when controls that measure job skill levels (including starting wages) and the area unemployment rate at the time of hire are added to the equation, the formerly significant coefficients on length of time to fill the last job are no longer so. When the various control variables were added individually to the basic equation (results not shown), the estimated effect of the length of time to fill the last job was driven below significance by each of the three variables that measure skill—starting wage, tasks required on the job, and time required to become competent on the job—and the effect was completely neutralized by inclusion of the starting wage.

The third measure of labor-market tightness, duration of longest noncollege vacancy, produces results more consistent with those from the first measure. The first row of table 4.3's bottommost panel indicates that tight labor markets, measured by this variable, increase an employer's probability of hiring a black person—specifically, a black woman. This gain seems to come primarily at the expense of Hispanics, who are less likely to be hired. In fact, the point estimates suggest that whites and Asians are also less likely to get the job, but only for Hispanics does the effect attain significance.

We added further controls to rule out alternative interpretations not based on labor-market tightness, again including formal recruiting procedures, starting wage, tasks required on the job, the time required to become competent on the job, and the area unemployment rate at the time of hire. All of these alternatives to a micro-labor-market-tightness interpretation have some plausibility, but besides driving the effect for Hispanics below significance, adding these controls nevertheless does not markedly change the results. Vacancy duration is still strongly related to the probability of hiring a black woman, so micro-labor-market tightness seems to be the underlying force. In addition, the increased probability of hiring a black woman does not generalize to greater probability of hiring women of other racial groups. Indeed, separate point estimates (not shown) indicate that greater vacancy duration decreases the probability of hiring a white or Hispanic woman more than it reduces the odds of hiring their male counterparts. (The reverse is true among Asians, but the coefficients for both Asian men and Asian women are far from statistical significance.)

Translating the estimated coefficients into odds ratios, a one-month increase in the duration of the longest vacancy corresponds to an increase in the probability of hiring a black woman of 13 to 14 percent (depending on the specification), or about 1.6 percentage points (since black women only represent 12 percent of hires); the estimated increase in black hiring overall is 8 to 9 percent (about 1.9 percentage points). This is comparable to the effect of a one-percentage-point decrease in the general unemployment rate, which is associated with a 12 percent increase in the odds of hiring a black woman, and an 11 percent increase in the probability of any black hire.

It is somewhat surprising that the two vacancy-duration variables, time required to hire for the job and duration of longest vacancy, have such disparate relations to the racial composition of hiring. However, time required for the most recent hire reflects the mean duration of a completed vacancy, whereas the longest vacancy represents the extreme. Perhaps mean time to hire is shaped primarily by firm selectiveness, while the extreme values owe more to labor-market tightness.

Table 4.4 shows the relation between labor-market tightness and employer attitudes toward stigmatized groups. Our general expectation is that when labor markets are tighter, employers will be more willing to hire workers that they otherwise would avoid. The chief finding here is that there is relatively little association between labor-market tightness and employer attitudes, as we measure them, for few coefficients show significance at all. However, two statistically significant coefficients bear out the expected relationship: employers are more willing to hire people with criminal records when the time to hire is longer, and employers are more likely to settle for less-qualified workers when vacancies are longer.

On the other hand, four statistically significant effects are opposite to what is expected. As in the pairwise correlations (but this time controlling for firm size), longer time required to hire corresponds to *reduced* willingness to settle for lower qualifications—indicating once more that time to hire may be reflecting pickiness rather than labor-market tightness. The other three unexpected effects are, at first glance, more baffling. Tighter labor markets are associated with less inclination to hire the long-term unemployed, welfare recipients, or GED/government-employment program graduates. However, there is a ready interpretation: when labor markets are tight, increasing numbers of workers can find work, and the average quality of these groups of workers—those who have been unemployed for a year or more, and those who must resort to welfare or government-

Table 4.4 Relation Between Measures of Labor-Market Tightness and Employer-Attitude Variables (t-Statistics in Parentheses; Bold = Significant at 10 Percent Level)

		"How Often Would You Hire Someone Who. . . ?"				
	Welfare Recipient	GED or Government Employment Program	Criminal Record	Unemployed One Year or More	Only Short-Term or Part-Time Experience	Less Qualified Because Need Workers Badly
Coefficient on metro-area unemployment rate at time of interview	**0.019** **(3.10)**	**0.012** **(2.24)**	0.009 (1.01)	−0.007 (1.05)	0.004 (0.47)	0.003 (0.50)
Coefficient on time required to hire	−0.0001 (0.05)	−0.0005 (0.23)	**0.007** **(2.01)**	−0.0005 (0.19)	−0.0006 (0.19)	−0.004 (1.64)
Coefficient on duration of longest noncollege vacancy	−0.002 (0.16)	0.005 (0.57)	0.000 (0.03)	**−0.021** **(2.05)**	−0.008 (0.68)	**0.046** **(5.24)**

Source: Multi-City Study of Urban Inequality Telephone Employer Survey. Authors' tabulations.

employment programs—plummets. (We would expect this effect to depend on the length of time that a labor market has been tight or slack, of which we have no measure, as well as on the degree of labor-market tightness.)

How does the state of the labor market change hiring methods? We surmise that when labor markets pinch, employers will more often cast a wider recruiting net and relax record-check requirements. Table 4.5 documents that the expected relationships hold for the longest-vacancy measure of labor scarcity. Firms that took longer to fill vacant noncollege positions show a much smaller affirmative-recruiting effect, and no record-check effect. Surprisingly, unemployment-rate differences do not seem to generate either effect.

Table 4.6 shows the impact of the mediating variables on the race of the last hire. Most of the employer-attitude variables ("How often would you hire someone who. . . ?") languish in statistical insignificance—and some of the hiring preferences that attain significance are puzzling. Why would employers who say they are more likely to hire a welfare recipient actually be more likely to hire a white person, when welfare recipients are disproportionately black and Hispanic? Why would those who state a greater willingness to hire

Table 4.5 Relation Between Measures of Labor-Market Tightness and Changes in Hiring Methods (z-Statistics in Parentheses; Bold = Significant at 10 Percent Level)

	Report Change in Hiring in Last Five to Ten Years	
	More Affirmative Recruiting	Less Use of Education or Criminal Record Checks
Coefficient on metro-area unemployment rate at time of interview	−0.019 (0.71)	0.013 (0.63)
Coefficient on time required to hire	**0.017** **(1.83)**	−0.003 (0.33)
Coefficient on duration of longest noncollege vacancy	**0.11** **(3.32)**	**0.06** **(2.17)**

Source: Multi-City Study of Urban Inequality Telephone Employer Survey. Authors' tabulations.

Table 4.6 Relation Between Employer Attitudes-Changes in Hiring Methods and Probability of Hiring a Member of a Given Racial Group (z-Statistics in Parentheses; Bold = Significant at 10 Percent Level)

	Race (and in Some Cases Gender) of Most Recent Hire					
	White	Black	Black man	Black woman	Hispanic	Asian
Coefficient on: "How often would you hire someone who . . . ?"						
Welfare recipient	**0.172**	−0.060	−0.058	0.027	−0.089	0.041
	(2.65)	(0.59)	(0.45)	(0.21)	(0.81)	(0.19)
GED or gov't employment program	0.052	0.012	0.230	−0.091	−0.126	−0.046
	(0.74)	(0.11)	(1.56)	(0.66)	(1.04)	(0.21)
Criminal record	0.028	0.073	**0.203**	−0.041	−0.042	−0.069
	(0.60)	(1.05)	**(2.34)**	(0.45)	(0.51)	(0.46)
Unemployed one year or more	**0.181**	**−0.210**	−0.179	−0.178	−0.003	−0.127
	(2.91)	**(2.26)**	(1.59)	(1.52)	(0.03)	(0.66)
Short-term, part-time experience	−0.017	−0.117	−0.064	−0.137	0.061	0.157
	(0.33)	(1.46)	(0.66)	(1.37)	(0.66)	(0.92)
Less qualified because need workers badly	**−0.213**	0.096	0.086	0.164	−0.119	−0.241
	(3.24)	(0.99)	(0.71)	(1.34)	(1.04)	(1.11)
Report change in hiring in last five to ten years						
More affirmative recruiting	**0.325**	−0.291	−0.008	**−0.442**	**−0.608**	0.098
	(2.67)	(1.53)	(0.03)	**(1.70)**	**(2.54)**	(0.27)
Less use of education or criminal record checks	**−0.163**	0.052	−0.100	0.140	0.166	0.231
	(1.74)	(0.37)	(0.56)	(0.77)	(1.04)	(0.80)

Source: Multi-City Study of Urban Inequality Telephone Employer Survey. Authors' tabulations.

a long-term unemployed person be more likely to hire a white person and less likely to hire a black one? These peculiar results suggest that employer responses to these queries might not be particularly useful predictors of actual actions. Indeed, in analyses of another data set, we found no statistically significant link between expressed employer attitudes toward black men and their probability of hiring black men (Moss and Tilly 1995), while in analyses of coded values from our qualitative in-depth data we found some mixed but still statistically weak links (Moss and Tilly 2000b).

Two of the employer attitude variables do yield expected results. Employers who are more prepared to hire someone who has a criminal record do hire more black men. And, as expected, employers who resort to hiring less-qualified workers hire fewer whites (although the positive-point estimate for hiring more black women falls short of significance).

The relationship of additional affirmative recruiting to the race of the last hire again runs counter to expectations. Employers who report more frequent use of affirmative-recruiting methods are more likely to hire whites, less likely to hire black women or Hispanics. The result for Hispanics is plausible, as immigrant Hispanics disproportionately obtain jobs through informal networks (Falcon and Melendez 2000). But we would expect more use of affirmative recruiting to yield fewer whites and more black women, not the opposite, as we find. Firms that decreased their use of educational criteria or criminal-record checks did hire fewer whites, as expected.

Note that if employer attitudes constitute the channel through which tighter labor markets affect the racial mix of hiring, we would expect significant coefficients both in equation 4.2 (vacancy duration → employer attitude) and equation 4.2' (employer attitude → race of hire). Similarly, if hiring methods are the key, we would look for action in equations 4.3 (vacancy duration → change in hiring method) and 4.3' (change in hiring method → race of hire). The only mediating variable that meets these conditions is "hire less-qualified workers," which is linked to longer vacancies and reduced probability of hiring a white person. Other variables measuring employer attitudes or changes in hiring methods do not appear to play important mediating roles.

Table 4.7 performs another check on the importance of the hypothesized mediating variables, inquiring whether incorporating any of these variables reduces the anticipated effect of labor-market

Table 4.7 Relation Between Labor-Market Tightness and Probability of Hiring a Member of a Given Racial Group, With and Without Controls for Employer Attitude and Changes in Hiring Method (z-Statistics in Parentheses; Bold = Significant at 10 Percent Level)

	Race (and in Some Cases Gender) of Most Recent Hire					
	White	Black	Black Man	Black Woman	Hispanic	Asian
Coefficient on unemployment rate at time of hire						
Basic controls only	**0.226**	**−0.141**	−0.148	−0.139	−0.072	−0.093
	(4.22)	**(1.71)**	(1.31)	(1.24)	(0.87)	(0.63)
Mediating variable controls	**0.203**	**−0.226**	−0.124	−0.252	−0.115	−0.024
	(3.21)	**(2.35)**	(1.03)	(2.02)	(1.25)	(0.15)
Coefficient on time required for most recent hire						
Basic controls only	**0.023**	−0.001	0.004	−0.014	**−0.036**	0.008
	(2.39)	(0.08)	(0.301)	(0.78)	**(1.92)**	(0.73)
Mediating variable controls	**0.021**	0.003	0.009	−0.013	−0.034	−0.001
	(1.94)	(0.26)	(0.55)	(0.69)	(1.61)	(0.03)
Coefficient on duration of longest noncollege vacancy						
Basic controls only	−0.039	**0.113**	−0.021	**0.152**	**−0.114**	−0.090
	(1.18)	**(2.54)**	(0.36)	**(3.14)**	**(1.74)**	(0.66)
Mediating variable controls	−0.057	**0.102**	−0.052	**0.169**	−0.087	−0.260
	(1.48)	**(2.12)**	(0.80)	**(3.21)**	(1.24)	(1.30)

Source: Multi-City Study of Urban Inequality Telephone Employer Survey. Authors' tabulations.
Note: "Basic controls" include applicants from this racial group, firm size, and city dummies. "Mediating variables" include all of the variables in table 4.6.

tightness on the probability of hiring someone from a given racial group. The answer, put briefly, is once more no. Even after adding the mediating variables as controls, white employment continues to be greater, and black employment reduced, where unemployment rates are higher, and the positive relationship between longer vacancies and employment of black women remains robust. (The association between time to hire and race of hire, which we have argued is driven by selectiveness rather than labor-market tightness, is essentially unchanged as well.) Estimated effects on Hispanic employment slip below significance, but the point estimates of these coefficients are not affected greatly by the addition of the mediating variables as controls. Tighter labor markets might indeed boost the probability of hiring blacks by affecting employer attitudes or hiring practices, but this does not show up with the measures of attitudes and hiring methods that we have employed.

QUALITATIVE EVIDENCE

During the in-depth interviews, employers were asked how difficult it was to attract and retain an adequate workforce for the sample entry-level job under discussion, and whether there had been changes in the supply of labor over time. Many employers reported problems with the available labor supply. Problems, in addition to simply a thin supply of applicants, included a lack of available skills, low work ethic, and high turnover. Many other employers indicated that sufficient workers were available, so that their major task was screening the available applicants. In both cases, quite a few managers contrasted the difficulty or ease of finding satisfactory workers with the conditions at a different point in the business cycle. For example, Boston and Los Angeles respondents often contrasted the slack market of the early 1990s with the taut one of the late 1980s, while Detroit employers often harked back to the early 1980s, when there was a glut of available workers.

Only a handful of respondents linked the relative ease or difficulty of finding workers to the racial composition of applicants or hires. However, some did make this connection, and others hinted at it. Following are a few excerpts from interviews that suggest a relation between relative abundance of workers and the resulting racial composition of hires. A white employer in Los Angeles was asked about the composition of his workforce, and responded that minorities are at the end of the queue and because things are slack, many selective firms won't hire them—though his firm is an exception to this:

> INTERVIEWER: The work force here is mostly minority. Do you have any insights on why?
>
> RESPONDENT: You mean why is it that they're here on our premises, as opposed to elsewhere? Our economy. I think we would have a very difficult time running our retail end of the business if we were in a good economy. Why are they here? Because they can't get jobs other [places] . . . What happens when you have a good economy? Boy, people bend ov—they have dropped all of their standards to get people hired in, OK? Now they can stand to be picky and choosy, because the economy is poor. When you drop those standards with a company that is . . . a very small employer, that doesn't know how to . . . [that doesn't] have a personnel department, doesn't know interviewing techniques, doesn't know how to select people, what do they do? The owner looks you up and down and says, "OK, I've got a position, come on in." Well who's that [position] going to today? Today [the owner] can be a little bit more selective in getting a higher-skilled person. In the past, he probably wouldn't have that ability and would go, "God, I need someone in here, I need a body. Let me get this person in—it does-n't matter that he doesn't have the skill level. I'll train him, I'll put the time in to teach him." You don't have to do that today. Our economy is solidly poor. . . . And so we end up getting in some instances quite capable peo-ple in here, because they can't find a job anyplace else. In a better economy, there would be more opportunities. And that's about what it is: there are less opportunities today than there were ten years ago.

If enough businesses functioned like this one—willingly hiring people of color when other firms choose not to—we would not expect to see any cyclical pattern in hiring rates for blacks, as Gary Becker (1957) pointed out decades ago. But if this manager is excep-tional (as he believes), then blacks will have a better chance of being hired when the labor market tightens and picky and choosy firms no longer have a choice.

The white human-resource director of a hospital in a predominantly minority inner-city section of Boston stated, conversely, that white nurses can be pickier about where they work when labor markets are tight:

> If you looked at RNs as a group, the minority here is Caucasian. . . . Now, is that a function of where we are? Perhaps. You know, I could also say it's because of our wonderful affirmative-action program, but it's probably more based on reality as to where we're located. But the marketplace has changed that, too. Five years ago, six years ago, we had major difficulties recruiting nurses here. . . . Within the last three years we'd go to job fairs and we'd be swamped with nice, brand-new graduates of all races. . . . All of a sudden it wasn't a problem with Caucasian nurses wanting to come here, because there were no jobs. I mean, they were being laid off at all of the other hospitals in the city. So now all of a sudden the neighborhood wasn't as big of a. . . . Economy, the economy has a wonderful way of equalizing neighborhoods. Now, when times are good and there are a number of jobs out there, maybe they don't want to come to Roxbury [the mainly black and Hispanic neighborhood where this hospital is located], but all of a sudden, when times get harder. . . .

This narrative does not necessarily imply that hospitals place white nurses higher on their hiring queues, but is certainly consistent with such a pattern.

When asked about why minorities in Atlanta are having a more difficult time in the labor market relative to whites, the white branch manager of an insurance company indicated that lack of skill was the issue. He went on to say, however, that things might be different were the economy not so slack at the time of our interview.

> INTERVIEWER: One of the things that I would be curious about is that when you look at a city like Atlanta, in the eighties particularly, it really grew—but you still have seen a disproportionate number of minorities that are unemployed, and we're kind of curious about why that is. Do you have any insight?
>
> RESPONDENT: Uh, just lacking skill. Lacking the basic skills for whatever the reason, just not having the basic . . . three R's skills . . . in a lot of situations to qualify for the job. I mean, being an employer now, you've got a lot to pick

> from. These days, when you put an ad in the paper, you almost have to bar the door, you know? And when we need to hire someone from the outside, we can really narrow exactly what we want in terms of skills, and we don't have to put out any kind of broad [searches], because, you know, they've got a thousand people walking down the street. . . . So, fortunately, we can really narrow in on what we want and there are enough. . . . It's largely a function of the market cycle that, that group that this is in, I think. Sometimes you have very different, for example, if the insurance business was just blowing and going and we just couldn't add enough people, we might, and had a lot of competition for the same workers . . . it would be a different story.

Thus, these examples from the qualitative data help to illustrate how labor-market tightness affects employer behavior.

CONCLUSION

What have we learned? The unemployment rate at the time of hire performs more or less as expected: higher unemployment corresponds to a greater probability of employers hiring whites and a reduced probability of their hiring blacks (though we note that the latter effect, like a number of our findings, attains significance only at the 10 percent level). The first of our micro-level indices, the time required to complete the most recent hire, appears to primarily reflect employer selectiveness rather than labor-market tightness. However, the duration of the longest noncollege vacancy does appear to bespeak the degree of labor-market tightness or slackness on a micro level. Vacancy duration has the expected correlations with other measures of labor-market tightness, the vacant jobs are fairly similar to the jobs for which we are gauging hiring, and the impact of vacancy duration on hiring persists after controlling for job tasks, training time, wage levels, and the presence of formal hiring procedures. In labor markets for jobs requiring no more than a high school degree in the four metro areas examined, this micromeasure of tighter labor markets increases the probability of hiring a black woman, after controlling for the percentage of the applicant pool made up by black women. Tighter micro-labor-markets are associated with lower hiring probabilities for Hispanics (again, after controlling for the applicant pool), suggesting that black women may gain at the expense of Hispanics when labor is scarce. We do not find significant effects of micro-labor-market tightness on the probability of hiring whites, black men, or Asians, though we estimate negative and insignificant effects in all three cases. The increased probability of hiring a black woman is not accompanied by heightened odds of hiring women of other ethnic groups.

One interpretation of the micro-level findings regarding the racial impact of labor-market tightness draws on the evidence from in-depth interviews with employers, which we discussed in the literature review. That literature suggests that for many, the racial queue from most-preferred to least-preferred workers goes from whites and Asians to Hispanics to black women to black men. Perhaps micro-labor-market tightness in the settings that we are studying most strongly affects the boundary between Hispanics (particularly Hispanic women) and black women in this ranking.

We hypothesized that labor-market tightness affects the racial composition of hires by acting on employer attitudes, making them more willing to hire from less-preferred groups, and/or on hiring methods, by encouraging employers to recruit more or differently and screen less rigorously. However, despite some statistically significant links between vacancy duration and attitudes and hiring methods, and some significant links between attitudes and hiring methods and the racial composition of hires, the cumulative evidence for these channels of influence for labor-market tightness is weak indeed. The only variable out of this set that links vacancy duration and the race of the most recent hire in two statistically significant spans is employers' reports of the frequency with which they hire workers with fewer qualifications due to needing workers badly. And controlling for this variable does not diminish the impact of vacancy duration on the race of the last hire, suggesting that other influences are at work.

In fact, the link between labor scarcity (as measured by unemployment rate or vacancy duration) and increased black women's employment is sufficiently sturdy that none of our controls does much to diminish it. Hence, two conclusions are possible. First, perhaps labor shortages do affect the racial composition of hiring via attitudes or hiring methods, but the measures of the mediating variables that we use are inadequate. Second, perhaps labor shortages act through some entirely different channel. The qualitative data from in-depth employer interviews, which we are continuing to explore, offer one potential source of new hypotheses corresponding to one or the other of these possibilities.

For funding to gather the data used in this paper, we thank the Russell Sage, Ford, and Rockefeller Foundations. Thanks to Tom Hertz for research assistance in preparing the telephone survey data for analysis, and to Laurie Dougherty, Ivy Kennelly, Joleen Kirschenman, Bob Smith, and Bryan Snyder for assistance in coding the in-depth survey data. We are grateful to William Julius Wilson and Robert Cherry, as well as other conference participants and two anonymous reviewers, for thoughtful comments on earlier drafts.

REFERENCES

Becker, Gary S. 1957. *The Economics of Discrimination.* Chicago: University of Chicago Press.

Bills, David B. 1988. "Educational Credentials and Hiring Decisions: What Employers Look for in New Employees." In *Research in Social Stratification and Mobility*, vol. 7, edited by Arne L. Kalleberg. Greenwich, Conn.: JAI Press.

Bound, John, and Richard B. Freeman. 1992. "What Went Wrong? The Erosion of the Relative Earnings and Employment of Young Black Men in the 1980s." *Quarterly Journal of Economics* 107(1): 201–32.

Bound, John, and Harry J. Holzer. 1996. "Demand Shifts, Population Adjustments, and Labor Market Outcomes During the 1980s." National Bureau of Economic Research working paper 5685. Cambridge, Mass.: National Bureau of Economic Research.

Cain, Glen G., and Ross E. Finnie. 1990. "The Black-White Difference in Youth Employment: Evidence for Demand-Side Factors." *Journal of Labor Economics* 8(1, Part 2): S364–95.

Falcon, Luis M., and Edwin Melendez. 2000. "The Effects of Ethnic Differences in Job Searching in Urban Centers." In *Urban Inequality: Evidence from Four Cities*, edited by Lawrence Bobo, Alice O'Connor, and Chris Tilly. New York: Russell Sage.

Freeman, Richard B. 1989. "Help Wanted: Disadvantaged Youths in a Labor-Shortage Economy." Mimeo. Cambridge, Mass.: National Bureau of Economic Research.

————. 1990. "Labor-Market Tightness and the Mismatch Between Demand and Supply of Less-Educated Young Men in the United States in the 1980s." Mimeo. Cambridge, Mass.: National Bureau of Economic Research.

Hamermesh, Daniel S., and Albert Rees. 1988. *The Economics of Work and Pay*, 4th ed. New York: Harper & Row.

Holzer, Harry J. 1996. *What Employers Want: Job Prospects for Less-Educated Workers*. New York: Russell Sage Foundation.

Kirschenman, Joleen, and Kathryn M. Neckerman. 1991. "'We'd Love to Hire Them, But. . .': The Meaning of Race for Employers." In *The Urban Underclass*, edited by Christopher Jencks and Paul E. Peterson. Washington, D.C.: Brookings Institution.

Lester, Richard A. 1954. *Hiring Practices and Labor Competition*. Princeton, N.J.: Princeton University, Industrial Relations Section.

Moss, Philip, and Chris Tilly. 1991. "Why Black Men Are Doing Worse in the Labor Market: A Review of Supply-Side and Demand-Side Explanations." New York: Social Science Research Council.

————. 1995. "Skills and Race in Hiring: Quantitative Findings from Face-to-Face Interviews." *Eastern Economic Journal* 21(3): 357–74.

————. 1996. "'Soft' Skills and Race: An Investigation of Black Men's Employment Problems." *Work and Occupations* 23(3): 252–76.

————. 2000a. "Why Opportunity Isn't Knocking: Racial Inequality and the Demand for Labor." In *Urban Inequality: Evidence from Four Cities*, edited by Lawrence Bobo, Alice O'Connor, and Chris Tilly. New York: Russell Sage.

————. 2000b. *Stories Employers Tell: Race, Skill, and Hiring in America*. New York: Russell Sage Foundation.

Osterman, Paul. 1991. "The Underside of Full Employment: Poverty in Boston." In *The Urban Underclass*, edited by Christopher Jencks and Paul E. Peterson. Washington, D.C.: Brookings Institution.

Reder, Melvin. 1955. "The Theory of Occupational Wage Differentials." *American Economic Review* 45: 833–52.

Waldinger, Roger. 1993. "Who Makes the Beds? Who Washes the Dishes? Black/Immigrant Competition Reassessed." Working paper 246. Los Angeles: Institute of Industrial Relations, University of California, Los Angeles.

Chapter 5

EXCLUSIONARY PRACTICES AND GLASS-CEILING EFFECTS ACROSS REGIONS: WHAT DOES THE CURRENT EXPANSION TELL US?

HEATHER BOUSHEY AND ROBERT CHERRY

The wage gap between African Americans and whites lessened during the 1970s, but began to increase again during the 1980s (Bound and Freeman 1992). The 1990s expansion modestly reduced racial inequality in employment among men and slightly widened it among women. Thus, racial earnings ratios at the end of the century are not very different from what they were fifteen years earlier. Conventional analysis of this phenomenon has focused on human-capital variables or changes in the industrial mix of jobs. The explanation for continuing inequality between African American and white workers, however, might lie in racial differences in occupational distributions, which vary across regional labor markets.

The labor market in the United States is not homogenous across the nation but is in fact an amalgam of a multitude of small, regional, and local labor markets. Because of this, statistics and analyses of labor-market outcomes at the national level hide important regional differences. Patterns of labor-force participation, employment-to-population ratios, unemployment, and pay gaps vary across regions. Regional employment patterns, moreover, affect national earnings-ratio trends. For example, the earnings ratio of African American males relative to white males between 1979 and 1989 would have declined by a somewhat larger percentage than it actually did had there not been a shift in regional employment patterns toward regions with smaller wage gaps (Saunders 1995). While human-capital and industrial variables certainly are important in explaining regional patterns, these differences among regions might also reflect variations in the extent of discrimination and the forms discrimination takes across regional labor markets.

160

Discrimination is a particularly important issue in the South Atlantic and Midwest regions of the United States.[1] The majority of African Americans live in these two regions, and, therefore, anti-discrimination policies, along with economic policies more generally, affect more African Americans here than anywhere else in the United States. Furthermore, the historical importance of these regions cannot be underestimated: the history of slavery and Jim Crow in the South and the Midwest's importance as the primary destination of African Americans during the post-World War II Great Migration indicate that the trajectory of discrimination in these regions is essential for an understanding of racial inequality in America.

In this chapter, we assess how tight labor markets during the 1990s economic expansion have affected the size and source of racial earnings differences in the Midwest and South Atlantic regions. In particular, we focus on three sources of earnings disparities: premarket discrimination, in which educational credentials limit African American access to employment in occupations requiring a college education; occupational exclusion, which limits African American access to better-paying professions even when their credentials equal those of other applicants; and wage inequality within occupations. The prevalence of each source might differ by region, given differences in labor-market institutions and historical configurations.

In order to identify discrete credential effects, we split the labor market into two occupational groups, one of fourteen occupations that require some college (the "college" group), and the second of thirty-one occupations that do not (the "noncollege" group). Focusing on occupational data also allows us to assess the relative importance of two sources of racial earnings gaps, exclusion and glass ceilings. Exclusion occurs when African American workers are denied employment in better-paying occupations. Historically, for example, women were excluded from many occupations, causing them to crowd a limited number of other occupations. This was especially true for African American women, who, as late as the 1930s, were overwhelmingly concentrated into just two occupations: domestic or agricultural workers. Over time, however, exclusionary barriers have lessened, and today more concern is focused on glass ceilings. Glass ceilings exist when workers can enter occupations but despite their credentials are prohibited by discrimination from moving up the job ladder. The glass ceiling is most likely to be present in occupations where there is a large gap in pay between different levels, indicating that the upper levels are dominated by a non-discriminated-against group.

The remainder of this chapter is organized as follows. In the section immediately following, we discuss recent economic trends and explore how the African American labor-market experience differs between the Midwest and South Atlantic regions. Next, we compare African American and white occupational distributions and changes in the ratio of noncollege-to-college wages over the economic expansion. Our fourth section evaluates what proportion of the change in racial-earnings ratios over the expansion may be attributed to structural changes in the population, such as shifts in the share of workers in the college and noncollege groups, and changes in the average wages for each of these groups. We find that the most important sources of change in racial-earnings ratios among women and men in each region were deteriorations in the average black-to-white wage ratios in both the college group and the skilled-occupations subset of the noncollege group.

The fifth breaks down the wage gaps in the college-occupational group and among the skilled occupations in the noncollege-occupational group to identify the relative importance of exclusion and glass-ceiling effects. Here, our findings for male labor markets are consistent with those in Joyce Jacobsen and Laurence Levin (this volume): glass-ceiling effects are more important in the college group than they are in the noncollege group, while exclusionary effects are more important in the noncollege group. In contrast, with regard to female labor markets, glass-ceiling effects were small and did not change over the economic expansion. However, white women were able to enter higher-paying college occupations at a greater rate than were African American women. This suggests that over the economic expansion, white women were able to break down exclusionary barriers more successfully than were African American women.

While our findings for the college-occupational group were consistent across regions, we saw substantial regional differences in the noncollege-occupational group. Among both men and women, the ratio of the black-to-white wages in this group declined in the Midwest but increased in the South Atlantic region. The decline in the Midwest reflects the more limited access of African American workers to employment in better-paying jobs within this occupational group. This paper suggests that the reduction in African American nonemployment rates over the expansion can help to explain these regional differences.

RECENT TRENDS

The Midwest and South Atlantic regions have had similar experiences with regard to overall trends in unemployment and employment over the current economic expansion. In both regions, the labor market bottomed out in 1992, and in that year their aggregate unemployment rates hit similar highs, rising to 7.2 percent in the Midwest and 7.3 percent in the South Atlantic.[2] Over the next four years, both regions experienced substantial growth, and the aggregate unemployment rate fell to 4.7 percent in the Midwest and 5.0 percent in the South Atlantic region. Concurrently, employment grew by 6.6 in the Midwest and 9.3 percent in the South Atlantic.

The correspondence in overall economic trends has not been mirrored by trends in African American labor-market outcomes in the two regions, however. As table 5.1 indicates, in 1992, African American workers across the South Atlantic region had employment rates that were nearly ten percentage points higher than those of blacks in the Midwest. Though the expansion reduced these regional differences, the regional gap nevertheless remained substantial: 8.5 percentage points among men and 4.8 among women.[3] In contrast, table 5.2 indicates that white employment rates are higher in the Midwest, and thus racial employment-rate differences in the two regions are dissimilar.[4] Among women in 1996, there was virtual racial equality in employment rates in the South Atlantic region, while in the Midwest there was a six-percentage-point gap separating blacks and whites. Among men, the gap was 17.7 percentage points in the Midwest but only 4.8 points in the South Atlantic region.

The regional disparity in African American employment rates possibly results from the deindustrialization of the so-called midwestern Rust Belt during the 1970s and '80s and accompanying spatial mismatches between the location of manufacturing firms and residency of blue-collar workers. These mismatches disproportionately affected African American workers (Bluestone and Harrison 1982; Seitchik 1989; Wilson 1996). Chinhui Juhn (1992) estimated that one-half of the black-white employment rate gap is due to the inability of African American workers to find jobs. Because white employment rates are essentially the same across the two regions, one-half of the regional difference among African Americans probably owes to the inability of midwestern African American workers to find jobs in the formal labor market relative to their counterparts in South Atlantic-region states.[5]

Table 5.1 Black Employment, 1992 and 1996

	Total Employment (Thousands)				Employment Rate (Percentage)			
	Male		Female		Male		Female	
	1992	1996	1992	1996	1992	1996	1992	1996
Maryland	321	309	331	340	66.6	69.7	61.3	65.4
Florida	415	461	432	467	61.9	65.7	54.7	57.8
Virginia	302	308	276	343	69.3	65.3	60.9	58.3
Georgia	335	299	353	350	63.8	64.6	55.2	58.1
N. Carolina	410	460	471	509	62.2	65.3	53.5	56.4
S. Carolina	218	222	213	235	62.8	62.3	51.3	53.0
Delaware	24	31	34	38	62.2	64.3	62.7	64.5
District of Columbia	69	69	75	78	52.5	53.0	49.8	47.7
West Virginia	10	11	11	12	*na*	*na*	*na*	*na*
Total	2,104	2,170	2,196	2,370	63.9	65.1	55.6	57.6
Illinois	302	315	346	363	53.6	56.6	47.4	51.5
Michigan	213	209	211	257	53.4	57.2	41.5	52.5
Ohio	195	254	227	261	55.0	58.8	50.4	54.0
Wisconsin	35	47	41	53	57.4	52.8	46.6	56.4
Indiana	75	86	99	91	48.8	59.3	46.7	51.8
Total	820	911	924	1,025	53.5	56.6	46.5	52.8

Source: United States Department of Labor, Bureau of Labor Statistics, *States: Employment Statistics of the Civilian Non-Institutional Population,* table 12 (Washington: U.S. Government Printing Office).

Higher white employment rates in the Midwest, despite declining employment opportunities in manufacturing, also suggest that the effect of exclusionary practices could be substantial. Research on employers' job-search procedures indicates that midwestern employers are hesitant to hire African Americans, especially in urban areas (Kirschenman and Neckerman 1991; Moss and Tilly, in this volume). Such discrimination might lead to higher levels of discouragement among black men, which with other factors such as high incarceration rates, census undercounting, and military enlistment, lowers black men's participation in the labor force. This points to racial exclusion, especially as perpetrated against African American men in the low-wage-labor market, playing an important role in the Midwest.

Table 5.2 State Employment Rates by Gender and Race, 1996

	Men		Women	
	Black	White	Black	White
Maryland	69.7	74.8	65.4	62.5
Florida	65.7	66.5	57.8	50.8
Virginia	65.3	72.6	58.3	57.7
Georgia	65.3	76.5	58.1	57.3
North Carolina	64.6	74.7	56.4	59.1
South Carolina	62.3	71.3	53.0	54.9
Delaware	64.3	70.8	64.5	60.1
District of Columbia	53.0	80.3	47.7	72.6
West Virginia	*na*	59.3	*na*	44.8
Total	65.1	70.9	57.6	55.5
Illinois	56.6	75.8	51.5	58.6
Michigan	57.2	72.4	52.5	56.6
Ohio	58.8	72.2	54.0	56.2
Wisconsin	52.8	78.2	56.4	68.1
Indiana	59.3	74.9	51.8	59.8
Total	56.6	74.3	52.8	58.8

Source: United States Department of Labor, Bureau of Labor Statistics, *States: Employment Statistics of the Civilian Non-Institutional Population,* table 12 (Washington: U.S. Government Printing Office).

These regional differences in blacks' employment rates may be interpreted to indicate that unemployment rates substantially understate the employment difficulties of African American men in the Midwest more than in the South Atlantic region. This has important implications for our analysis. First, these differences suggest that exclusionary barriers may be more prevalent in the Midwest than in the South Atlantic region. Second, they suggest that over the economic expansion, the closing of the regional employment-rate gap reflected a disproportionate entrance of previously excluded African American workers in the Midwest. Third, they should caution against the use of results based solely on employment data. Regional disparities in pay might be the result of disparities in employment rates and different occupational distributions of African American and white workers in the Midwest and the South Atlantic. Prior research on racial employment disparities by region has found that African Americans enjoy higher wages in the Midwest, but lower employment rates. Jeremiah Cotton (1993) found that not only did African American men suffer from higher unemployment rates in the Midwest, but they also had larger unexplained wage differentials there than in the South. In another study, Charles Carlstrom and Christy Rollow (1998) found that African Americans in the South are underrepresented in the highest-paying occupations, but these differences are virtually nonexistent in the rest of the country. Bound and Freeman (1992) found that between 1974 and 1989, among male workers with no more than a high school degree, the racial wage gap rose from 0.6 to 20.9 percent in the Midwest but only from 16.8 to 18.3 percent in the South. Our analysis explores the black-white earnings disparities that these past studies have found, and emphasizes the impact of the racial distribution of workers between and within the college- and noncollege-occupational groups over the recent economic expansion.

OCCUPATIONAL AND EARNINGS DATA

We begin our analysis by identifying racial differences in the distribution of workers across occupational groupings. Disparate educational credentials could result in differences in the shares of African American and white workers in the college-occupational group. Within the noncollege-occupational group, African American workers might be crowded out of better-paying occupations and into low-waged manual ones. These structural differences will influence racial-earnings ratios and explain why they differ across regions and change over time. We use the Outgoing Rotation Group files of the Current Population Survey (CPS) to explore regional differences in racial inequality. This data set is the most appropriate to use when exploring wage inequality (Bernstein and Mishel 1997). These data have been used for regional analysis as well, but prior research has also used the Public Use Microsample of the U.S. Census, which has the advantage of being large enough to generate reliable estimates by region and race. However, census data cannot be used here since they are only available by decade. In order to ensure a large enough sample of African American workers in the Outgoing Rotation Group data, we pool our sample into two time periods, 1992 through 1994 and 1995 through 1997. Pooling across years in this manner allows us to divide workers into two groups: a college group comprising fourteen occupations, in which at least 70 percent of those employed have some education beyond a high school degree, and a noncollege group of ten low-wage manual and twenty-one skilled occupations.[6] (See appendix 5A for the individual occupations in each of the three groups.)[7]

Table 5.3 summarizes male and female employment shares by race in the three occupational groupings. Relative to their counterparts in the South Atlantic, African American women and men in the Midwest were more likely to be in college occupations and less likely to be in manual occupations. By contrast, white women and men in the South Atlantic region were more likely to be in the college-occupational group and less likely to be in manual occupations. As a result, it appears that the labor market is more favorable for

Table 5.3 Occupational Employment Shares by Race and Gender

	Black (Percentage)		White (Percentage)		Black-to-White Ratio	
	1992 to 1994	1995 to 1997	1992 to 1994	1995 to 1997	1992 to 1994	1995 to 1997
Men						
South Atlantic						
College	15.81	18.19	29.47	30.79	0.54	0.59
Skilled	55.54	55.65	56.77	55.81	0.98	1.00
Manual	28.65	26.16	13.76	13.40	2.08	1.95
Midwest						
College	21.54	22.28	25.42	26.68	0.85	0.84
Skilled	55.58	56.26	60.05	59.92	0.93	0.94
Manual	22.88	21.46	14.53	13.40	1.57	1.60
Women						
South Atlantic						
College	23.68	26.33	35.19	37.27	0.67	0.71
Skilled	49.22	49.32	49.85	47.80	0.99	1.03
Manual	27.10	24.35	14.96	14.93	1.81	1.63
Midwest						
College	26.87	27.88	30.91	33.15	0.87	0.84
Skilled	50.68	50.19	51.03	49.33	0.99	1.02
Manual	22.45	21.93	18.06	17.52	1.24	1.25

Source: Authors' calculations from the United States Bureau of the Census, Current Population Survey Outgoing Rotation Group Files (Washington: U.S. Government Printing Office, 1992–1997).

African American workers in the Midwest while being more favorable for white workers in the South Atlantic states. Over the economic expansion, however, African American men and women increased their relative share of employment in the college group in the South Atlantic but not Midwest, reducing these regional disparities.

Looking more closely, we find that between 1992 and 1994, the share of African American men employed in manual occupations in the South Atlantic was 5.88 percentage points higher than it was in the Midwest. In contrast, the share of white men in this occupational subgroup was 0.77 percentage point higher in the Midwest than in the South Atlantic region. Looking at the three heavy manual occupations (construction laborers, handlers, and freight) during the 1992-to-1994 time period, the portion of African American men in these occupations was dramatically lower in the Midwest than South Atlantic, 7.98 versus 11.10 percent. However, among white men it was substantially higher in the Midwest: 6.82 versus 5.41 percent. In addition, for farm and forestry workers, employment shares were lower in the Midwest for both African American and white men. The regional gap, however, was much larger for African American men—3.67 to 1.19 percent—than for white men, for whom it was 2.59 to 1.86 percent. Similar differences were found during the 1995 to 1997 period.

The fact that African Americans are less likely to be in manual occupations in the Midwest could relate to the higher African American nonemployment rate there. A disproportionately large share of African American men who have dropped out of the labor force have low levels of education attainment and work experience. As a result, these men would most likely have been employed in manual occupations had the job market been stronger. Thus, their exclusion from employment artificially reduces the cohort of African American men in manual occupations in the Midwest.

In addition, a number of studies (Moss and Tilly, this volume; Kirschenman and Neckerman 1991; Holzer 1996) have found that firms will employ educated, "articulate" African Americans, but not low-skilled ones. Consequently, Hispanics and white immigrants might be offered these jobs in the Midwest but not in the South Atlantic, where there are generally fewer immigrants. Further, African American men are overwhelmingly concentrated in midwestern metropolitan areas, and, therefore, agricultural and heavy manual jobs in nonmetropolitan midwestern areas are filled, by default, by white men.

Higher African American nonemployment potentially creates a bias in the official labor-market tabulations because African American men "missing" from official labor market tabulations are more likely to have less human capital than African American men in the labor market. Consistent with this view, the regional gap in African American employment shares in the manual occupations has declined over the current economic expansion. For African American men, it has fallen from 5.77 to 4.60 percent, while among African American women it was almost halved, from 4.65 to 2.42 percent. Thus, over the expansion, African American men who were formerly out of the official labor market were pulled in, and were disproportionately pulled in to manual occupations. This indicates that assumptions about the more favorable labor market for African Americans in the Midwest during the 1992 to 1994 period might have underestimated the true labor-market difficulties of African American male workers there. Appendix 5B assesses the ways in which the especially high nonemployment rate of African Americans might have affected occupational distributions and racial-earnings ratios in the Midwest.

Wage ratios, as well as employment distributions, vary across the college- and noncollege–occupational groups. In both the Midwest and South Atlantic regions (see table 5.4), wages in noncollege occupations averaged between 52 and 62 percent of the wages paid in college occupations. Among men, the ratios were higher in the Midwest, which probably reflects the power of unions there to raise the wages of workers in noncollege occupations. Similar fluctuations were observed for African American women. Among white women, however, there was no clear regional difference. Wages in each occupational group were higher in the Midwest than in the South Atlantic region, and, within each occupational group, white wages were higher than African American wages.

Because wages are higher in the college than in the noncollege group, a relative shift of African American workers into the college group would reduce racial-earnings ratios. However, African Americans continue to be disproportionately employed in the noncollege group, meaning that a decrease in the ratio of the average noncollege to average college wage would reduce racial-earnings ratios.

Table 5.4 Average Weekly Wage in College and Noncollege
Occupational Groups, by Gender and Region, 1992 to 1994
and 1995 to 1997

	1992 to 1994			1995 to 1997		
	Non-college	College	Ratio	Non-college	College	Ratio
Men						
South Atlantic						
Black	$ 368.06	$ 672.41	54.74	$ 403.75	$ 727.85	55.47
White	$ 473.52	$ 826.02	57.33	$ 513.44	$ 905.85	56.68
Midwest						
Black	$ 423.25	$ 691.15	61.24	$ 459.32	$ 782.54	58.70
White	$ 506.59	$ 835.67	60.62	$ 562.01	$ 926.45	60.66
Women						
South Atlantic						
Black	$ 291.90	$ 563.85	51.77	$ 315.37	$ 575.81	54.77
White	$ 311.80	$ 557.09	55.97	$ 338.83	$ 617.00	54.92
Midwest						
Black	$ 322.15	$ 578.08	55.73	$ 340.46	$ 600.73	56.67
White	$ 282.38	$ 539.48	52.34	$ 328.04	$ 593.59	55.26

Source: Authors' calculations from the United States Bureau of the Census, Current
Population Survey Outgoing Rotation Group Files (Washington: U.S. Government
Printing Office, 1992–1997).

During the current expansion, the college–noncollege wage ratio
in the South Atlantic region increased for African Americans of both
genders while decreasing for white men and women. In specific race-
gender breakdowns, there was a relatively large increase in the earnings of African American men in noncollege occupations and those
of white women in college occupations. In the Midwest, meanwhile,
the wage ratio rose slightly among both white men and women, and
reflected a substantial improvement in the wages of white men and
women in noncollege occupations. Contrastingly, among African
American men, the wage ratio declined substantially, in response to
a relatively small wage increase in the noncollege occupations.

RACIAL-EARNINGS RATIOS

The previous section identified changes in the shares of African
American and white workers across two occupational groups, college

and noncollege, and explored how wages changed in those groups. This section will estimate how these share and wage effects influenced racial-earnings ratios by gender in each region.

Over the economic expansion, the racial-earnings ratio rose modestly from 72.07 to 73.24 percent in the South Atlantic and declined modestly from 81.49 to 80.51 percent in the Midwest. For women, the racial earnings ratio declined in both regions, from 89.49 to 86.72 percent in the South Atlantic and from 104.00 to 99.27 percent in the Midwest.[8] The finding that racial-earnings ratios are highest in the Midwest while racial earnings disparities among men are improving in the South Atlantic is consistent with other studies (Carlstrom and Rollow 1998; Murphy and Welch 1990).

To explore changes over the economic expansion, we decompose racial-earnings ratios in each region into three distinct components for each gender. The "group-shares" effect measures how much of the change derives from changes in the distribution of African American and white workers between the two occupational groups. As previously noted, African American workers, disproportionately gaining employment in college occupations, would increase the racial-earnings ratios, assuming that average African American and white wages in each occupational group were constant. The "college-wage" effect measures how much of the racial-earnings ratio change is due to changes in the average wage of African American and white workers in the college group. The "noncollege-wage" effect measures how much of the change comes from changes in the average wage of African American and white workers in the noncollege group. To measure how much of the total change in the racial earnings ratio is due to each of these components, we use an iterative procedure. For each gender in each region, we start with the actual racial-earnings ratio for the 1992 through 1994 time period, denoted *R92*. We then estimate a racial-earnings ratio, *R1*, that would have characterized the 1995 through 1997 time period had the only change over the expansion occurred in the proportions of African American and white workers in the two occupational groups.

Hence, to determine the group-shares effect:

$$\text{group-shares effect} = R1 - R92$$

Next, we add the change in average African American and white wages in the college group, computing a second adjusted racial earnings ratio, *R2*.

$$\text{college-wage effect} = R2 - R1$$

Then, adding the change in average African American and white wages in the noncollege group yields the actual 1995 to 1997 racial-earnings ratio, $R95$. (For calculations of the various ratios, see appendix 5C.)[9]

$$\text{noncollege-wage effect} = R95 - R2$$

Table 5.5 presents our estimates of how much of the change in racial-earnings ratios results from each of the three components.[10] Among women in the South Atlantic region, the college-wage effect caused the racial-earnings ratio to decline by 3.99 percentage points. Calculated using the favorable group-shares effect, which increased the ratio by 0.66 percentage point, and using the favorable noncollege-wage effect, which increased the ratio by 0.56 percentage point, the decline was only 2.77 percentage points. The decline in the racial-earnings ratio among women in the Midwest was even larger, not only because the college-wage effect there was large and negative, at 3.05 percentage points, but also, unlike in the South Atlantic region, the other two components also had adverse effects.

Changes in the racial-earnings ratio in male labor markets were smaller, owing primarily to more-modest college-wage effects. In the South Atlantic states, the change in the average African American and white wages in the college group reduced the racial-earnings ratio by only 1.01 percentage points, so the favorable noncollege-wage and

Table 5.5 Decomposition of Changes in the Black-White Earnings Ratio by Gender and Region, 1992 to 1994 and 1995 to 1997

| | Racial Earnings Ratio | | Decomposition into | | | |
	1992 to 1994	1995 to 1997	Total Change	Group shares	College wage	Non-college wage
Male						
South Atlantic	72.07	73.24	1.17	0.68	−1.01	1.48
Midwest	81.49	80.51	−0.98	−0.25	0.11	−0.84
Female						
South Atlantic	89.49	86.72	−2.77	0.66	−3.99	0.56
Midwest	104.00	99.27	−4.73	−0.78	−3.05	−0.90

Source: Authors' calculations from the United States Bureau of the Census, Current Population Survey Outgoing Rotation Group Files (Washington: U.S. Government Printing Office, 1992–1997).

group-shares effects dominated. In the Midwest, the college-wage effect was virtually zero. However, both the noncollege-wage and group-shares effect were negative, causing the racial-earnings ratio to decrease slightly.

As discussed, changes in average African American and white wages in the noncollege group reduced racial-earnings ratios in the Midwest, but increased them in the South Atlantic. We performed decompositions in the noncollege group to explore these disparate noncollege-wage effects.[11] The noncollege group is divided into two occupational groupings of twenty-one skilled and ten manual occupations. Changes in the average black-to-white wage ratio in the noncollege group can result from any of three factors: subgroup-shares effects, which reflect changes in the distribution of workers between the two noncollege occupational subgroups; skilled effects, which reflect the changes in average African American and white wages in the skilled noncollege occupational subgroup; and manual effects, which reflect the change in average African American and white wages in the manual occupational subgroup. (This is the same method as the previous decomposition, except that the two occupational groups are skilled and manual rather than college and noncollege.)

Table 5.6 presents our estimates of how much of the change in the average black-to-white wage ratio in the noncollege group may be

Table 5.6 Decomposition of Changes in the Black-White Earnings Ratio in the Noncollege Labor Sector by Gender and Region, 1992 to 1994 and 1995 to 1997

	Racial Earnings Ratio			Decomposition into		
	1992 to 1994	1995 to 1997	Total Change	Group shares	Skilled wage	Manual wage
Men						
South Atlantic	77.56	78.71	1.15	0.50	−1.07	1.62
Midwest	83.55	81.58	−1.97	0.13	−4.30	2.20
Women						
South Atlantic	93.62	93.08	−0.54	1.04	−3.93	2.35
Midwest	106.69	103.94	−2.75	0.13	−3.31	0.43

Source: Authors' calculations from the United States Bureau of the Census, Current Population Survey Outgoing Rotation Group Files (Washington: U.S. Government Printing Office, 1992–1997).

accounted for by each of the three components. Among men and women in both regions, changes in average African American and white wages in the skilled occupations had an adverse effect. For example, among men in the Midwest, the change in average African American and white wages in the skilled occupations caused the average black-to-white wage ratio in the noncollege group to decline by 4.30 percentage points. Meanwhile, among men and women in both regions, the average black-to-white wage ratio in the noncollege group was affected positively by the other two components: the change in average African American and white wages in the manual group and the disproportionate growth of black employment in the skilled occupations. In the South Atlantic male-labor market, these two positive effects were dominant such that the average black-to-white wage ratio in the noncollege group rose. However, adverse wage changes in the skilled-labor market were so substantial that the average black-to-white wage ratio in the noncollege group declined among men in the Midwest and among women in both regions.

Over the economic expansion, we found that there were improvements in the numbers of African Americans in college occupations. In addition, among African Americans in the noncollege group we observed gains in skilled-occupation employment share. These favorable group- and subgroup-share effects improved racial-earnings ratios. However, essential to understanding why racial-earnings ratios did not improve over the economic expansion among women in both regions and men in the Midwest was the decline in the average black-to-white wage ratios in the college group and among skilled occupations within the noncollege group. The next section will look more closely at why average black-to-white wage ratios deteriorated in each of these two occupational groupings.

SOURCES OF AVERAGE WAGE-RATE CHANGES

This section explores the reasons for the deterioration of the average black-to-white wage ratio in both the college group and among skilled occupations in the noncollege group. Within each of these two occupational groupings, racial wage gaps can be decomposed into the share explained by differences in African American and white wages within occupations and the share due to differences in the distribution of African American and white workers across the occupations. The racial wage gap is:

$$W_w - W_b = \Sigma[(S_{wi})(W_{wi})] - \Sigma[(S_{bi})(W_{bi})]$$
$$= \Sigma[(W_{wi} - W_{bi})(S_{wi})] + \Sigma[(S_{wi} - S_{bi})(W_{bi})]$$

where:

$\Sigma[(W_{wi} - W_{bi})(S_{wi})]$ is the "within-occupations" effect

$\Sigma[(S_{wi} - S_{bi})(W_{bi})]$ is the "across-occupations" effect

For each region, gender, and occupational grouping S_{wi} represents the share of all white workers in the ith occupation, while S_{bi} does the same for blacks. Likewise, W_{wi} and W_{bi} designate the average wage of white and African American workers employed in the ith occupation. The first term, the "within-occupations" effect, indicates the share of the racial wage gap due solely to differences in African American and white wages within occupations. To the extent that African American and white workers are equally qualified, this reflects a glass-ceiling effect that imposes limitations on black workers' opportunities to make salary advances within occupations. If the level of relative skills remains constant over the expansion—a much less restrictive assumption—a growth in this component implies that white workers were able to obtain salary advancements within occupations more rapidly than were African American workers.

The second term, the "across-occupations" effect, reflects the share of the racial wage gap attributable to differences in the distribution of African American and white workers across the occupational grouping, and measures the degree to which African American workers have less access to higher-paying occupations than do white workers. Its growth over the expansion would indicate that white workers were able to shift to the higher-paying occupations within each occupational group more rapidly than were African American workers.

Table 5.7 presents this breakdown of Midwest and South Atlantic racial wage gaps among men and women in both occupational groupings at each point in the economic expansion. Glass-ceiling effects—promotions within occupations, or lack thereof—rather than exclusionary barriers seem to be the greatest obstacles to the advancement of African American men in the college group, as across-occupation differences were completely eliminated over the economic expansion. In the skilled occupational grouping, the share of the racial wage gap due to differences in the African American and white occupational distributions were larger in the Midwest than in the South Atlantic region in both time periods. This suggests that in

Table 5.7 Decomposition of Racial Wage Gaps by Gender and Occupational Grouping, 1992 to 1994 and 1995 to 1997

	Total Wage Gap		Within-Occupation		Across-Occupation		Share of total gap (percent):	
	1992 to 1994	1995 to 1997	1992 to 1994	1995 to 1997	1992 to 1994	1995 to 1997	1992 to 1994	1995 to 1997
College								
Men								
South Atlantic	153.61	168.07	130.75	168.46	22.86	−0.39	14.9	−0.2
Midwest	144.52	143.91	126.15	145.03	18.37	−1.12	12.7	−0.8
Women								
South Atlantic	−6.79	41.19	1.09	6.02	−7.88	35.17	116.1	85.4
Midwest	−38.80	−7.24	−0.95	−1.11	−37.65	−6.13	97.5	84.7
Skilled								
Men								
South Atlantic	98.68	109.76	78.30	94.61	20.38	15.16	20.7	13.8
Midwest	71.17	107.93	55.15	85.74	16.02	22.19	22.5	20.6
Women								
South Atlantic	7.91	24.93	−2.01	6.48	9.92	18.45	125.4	74.0
Midwest	−21.46	−10.52	−10.46	−12.46	−5.00	1.94	22.3	−9.0

Source: Authors' calculations from United States Bureau of the Census Current Population Survey Outgoing Rotation Group Files (Washington: U.S. Government Printing Office, 1992–1997).

this occupational grouping, with greater job competition in the Midwest, white men had greater access to higher-paying occupations than did African American men. Consistent with this thesis, the share of the racial wage gap due to across-occupational differences was larger for all occupational groups at the beginning of the expansion, when job competition was greatest, than after the expansion occurred.

Among women, the most striking finding is in the college group. Over the economic expansion, the racial wage gap grew by $47.98 in the South Atlantic and $31.34 in the Midwest. For African American women, these amounts constitute approximately 5 to 8 percent of the average, usually weekly, wage. In the Midwest region, this enabled white women to approach pay equity; in the South, there was a movement from pay equity to a substantial advantage for white women. Most importantly, changes in the racial wage gap among women in the college group were entirely produced by growth of the across-occupations component.

In the South Atlantic region during the economic expansion, both African American and white women increased their representation in teaching, officials, and other executive occupational categories. However, there were important differences in the races' experiences. White women, for instance, experienced a more dramatic shift out of the lower-wage technician categories than did African American women. In addition, only white women significantly increased their representation in mathematical and hospital-administration occupations, which are among the highest-paying college occupations for women. In contrast, African American women lowered their representation in hospital administration by almost as much as they increased their representation in the lower-paid management category. As a result, the share of the racial wage gap engendered by changes in the occupational distribution increased from $7.88 to $35.17. Thus, it seems that over the economic expansion, exclusionary barriers weakened in the South Atlantic region substantially more for white than for African American professional women.

CONCLUDING REMARKS

Understanding regional differences in racial inequity can help explain national trends and also provide a map to indicate where different types of antidiscrimination policy need to focus. Statistics reveal that during the 1990s, as in previous decades, African American employment rates were dramatically lower in the Midwest than in the South Atlantic region, and that employed African American women outnumbered employed African American men. Over the 1990s expansion, African American employment rates grew in both regions. However, for women in both regions, and men in the Midwest, racial-earnings ratios declined.

High nonemployment rates reduce the share of African American workers in manual occupations in the Midwest relative to the South Atlantic, distorting regional comparisons. In addition, increased Midwestern employment over the expansion should have increased disproportionately the share of black workers in manual occupations, making the expansion appear less favorable. This is most clearly the case where welfare reform thrust large numbers of poorly skilled African American women with limited work experience into the labor market. Their entry could be expected to worsen the African American occupational distribution and racial-earnings ratios in the Midwest relative to the South Atlantic region.

Racial-earnings ratios deteriorated primarily as a result of the decline in the average black-to-white wage ratios in the college group and in the skilled noncollege occupations. In general, these wage effects dwarfed the positive effects of a rise in the average black-to-white wage ratio in manual occupations and the group-shares effects. Only for men in the South Atlantic region did these positive effects offset the adverse wage effects.

Additional decompositions sought to better understand why African American wage growth, both in the college group and in the skilled occupations in the noncollege group, lagged behind white wage growth. In each of these occupational groups, wage gaps result from either differences in African American and white wages within occupations, or differences in the distribution of African American and white workers across the occupations. Among men in both regions, the entire wage gap in the college group could be attributed to within-occupation wage differences. We associate this finding with glass-ceiling effects. For women in both regions, the main conclusion is that the racial wage gap in the college group grew over the expansion solely as a result of an increase in across-occupation differences. We associate this with white women being able to surmount exclusionary barriers in professional-labor markets more rapidly than African American women could.

Finally, in skilled occupations in the noncollege group, more of the racial wage gap among men in the Midwest owed to across-occupation differences than in the South Atlantic region. As might be expected, with the lessening of job competition over the expansion, the share of average wage differences due to across-occupation differences declines in both regions, indicating the weakening of exclusionary barriers.

It should not be surprising that for men in the college group, glass-ceiling effects have become more significant than exclusionary barriers. For while exclusionary barriers are the first to go, the promotion ladder takes longer to change. When both African American and white women become more integrated into professional occupations, gender wage gaps will also become dominated by glass-ceiling effects. Thus, it may be premature to focus solely on glass-ceiling effects as long as African American women continue to have more-limited access to higher-paying professions than white women.

The results of this study must be tempered by a number of factors. High African American nonemployment rates have a substantial impact on regional comparisons and racial-earnings ratios. As a preliminary test of this hypothesis, appendix 5B presents one possible adjustment procedure, which suggests that virtually all of the regional differences in the occupational distribution of African American workers can be explained by their higher nonemployment rate in the Midwest. This adjustment procedure also indicates that reductions in the nonemployment rate over the economic expansion explain why the group-shares effects are negative in the Midwest. Further research should explore this issue.

This study has identified occupational sectors in which glass-ceiling effects and/or exclusionary barriers persist and the degree to which they have changed over the economic expansion. Such findings can be quite useful in determining where policy-makers should focus their efforts to reduce racial earnings gaps. However, this study has not assessed to what extent these practices reflect human-capital discrepancies. Despite separating labor markets into those that generally require college educations and those that do not, human-capital disparities between black and white workers exist.[12] Only in the Midwest in the noncollege group are there no racial differences in educational attainment among men or women. Otherwise, whites have somewhat higher levels of educational attainment than do African Americans. However, over the economic expansion, human-capital disparities did not change significantly from earlier levels, thus they cannot explain fluctuations in racial-earnings ratios.

APPENDIX 5A: OCCUPATIONS IN EACH OCCUPATIONAL GROUPING

College Occupations (14)

Official, executive, or owner; other executive; manager; engineer; mathematical professional; natural scientist; health director; health administrator; teacher—postsecondary; teacher—primary or secondary; lawyer; other professional; health technologist or technician; technician

Skilled Noncollege Occupations (21)

Engineering and science technicians; supervisors and proprietors, sales occupations; sales representatives; sales workers, retail and personal-services workers; sales-related occupations; supervisors, administrative-support personnel; computer-equipment operators; secretaries, stenographers, and typists; financial records, processing occupations; mail and message distributors; other administrative-support personnel, including clerical workers; protective-service personnel; mechanisms and repairers; construction trades; other precision production occupations; machine operators and tenders, excluding precision machinists; fabricators, assemblers, inspectors, and samplers; motor-vehicle operators; other transportation personnel and material moving; farm operators and managers

Manual Occupations (10)

Private-household service personnel; food-service personnel; nonskilled health-service worker; cleaning and building-service personnel; personal-service personnel; construction laborer; freight, stock, or material handler; other handler, equipment cleaner, or laborer; farm or related agricultural worker; forestry or fishing personnel

APPENDIX 5B: ADJUSTMENTS FOR AFRICAN AMERICAN NONEMPLOYMENT RATES

If African American workers in the Midwest are less able to obtain employment than are African American workers in the South Atlantic region, the Midwest's favorable occupational distribution may be illusionary. To judge the impact of African American nonemployment rates in the Midwest on the occupational distribution, we made the following adjustments to the Midwest African American occupational distribution: During each time period, we added one-half of the regional African American employment-rate difference to the African American Midwestern employment rate. Following Juhn (1992), we assumed that this would account for African American workers who would have been employed had the job market been stronger there. For the 1992 through 1994 time period, this adjustment added an additional 10 percent to both male and female employment. In the 1995 through 1997 time period, this adjustment increased African American employment in the Midwest among men by an additional 7.5 percent and among women by 5 percent.

It is quite likely that the high nonemployment rate overwhelmingly reflected individuals seeking employment in occupations located in the noncollege group, especially among the manual subset. As a result, African American workers were added to the noncollege group in the following manner: one-fifth to the skilled occupations and the remaining four-fifths to the manual occupations. While arbitrary, we believe that this adjustment gives us a reasonable benchmark from which to assess the extent to which nonemployment rates might distort the African American occupational distribution in the Midwest region. Table 5B.1 displays the estimated impact of these adjustments on the distribution of African American workers.

After these adjustments, regional occupational differences among African American women were eliminated, suggesting that current differences are entirely due to regional variations in nonparticipation rates. Nonparticipation-rate variations also seem to explain the regional differences in the share of African American male workers in manual occupations. Only among African American men in the college group does a significant regional difference remain.

Without the adjustment, it appeared that white men and women moved disproportionately into noncollege occupations in the Midwest, resulting in a negative group-shares effect. After our adjustment for nonemployment rates is made, however, the group-shares effect is completely eliminated. (See table 5B.2.) Before our adjustment, the wages of white workers in the noncollege group increased more rapidly than the wages of their African American counterparts. After our adjustment, however, this difference disappears, indicating that changes in average African American and white wages in the noncollege group had no impact on racial-earnings ratios. Among

Table 5B.1 Adjusted and Actual Black Midwest Employment Distribution by Occupational Classification and Gender, 1992 to 1994 and 1995 to 1997

| | Actual Shares | | | Difference Between South Atlantic and Midwest | |
	South Atlantic	Midwest	Adjusted Midwest	Actual	Adjusted
College					
Men					
1992 to 1994	15.81	21.54	19.58	5.73	4.07
1995 to 1997	18.19	22.28	20.73	4.09	2.53
Women					
1992 to 1994	23.68	26.87	24.43	3.19	0.75
1995 to 1997	26.33	27.88	26.55	1.55	0.22
Manual					
Men					
1992 to 1994	28.65	22.88	28.07	−5.77	−0.58
1995 to 1997	26.16	21.46	25.54	−4.70	−0.62
Women					
1992 to 1994	27.10	22.45	27.68	−4.65	0.58
1995 to 1997	24.35	21.93	24.70	−2.42	0.35

Source: Authors' calculations from United States Bureau of the Census, Current Population Survey Outgoing Rotation Group Files (Washington: U.S. Government Printing Office, 1992–1997).

Table 5B.2 Decomposition of Changes in the Midwest Black-White Earnings Ratio by Gender, 1992 to 1994 and 1995 to 1997

| | Racial Earnings Ratio | | Decomposition into: | | | |
	1992 to 1994	1995 to 1997	Total Change	Group shares	College wage	Non-college wage
Men						
Actual	81.49	80.51	−0.98	−0.25	0.11	−0.84
Adjusted	79.11	78.85	−0.26	−0.02	−0.03	−0.21
Women						
Actual	104.00	99.27	−4.73	−0.78	−3.05	0.90
Adjusted	101.02	97.83	−3.19	0.12	−3.03	−0.28

Source: Authors' calculations from United States Bureau of the Census, Current Population Survey Outgoing Rotation Group Files (Washington: U.S. Government Printing Office, 1992–1997).

men, this suggests that the modest decline in the racial-earnings ratio over the economic expansion resulted entirely from changes in nonemployment rates. Among women, changes in average African American and white wages in the college group would continue to have a strong negative effect. Thus, while reduced, the decline in the racial-earnings ratio among women would still be substantial.

APPENDIX 5C: CALCULATING THE DECOMPOSITIONS OF RACIAL-EARNINGS RATIOS

The actual racial-earnings ratio in each region for each gender in 1992 through 1994 can be determined thusly:

$$R92 = [(W_{92wc})(S_{92w}) + (W_{92wn})(1-S_{92w})] / [(W_{92bc})(S_{92b}) + (W_{92bn})(1-S_{92b})]$$

where W_{bc} represents the average African American wage in the college group and W_{bn} the average African American wage in the noncollege group; W_{wc} and W_{wn} the same for white males; and S_b and S_w respectively the portions of all African American and all white workers in the college group. Inclusion of "92" and "95" in the subscripts indicates the periods that yielded those values: 92 for 1992 through 1994; 95 for 1995 through 1997.

We first estimate the racial-earnings ratio had only the share of African American and white workers in each occupational group changed:

$$R1 = [(W_{92wc})(S_{95w}) + (W_{92wn})(1-S_{95w})] / [(W_{92bc})(S_{95b}) + (W_{92bn})(1-S_{95b})]$$

Next, we estimate what regional racial-earnings ratios would be if in addition to the share of workers in each of the two occupational groups changing, the average wage of African American and white workers in the college group changed as well:

$$R2 = [(W_{95wc})(S_{95w}) + (W_{92wn})(1-S_{95w})] / [(W_{95bc})(S_{95b}) + (W_{92bn})(1-S_{95b})]$$

Finally, by including the change in average wages for African Americans and whites in the noncollege group, we compute the actual earnings ratio for the 1995 through 1997 time period:

$$R95 = [(W_{95wc})(S_{95w}) + (W_{95wn})(1-S_{95w})] / [(W_{95bc})(S_{95b}) + (W_{95bn})(1-S_{95b})]$$

NOTES

1. For this paper, the Midwest comprises the eastern north-central region of the United States: Illinois, Indiana, Michigan, Ohio, and Wisconsin.

The South Atlantic region includes Delaware, the District of Columbia, Florida, Georgia, Maryland, North Carolina, South Carolina, Virginia, and West Virginia.

2. Labor-market difficulties are sometimes measured by differences between the natural and official unemployment rates. According to Mark Zandi and John Hancock (1996), the natural rate was 5.48 for the Midwest and 5.42 in the South Atlantic.

3. Robert Cherry (forthcoming) looks at the 1992 to 1996 annual employment-growth rates of African American workers relative to white workers in each of the seventeen states with the highest levels of African American employment. He finds that each state's relative African American employment growth was inversely related to its unemployment rate. Thus, relative African American employment-rate growth seemed to slow down as the current expansion matured between 1992 and 1996.

4. Owing to its large retirement-age population, white employment rates are relatively low in Florida. If we exclude Florida from South Atlantic calculations, white-male and -female employment rates in that region would be 73.0 and 57.8 percent respectively, still lower than the rates in the Midwest.

5. Cherry (forthcoming) contends that if reasonable adjustments are made for the higher African American nonemployment rate, the "true" 1997 unemployment rate for twenty- to sixty-four-year-old African American men would have been 17 percent.

6. The Outgoing Rotation Group files provide detailed occupational data and weekly wages for nonself-employed workers eighteen to sixty-four years old. The sample includes all workers identified as either "African American" or "white" who have weekly earnings data.

7. Another method of exploring occupational distribution is to use dissimilarity indices measuring the percentage of African American workers who must switch occupations in order to have the same occupational distribution as white workers. We find that the racial occupational dissimilarity indices are greatest among men in the South Atlantic region, where they were 0.28 in the 1992 to 1994 period and 0.25 from 1995 to 1997. They were lowest among women in the Midwest region: 0.16 in 1992 to 1994 and 0.14 in 1995 to 1997. Men in the Midwest had

dissimilarity indices of 0.19 for 1992 to 1994 and 0.20 in 1995 to 1997, while for women in the South Atlantic region, they were 0.21 and 0.19 for the two respective periods.

8. Findings in appendix 5B suggest that in the Midwest, the entire decline in the racial-earnings ratio among men and more than one-half of the decline among women can be attributed to changes in the African American nonemployment rate.

9. This method (Blau, Simpson, and Anderson 1998, table 1) is a general approximation. In particular, the size of each effect is influenced by the order in which they are added, a variation occurring because each component's effect is dependent upon the levels of the other components.

10. These results would have been slightly different if the change in the average African American and white wages in the noncollege group had been entered before the changes in the college group. For example, the noncollege-wage effect in the Midwest would have been slightly more adverse among women, at −1.04 rather than −0.90, but slightly less adverse among men, at −0.84 instead of −0.87.

11. Adjustments discussed in appendix 5B suggest that the negative group-shares and noncollege-wage effects for both men and women in the Midwest are due to changes in the nonemployment rate there.

12. For the college group in both the Midwest and South Atlantic, as well as for the noncollege group in the South Atlantic, the average educational level of African American workers was lower than that of white workers. This suggests that in those occupational groupings, supply-side factors can explain a portion of the exclusionary and glass-ceiling effects. However, in the noncollege group in the Midwest, there were virtually no racial differences in educational attainment among women or men. This strongly suggests that the substantial racial wage gap among men in this labor grouping, which grew over the economic expansion, was not a result of human-capital differences.

REFERENCES

Bernstein, Jared, and Lawrence Mishel. 1997. "Has Wage Inequality Stopped Growing?" *Monthly Labor Review* 120(12): 3–16.

Blau, Francine, Patricia Simpson, and Deborah Anderson. 1998. "Revisiting Occupational Crowding in the United States: A Preliminary Study." *Feminist Economics* 4(Fall): 29–72.

Bluestone, Barry, and Bennett Harrison. 1982. *The Deindustrialization of America: Plant Closings, Community Abandonment, and the Dismantling of Basic Industry.* New York: Basic Books.

Bound, John, and Richard Freeman. 1992. "What Went Wrong? The Erosion of Relative Earnings and Employment Among Young Black Men in the 1980s." *Quarterly Journal of Economics* 107(February): 201–32.

Carlstrom, Charles T., and Christy D. Rollow. 1998. "Regional Variations in White-Black Earnings." *Federal Reserve Board of Cleveland Economic Research* 34(2): 10–22.

Cherry, Robert. Forthcoming. "Black-Male Employment and Tight Labor Markets." *Review of Radical Political Economy.*

Cotton, Jeremiah. 1993. "A Regional Analysis of Black-Male–White-Male Wage Differences." *Review of African American Political Economy* 22(Summer): 55–72.

Deming, William G. 1996. "A Decade of Economic Change and Population Shifts in U.S. Regions." *Monthly Labor Review* 119(11): 3–14.

Freeman, Richard. 1991. "Employment and Earnings of Disadvantaged Young Men in a Labor-Shortage Economy." In *The Urban Underclass,* edited by Christopher Jencks and Paul E. Peterson, 103–21. Washington, D.C.: Brookings Institution.

Holzer, Harry. 1996. *What Do Employers Want?* New York: Russell Sage Foundation.

Juhn, Chinhui. 1992. "Decline of Male Labor-Market Participation." *Quarterly Journal of Economics* 107(February): 79–121.

Kirschenman, Joleen, and Kathryn Neckerman. 1991. "'We'd Love to Hire Them, But. . .': The Meaning of Race for Employers." In *The Urban Underclass,* edited by Christopher Jencks and Paul E. Peterson. Washington, D.C.: Brookings Institution.

Murphy, Kevin M., and Finis Welch. 1990. "Empirical Age-Earnings Profiles." *Journal of Labor Economics* 8(2): 202–29.

Saunders, Lisa. 1995. "Relative Earnings of Black Men to White Men by Region, Industry." *Monthly Labor Review* 118(April): 68–73.

Seitchik, Adam. 1989. "Who are the Displaced Workers?" In *From One Job to the Next: Worker Adjustment in a Changing Labor Market,* edited by A. Seitchik and J. Zornitsky. Kalamazoo, Mich.: W. E. Upjohn Institute for Employment Research.

U.S. Department of Commerce, Bureau of Labor Statistics. Various years. Table 12: States: Employment Statistics of the Civilian Non-Institutional Population. Washington: U.S. Government Printing Office.

Wilson, William J. 1996. *When Work Disappears*. New York: Vintage.

Zandi, Mark, and John Hancock. 1996. "A Wager on Wages." *Regional Financial Review* (Financial Research Associates, Westchester, Penn.) 5(August): 2–8.

Chapter 6

WHAT DO WE NEED TO EXPLAIN ABOUT AFRICAN AMERICAN UNEMPLOYMENT?

WILLIAM E. SPRIGGS AND RHONDA M. WILLIAMS

After a long period in the 1980s when African American communities experienced double-digit unemployment rates, the post-1992 economic expansion has consistently produced black adult-unemployment rates of less than 10 percent. When the African American unemployment rate dipped to 8.2 percent in 1998, it reached its lowest level since 1972, the first year for which the Bureau of Labor Statistics broke down unemployment figures into white, black, non-white, and nonblack categories. When African American joblessness remained intractably high during the 1980s, theories of labor deficiencies in the African American community became the preferred policy shorthand for explaining African American unemployment. However, some analysts offered a simpler explanation of the double-digit black unemployment rate: African American unemployment rates have historically been twice those of whites, and until the 1992 recovery, the national unemployment rate had drifted upward from economic peak to economic peak.

Most recent research on African American unemployment has been microeconomic in nature and based on the assumption that some form of labor-market deficiency persists in African American communities. Advocates of the deficiency thesis generally argue that premarket forces are the causal determinants of observed racial employment disparities: some analysts suggest that inadequate public investment in education and worker training disproportionately affects African Americans; others assert that deficiencies lie in the cultural norms and choices of African Americans. Their differences notwithstanding, these two variants of the deficiency, or supply side, thesis share an underlying view of labor markets as efficient and just machines that allocate jobs fairly and tend to reward equals equally. Accordingly, most economists explain wage and employment disparities between individuals as the results of pre-market phenomena. Moreover, in this paradigm, "race" is a focus of inquiry only to the extent that, as represented in its quantified form (the well-known dummy variable), it correlates with premarket factors and employment outcomes. "Race" as a social construct used to define and maintain economic privilege and political power disappears in such an analysis, as do the connections among racially mediated meanings, economic and political decision making, and macroeconomic outcomes.

Proponents of recovering and reconceptualizing the nexus of markets, race, and social outcomes continue to explore alternative means to the end of theorizing race and economic life. Specifically, economists William Darity Jr., Patrick L. Mason, James Stewart, and Rhonda M. Williams argue for a paradigm that locates racial economic inequalities within a larger context, one wherein market agents contest the meanings of race and organize racialized economic outcomes.[1] Notions of "race" inform market actors' understandings of class, gender, ability, and community, and so, within this context, race-based economic discrimination is a form of institutionalized racism that creates economic privilege in the dominant community and economic want in the subordinated community.

Because United States economic history abounds with examples of white discrimination, perpetrated in the interest of white economic privilege, against persons and communities of color, this paradigm thus suggests a different approach to the analysis of the relationship between race and labor-market outcomes.[2] Social scientists must seek more than explanations of the absolute levels of black joblessness; they should also attempt to explain why the African American unemployment rate is twice the white unemployment rate and why black unemployment rates decline more slowly than white rates during economic recoveries. The failure to explain persistent gaps between black and white unemployment rates trivializes and underestimates the high cost that unemployment exacts on African American communities. This paper revisits the economics of African American unemployment and asks again: what needs to be explained? We answer that it is the black-white unemployment gap which requires explanation. To that end, we begin with an examination of the macroeconomy and its relationship to black and white unemployment rates and ask why the unemployment ratio remains relatively constant despite changes in the economy and after controlling for education. We use spectral analysis to comparatively assess the business cycle's impact on black and white unemployment rates, and present a human-capital analysis that explores the extent to which black-white education gaps account for black-white unemployment gaps. The conclusion argues in favor of a macroeconomic account of African American unemployment in which racial employment inequalities are endogenous labor-market outcomes generated by race-conscious market agents competing for jobs and profits.

THE MACROECONOMY AND THE BLACK-WHITE UNEMPLOYMENT RATIO

Beginning with the business-cycle peak in 1957, table 6.1 shows the civilian unemployment rate, seasonally adjusted, for each business cycle peak and trough through the present.[3] Between 1970 and 1982, trough to trough and peak to peak, unemployment levels increased.

Table 6.1 Peak-to-Peak and Trough-to-Trough Unemployment Rates
(All Civilian Workers Seasonally Adjusted)

Business-Cycle	Unemployment Rate
Peak	
August 1957	4.1
April 1960	5.2
December 1969	3.5
November 1973	4.8
January 1980	6.3
July 1981	7.2
July 1990	5.5
Trough	
April 1958	7.4
February 1961	6.9
November 1970	5.9
March 1975	8.6
July 1980	7.8
November 1982	10.8
March 1991	6.8[a]

Source: National Bureau of Economic and Bureau of Labor Statistics.
[a]The unemployment rate did not reach its highest level at the trough of the 1990 recession. The unemployment rate continued to increase, reaching 7.7 percent in June 1992.

Starting with the recovery of 1982, unemployment rates decline in periods between business-cycle peaks. However, if the ratio of African American to white unemployment rates remains at the September 1998 ratio of 2.4 to 1, then the African American community will continue to suffer unemployment rates typical of what whites suffer only during economic recessions.

The notion that African American unemployment is particularly sensitive to economic growth is rooted in economists' cursory examination of statistics and the unique experience of growth in the 1960s. The 1982 recession and its early recovery reinforced the view that the African American unemployment rate is sensitive to macroeconomic dynamics. Figure 6.1 shows the seasonally adjusted monthly unemployment rates for adult men (men twenty years old and older) twelve months before that business cycle trough and twelve months after. As illustrated, the recovery dramatically lowered the unemployment rate for adult African American men and

Figure 6.1 Monthly Unemployment During the 1982 Recession

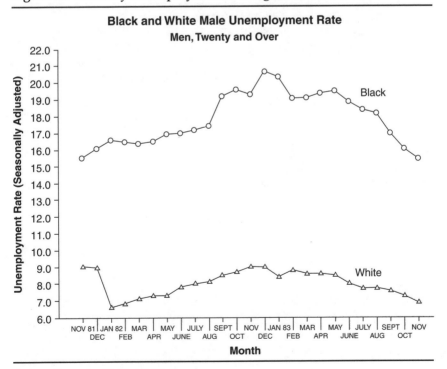

Source: Bureau of Labor Statistics.

did so faster than it lowered the rate for white men. Those who believe that that the African American unemployment rate might not be very sensitive to economic growth cite the consistency of the black-to-white unemployment-rate ratio. Throughout the post–World War II era, this ratio has hovered around two to one. During periods of economic recovery, the ratio increases, and during periods of recession, the ratio declines.

Data from the three most recent recession-recovery cycles generally support this view, the one exception to the pattern being the 1960s expansion. Similar to figure 6.1's depiction of 1982, figures 6.2, 6.3, and 6.4 show peaks and troughs for the recessions of 1975, 1980, and 1990. In 1975 (figure 6.2) and 1980 (figure 6.3), the white-male unemployment rate rises and falls with the business cycle. Meanwhile, the African American men's unemployment rate did not fall as quickly during those recoveries, and so the relative position of African American men declined. During the first twelve months of the 1975 recov-

Figure 6.2 Monthly Unemployment During the 1975 Recession

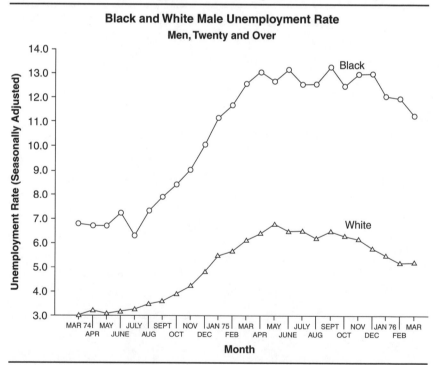

Source: Bureau of Labor Statistics.

Figure 6.3 Monthly Unemployment During the 1980 Recession

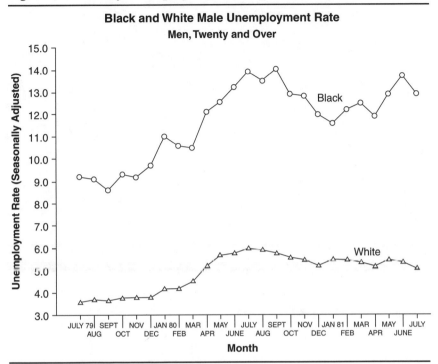

Source: Bureau of Labor Statistics.

ery, the African American–male unemployment rate did not fall (figure 6.2); instead, it bounced around the high level it had reached during that business cycle's trough. After the trough of the 1980 recession, the African American–male unemployment rate fell, but soon turned up again just before the nation entered its next recession (figure 6.3). At the same time, the white-male unemployment rate continued to decline during the aborted economic recovery. In the most recent recession, that of 1990 (see figure 6.4), the white-male unemployment rate slowly rose after the beginning of the recovery in March 1991. The path of the African American unemployment rate, however, is striking: it first drifts down before racing up in late 1991.

Table 6.2 displays the annual unemployment rate for men twenty-five and older for the period 1974 to 1994. The relative unemployment rate—the ratio of black to white unemployment—was at its lowest points in 1972 (not shown), 1973 (not shown), 1975 through 1977, and 1991. Except for 1972, each of these years included at least some

Figure 6.4 Monthly Unemployment During the 1990 Recession

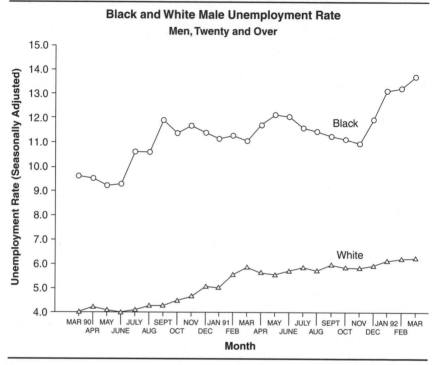

Source: Bureau of Labor Statistics.

months of economic downturn. Conversely, the ratio was at its highest in 1979 and 1989—both years in which the economy was at a peak. During the 1970s, the ratio averaged 2.2, and rose to 2.4 during the 1980s. The upward drift in the ratio also is evident if the period is broken into segments spanning 1972 to 1982 and 1983 to 1990 in order to highlight the recovery.

Thus, our back-of-the-envelope assessment of these four figures and two tables constructed from actual unemployment rates is consistent with the view that the African American unemployment rate is less sensitive to changes in the economy than is the white unemployment rate. Table 6.2, for instance, specifically shows that the African American adult-male unemployment rate increases during recessions and falls during expansions. However, the African American unemployment rate generally falls more slowly during recoveries than does the white rate.[4] Of course, in absolute terms, African Americans do not benefit from economic downturns.

Table 6.2 Unemployment Rate for Black and White Males, Twenty-Five and Over, March of Each Year

	(1) Actual White (Percentage)	(2) Actual Black (Percentage)	(3) Holding Unemployment Rate Constant (Percentage)	(4) Actual Ratio (2)/(1)	(5) Nondiscriminatory Ratio (3)/(1)
1974	3.5	7.7	4.1	2.2	1.2
1975	7.3	15.1	8.5	2.1	1.2
1976	6.1	13.2	7.3	2.1	1.2
1977	5.8	12.0	6.9	2.1	1.2
1978	4.7	10.2	5.6	2.2	1.2
1979	4.1	11.2	8.0	2.7	1.9
1980	5.3	11.6	6.4	2.2	1.2
1981	6.3	14.5	7.5	2.3	1.2
1982	8.5	18.2	10.0	2.1	1.2
1983	9.8	21.3	11.6	2.2	1.2
1984	6.4	16.9	7.8	2.6	1.2
1985	6.1	15.3	7.3	2.5	1.2
1986	6.4	13.7	7.6	2.1	1.2
1987	5.9	12.7	6.8	2.2	1.2
1988	4.8	12.6	5.7	2.6	1.2
1989	4.3	11.5	5.0	2.7	1.2
1990	4.6	10.9	5.4	2.4	1.2
1991	6.7	13.2	7.7	2.0	1.2
1992	7.3	16.2	8.6	2.2	1.2
1993	7.1	15.3	8.2	2.2	1.2
1994	6.2	12.4	7.0	2.0	1.1

Source: Authors' calculations based on data from the Bureau of Labor Statistics.

In order to more fully substantiate our claim that economic growth benefits black workers different than it does their white counterparts, we next present the results from a spectral analysis of business cycles. Spectral analysis allows a researcher to quantify the extent to which two time series move together.[5] In this case, the time series in question are the race-specific unemployment rates and the economy's growth rate, and the objective is to quantify growth rate's differential impact upon the black and white unemployment rates. Table 6.3 shows the cross spectra of unemployment rates for black and white adult males with the growth of the U.S. economy. The spectral analysis uses quarterly data for the period from 1954 to 1989 and unemployment rates that are seasonally adjusted quarterly averages. We adjusted both the black and white series for a linear trend. The growth in the economy is the trend-adjusted difference in the natural logarithm of seasonally adjusted quarterly real gross domestic product (GDP) (using 1982 price weights).

Table 6.3 Cross-Spectra-Analysis of Black and White Adult Male (Twenty Years and Older) Unemployment Rates with Growth of Log Gross Domestic Product (Seasonally Adjusted Quarterly Data [Detrended] 1954 to 1989)

	Whites			African Americans		
Period	Coherence	Gain	Phase	Coherence	Gain	Phase
24.00	0.0782	2529.0	2.00	0.0657	2127.0	0.65
12.00	0.2658	10430.0	37.96	0.1703	6686.0	30.94
8.00	0.3234	10870.0	17.09	0.2210	7429.0	14.35
6.00	0.4598	15520.0	10.64	0.3300	11400.0	8.92
4.80	0.4742	15740.0	8.12	0.3344	11000.0	6.91
4.00	0.7908	27050.0	6.35	0.6770	23160.0	5.98
3.43	0.7720	24270.0	5.08	0.6477	20360.0	4.82
3.00	0.7806	26870.0	4.19	0.6548	22540.0	4.04
2.67	0.8050	27030.0	3.76	0.7093	23820.0	3.70
2.40	0.8406	28800.0	3.17	0.7554	25880.0	2.97
2.18	0.8985	31100.0	2.77	0.8215	28440.0	2.59
2.00	0.8610	37660.0	2.56	0.7606	33270.0	2.40
1.85	0.8514	39630.0	2.25	0.7380	34350.0	2.14
1.71	0.8577	40420.0	2.12	0.7499	35340.0	2.07
1.60	0.8434	40450.0	1.88	0.7621	36550.0	1.72
1.50	0.7737	45080.0	1.81	0.6367	37100.0	1.67

Source: Authors' calculations using data from the Bureau of Labor Statistics and Bureau of Economic Analysis.

Table 6.3 presents race-specific coherence, gain, and phase statistics for the spectral analysis. Consider first the coherence statistic, which measures the strength of the linear association between the unemployment series and the growth in the economy for cycles of various lengths. Our hypothesis is that for cycles of various periods, the white coherence statistic is greater than the black coherence statistic. The greatest association for both unemployment series with growth in the economy is for cycles lasting six and one-half months (2.18 quarters). Another peak in the correlation occurs for cycles of almost five months in length. For all cycles, the coherence statistic for the white unemployment rate and economic growth is greater than the coherence statistic for African American unemployment rates. This part of the spectral analysis supports the view that unemployment for African Americans is less sensitive than white unemployment to macroeconomic growth.

Careful examination of the gain in the spectra strengthens this argument. The gain statistic measures the "amplification" of a series. We note that economic growth amplifies the unemployment rates according to a discernible pattern, increasing them with the cycle frequencies. This makes the unemployment rate appear to be more sensitive to economic growth in the short run, but less variable over the longer term. At all frequency levels, economic growth amplifies the white unemployment rate more than it moves the African American unemployment rate. So, economic fluctuations tend to change the white unemployment rate more than they do the African American rate, hence increasing the disparity in the two unemployment rates. Thus, policy interventions aimed at economic growth will tend to reduce white unemployment rates more than black rates, and thereby increase the black-white unemployment gap. Table 6.2, as well as figures 6.3 and 6.4, show that was indeed the case for the 1980s.

The phase statistic of the cross spectra shows the number of periods in which one series' spectral-density function leads, lags behind, or changes direction before another. Here, the results indicate that both unemployment series lead the change in the economy for cycles with long periods. The phase for the initial period (not shown) is negative for both unemployment series, signifying that they lag current economic growth. In this case, the fact that the white phase statistics exceed the black phase statistics simply suggests that changes in the white unemployment rates more strongly indicate the economy's direction than the black rates do. This result is not surprising, given the relative size of the white labor force. The differences in the cross-spectra statistics for the two unemployment series highlight the differential impact of economic growth on black and white unemployment. These statistics provide empirical support for our claim that white-male unemployment rates are more responsive to economic growth than are their black-male counterparts, but, of course, economic growth does not perfectly predict unemployment rates. Clearly, GNP growth does not perfectly predict unemployment levels; other factors matter as well. Our analysis suggests that these other determinants matter more for African Americans than for whites.

To address this issue, we now turn to microeconomic determinants of racial disparities in unemployment: can human-capital differences provide a consistent explanation for the relative unemployment-rate difference?

HUMAN CAPITAL AND BLACK-WHITE UNEMPLOYMENT DISPARITIES

Robert J. Flanagan (1976) found that in 1960, the unemployment rate of African American men relative to white men was greatest among those with more years of education. During the 1960s, however, the decline in the relative unemployment rate of African Americans with more years of schooling made their rates of joblessness almost equal to those of equally educated whites. Between 1968 and 1988, the relative unemployment of African American men was lowest in non–central-city areas in the West and South. Franklin D. Wilson, Marta Tienda, and Lawrence Wu (1991) found that after controlling for age and year, the black-white unemployment ratio during that period increased with educational attainment in both regions. The ratio for high school dropouts was 1.3 to 1, for high school graduates 1.8 to 1, and for those with some college 2.1 to 1; moreover, this pattern was repeated for all regions and across inner-city and non-central-city groupings of the data. Beginning in 1994, the unemployment rate for recent African American college graduates again almost equaled that of their white peers. Nevertheless, we have two decades' worth of data suggesting that relative employment outcomes worsened for blacks with the most human capital.

Like Franklin Wilson, Marta Tienda, and Lawrence Wu (1991), Lee Badgett (1990, 1994) suggests that African American educational achievement in the 1970s and 1980s did not yield significant payoffs in employment outcomes. Decomposing changes in the unemployment rate for African Americans by comparing unemployment in March 1971 with 1987, Badgett calculated that while the white unemployment rate was roughly the same in each year, registering 5.8 percent in 1971 and 5.9 percent in 1987 the black-white unemployment ratio increased from 1.7 to 1 to 2.4 to 1. Because almost all of the change in relative unemployment came from the change in jobless rates for African Americans, Badgett limited the substance of her analysis to changes in black unemployment. (Badgett also included both genders, and adults and teenagers, in her study, in contrast to our focus on men.)

The results of Badgett's decomposition analysis of the relationship between unemployment and education are telling. Between 1971 and 1987, the share of the African American workforce that had four or more years of college doubled, and the share of high school dropouts declined by half. Yet the unemployment rate for African Americans increased by 4.4 percentage points, from 9.6 to 14.0 percent. Absent a structural shift in African American unemployment rates, Badgett found that the substantial improvement in the educational credentials of the work force would have cut the increase in the unemployment rate for African Americans from 4.4 to 3.8 percentage points. Thus, increases in the unemployment rate for African Americans at each education level can explain all of the increase in the total unemployment rate.

Other research on labor markets in the 1980s makes a similar point. Economic outcomes for high school–educated workers fell during the 1980s in absolute terms as well as relative to workers with more education. Still, David R. Howell (1991) finds that from 1979 to 1989, the industry- and occupation-mix change was less favorable to young, high school–educated African American men nineteen to thirty-five years old than it was to similarly educated whites. Young, white, high school–educated men were much more successful in increasing their share of the dynamic sectors of the economy, while black men actually lost employment share in two of the three most dynamic sectors. McKinley Blackburn, Richard Freeman, and David Bloom (1991) found that during the 1980s, the earnings of African American males relative to white males fell by the largest amount for college graduates, followed successively by high school graduates and high school dropouts. John Bound and Richard Freeman (1992) also found that African Americans' relative employment–to-population ratio fell for all three education categories, though the greatest drop was for high school dropouts, followed by high school and then college graduates.

Table 6.2 shows March unemployment rates from 1974 to 1994 for black and white men twenty-five years old and older (first and second columns). The third column shows what the unemployment rate for American American men would have been if at each education level (less than high school, high school graduate, some college, college graduate) their unemployment rates mirrored those of white men. Recalling the Oaxaca-Blinder decomposition technique, this manipulation is equivalent to holding the human-capital variables fixed and looking at the difference in returns to human capital. So, table 6.2 shows the "actual" ratio of black to white unemployment and what that ratio would be if returns to education, here measured as unemployment rates, were made equal across the two groups. The actual ratio varies with the economic cycle, while the ratio with equal educational returns remains remarkably stable. As a result, the share of the ratio of black to white unemployment that can be explained by human-capital differences varies with the business cycle. This is surprising, given that in 1974 about half of the African American workforce included high school dropouts, but that by 1994 that number had dropped dramatically to about one-sixth.

Our analysis suggests that a cross-section examination of labor-supply issues—one that focuses on the skills of African Americans, labor-demand issues, or the skills that employers say they want—explains only a portion of the black-white unemployment gap and is unlikely to account for the persistence of the two-to-one ratio. These results, again, suggest that dramatic improvements in the human-capital stock of African Americans are insufficient to reduce substantively the racial disparity in unemployment. Differences in employment opportunity persist, even after controlling for education.

AN ALTERNATIVE LINE OF INQUIRY: UNEMPLOYMENT DISPARITIES AND RACE-BASED JOB COMPETITION

Thus far, this chapter has suggested two stylized facts about African American unemployment: first, that the African American–male unemployment rate is sensitive to changes in the general economy, but less so than whites', and, second, that the percentage of the black-white unemployment-rate gap that can be explained by skill differences also is sensitive to the state of the general economy.

We suggest that the job-competition literature provides an alternative and more robust explanation for African American unemployment.[6] Their differences notwithstanding, the models developed in this literature share two core premises. The first is that competition between employers creates a dynamically differentiated set of employment conditions for working people; at any given moment, workers confront employment hierarchies among and within industries, and these hierarchies are not simply manifestations of job-skill requirements. These hierarchies mean that working people in search of favorable employment outcomes have ample incentive to restrict access to preferred job niches via the control of job definitions, training, and information—but they do so in the context of employers seeking profitable production at minimum cost. The first premise posits job competition as the norm and predicts that workers less able to secure and protect job niches will more often be unemployed; when employed, they will more likely be found in lower-paying jobs and industries.[7] The second premise incorporates the aforementioned notion of racialized market subjects: the cultural legacy of white racism is that "race" plays a large role in defining worker and employer identities. Alternatively stated, employers and workers enter the market as (gendered) members of racial, or ethnic, communities, and compete as such. In the United States, working people of European descent defined "whiteness" as the racial category of privilege and frequently have acted collectively to increase their own relative and absolute standing in various job markets, the result being that even today, when seeking to enter and climb the employment hierarchies, white workers can and do benefit from racial discrimination.[8]

Discrimination persists because employers confront nonzero costs for both continuing and ending discrimination. Employment discrimination implies increased employer search costs thus forgone profits in the immediate and possibly long-term future, because it reduces the pool of employable, qualified workers to choose from, and this provides employers with strong incentives to end discrimination. However, at the same time, ending discrimination disrupts established race-based job hierarchies and race-specific notions of employment entitlement, and this, too, can cost employers in the form of employee resistance.[9] Thus, if costs of discrimination outweigh the costs of ending discrimination, discrimination declines, but if ending discrimination is deemed more costly than allowing it to continue, discrimination will continue or even increase. In this discussion, we are particularly interested in how shifts in the macroeconomy affect the costs of ending versus perpetuating discrimination.[10]

Increased unemployment reduces the costs of employment discrimination because qualified white workers appear in job queues in greater numbers. Rising unemployment rates intensify job competition, as do increases in earnings inequality. Heightened job competition means that white employees feel more economically distressed and vulnerable; in a world of racialized job competition, white employees become more resistant to employment practices that benefit persons of color. When manifest as disruption in the social relations of the workplace, white resistance will lower worker productivity and increase employers' costs of ending discrimination. Therefore, during periods of economic contraction, the job-competition model predicts an increase in employment discrimination. Conversely, during periods of economic expansion, white workers' resistance to the hiring of African Americans should decline, as job growth increases employment opportunities for all.

Recalling the earlier discussion of the macroeconomy and black-white employment levels, we are trying to explain, first, why economic growth lowers unemployment more slowly for African Americans than for whites, and, second, why recessions increase white unemployment rates faster than black rates and thus reduce the black-white unemployment ratio. To approach these questions, consider a macroeconomic shock that raises white unemployment rates. Eventually, this shock will increase the costs of reducing discrimination and lower the costs of employment discrimination. However, the equilibrium level of discrimination will not rise until employers observe an increase in the number of whites in their labor queues; in the months immediately following the shock, employers are theoretically hiring blacks at the previously determined equilibrium rate. So, initially, the white unemployment rate will rise faster than the African American rate, and the black-white unemployment ratio will accordingly shrink. As the white unemployment rate continues to rise, however, the equilibrium level of discrimination will also rise, as will African American unemployment rates. Similarly, when the economy starts to recover, the white rate will fall, but discrimination will keep the African American unemployment rate high, and this will make the unemployment ratio grow. As the recovery continues, the equilibrium rate of discrimination will fall, and so will the African American unemployment rate. Note that a net effect of the model is that the black-white wage gap cannot close substantially as long as the black-white unemployment ratio remains at two to one.

This model also would help to explain why during the 1980s the wages of college-educated African Americans suffered the most of all black workers relative to whites of equal educational attainment. As the share of African Americans with college educations increased dramatically, the relative unemployment rate of African American college graduates increased: intensified job competition among the college educated increased the costs of ending discrimination more than economic growth could reduce the costs of continued discrimination. Employment discrimination thus increased among the college graduates, the wage gap between African American and white college graduates grew, as did the overall black-white unemployment ratio.

CONCLUSION

This chapter challenges skill-based explanations of black-white unemployment gaps and uses spectral analysis to evaluate the thesis that African American unemployment rates are less sensitive than white rates to fluctuations in the business cycle. Our analysis suggests that once established, neither economic growth nor black human-capital acquisition are sufficient to eradicate the two-to-one black-white unemployment gap. The fact that African American unemployment rates are consistently twice as high as white rates should be one of the greatest mysteries in labor economics, yet it is among the least-researched dimensions of racial economic inequality. In that light, attempts to decompose the absolute level of unemployment for African Americans, while interesting, do not address racial unemployment inequality per se. Onetime snapshots of labor supply or labor demand, though informative, might not provide an explanation for the persistence of the two-to-one ratio. At the very least, economists should offer their explanations of this injurious phenomena with the greatest of caution.

APPENDIX 6A: A NOTE ON METHODOLOGY

This appendix presents background information on the statistical methods discussed in this paper. Examining the relation between unemployment and economic growth requires the study of variables over time. Typically, such data series are described as having trend, seasonal, cyclical, and random components. The trend in a time series is the component that reflects changes in the average value of the series over long periods. The seasonal component shows changes related to the climate or the calendar (like Christmas buying), or institutional factors (like budgets), that take place within one year in a time series. The cyclical component represents long-run peaks and troughs in the series and shows the effects of such cyclical influences on the labor market as migration, building construction, and changing consumer-behavior patterns as the population ages. The random component is best thought of as "noise": erratic and containing no useful information.

Statistical methods that examine time series are of two types: those that study time domains and those that study frequency domains (for examples, see Box and Jenkins 1974; Fishman 1969; Koopmans 1974; Sargent 1979). The time-domain approach can be thought of as studying the effects of the time at which an event occurs, while the frequency-domain framework can be thought of as studying how regularly something takes place. Much of what economists do is discussed in the time domain. The frequency domain, however, gives economists their most useful tool for examining the intertemporal dependence of two series: the association of the past and present values of a series. Frequency-domain analysis is carried out using the spectrum of the time series created by applying sine and cosine waves to duplicate the rises and falls in the series. Because a series might have peaks and troughs caused by more than one cycle, spectral analysis helps economists to understand which cycles are most important.

NOTES

1. The following definition is offered by Patrick Mason and Rhonda Williams (1997): "By *racialization*, we mean the processes by which individuals learn to read specific phenotypes as indicative of discrete and naturally occurring breeding populations, or 'races.' "

2. See Rhonda Williams (1991a) for extended discussion on this subject.

3. This analysis uses only adult-male unemployment data; subsequent work will examine unemployment data for women and youth.

4. "More slowly" refers to percentage declines on a year-to-year basis.

5. Please see the note on methodology, which explains spectral analysis in greater detail, at the end of this chapter.

6. See, for example, Steven Shulman (1991), M. V. Lee Badgett and Rhonda Williams (1994), Patrick Mason (1995), Rhonda Williams and Robert Kenison (1996), and William Darity Jr. and Rhonda Williams (1985).

7. See Rhonda Williams (1991a, 1997) and Patrick Mason (1995) for fuller treatment and supporting evidence.

8. See Rhonda Williams (1991b) for more detail on white workers and racial consciousness. Historical scholarship in this field dates back to W. E. Burghardt DuBois (1968); David Roediger (1991) contributes to recent wave of scholarship.

9. Rhonda Williams (1991a), Steven Shulman (1991), M. V. Lee Badgett and Rhonda Williams (1994), and Patrick Mason (1995) provide fuller and more-detailed analyses of the costs incurred by ending discrimination.

10. There are multiple mechanisms through which workers resisting the reduction or termination of racial privilege can impose costs on capital. For example, employees can disrupt workplace cooperation and training, or, more directly, they can engage in overt or covert hostilities and harassment. All of these tactics increase the social costs of production and therefore increase the costs of ending discrimination. See Rhonda Williams (1991a), Steven Shulman (1991), and M. V. Lee Badgett and Rhonda Williams (1994).

REFERENCES

Badgett, M. V. Lee. 1990. "Racial Differences in Unemployment Rates and Employment Opportunities." Ph.D. diss., University of California, Berkeley.

———. 1994. "Rising Black Unemployment: Changes in Job Stability or in Employability?" *Review of Black Political Economy* 22(3): 55–75.

Badgett, M. V. Lee, and Rhonda M. Williams. 1994. "The Changing Contours of Discrimination: Race, Gender, and Structural Economic Change." In *Understanding American Economic Decline*, edited by Michael A. Bernstein and David E. Adler. Cambridge, Eng.: Cambridge University Press.

Blackburn, McKinley, Richard Freeman, and David Bloom. 1991. "Changes in Earnings Differentials in the 1980s: Concordance, Convergence, and Consequences." National Bureau of Economic Research Working Paper 3901. Cambridge, Mass.: National Bureau of Economic Research.

Blank, Rebecca M., and Alan S. Blinder. 1996. "Macroeconomics, Income Distribution, and Poverty." In *Fighting Poverty: What Works and What*

Doesn't, edited by Sheldon H. Danziger and Daniel H. Weinberg. Cambridge, Mass.: Harvard University Press.

Bound, John, and Richard Freeman. 1992. "What Went Wrong? The Erosion of Relative Earnings and Employment Among Young Black Men in the 1980s." *Quarterly Journal of Economics* 107(February): 201–32.

Box, George E. P., and Gwilym M. Jenkins. 1974. *Time Series Analysis: Forecasting and Control.* San Francisco: Holden-Day.

Bulow, Jeremy I., and Lawrence H. Summers. 1986. "A Theory of Dual Labor Markets with Application to Industrial Policy, Discrimination, and Keynesian Unemployment." *Journal of Labor Economics* 4: 376–414.

Darity, William Jr., and Rhonda M. Williams. 1985. "Peddlers Forever? Culture, Competition, and Discrimination." *American Economics Association Papers and Proceedings* 75: 256–61.

Donohue, John J. III, and James Heckman. 1991. "Continuous Versus Episodic Change: The Impact of Civil Rights Policy on the Economic Status of Blacks." National Bureau of Economic Research Working Paper 3894. Cambridge, Mass.: National Bureau of Economic Research.

DuBois, W. E. B. 1968 (c. 1935). *Black Reconstruction in America: An Essay Toward a History of the Part Which Black Folk Played in the Attempt to Reconstruct Democracy in America, 1860–1880.* Cleveland: Meridian.

Fishman, George S. 1969. *Spectral Methods in Econometrics.* Cambridge, Mass.: Harvard University Press.

Flanagan, Robert J. 1976. "On the Stability of the Racial Unemployment Differential." *American Economic Review* 66: 302–8.

Gilman, Harry J. 1963. "The White/Non-White Unemployment Differential." In *Human Resources in the Urban Economy,* edited by Mark Perlman. Washington, D.C.: Resources for the Future.

Gilroy, Curtis L. 1974. "Black and White Unemployment: The Dynamics of the Differential." *Monthly Labor Review* 97: 38–47.

Hashemzadeh, Nozar, and Burl F. Long. 1986. "Cyclical Aspects of Black Unemployment: An Empirical Analysis." *Review of Regional Studies* 20: 7–19.

Howell, David R. 1991. "Economic Restructuring and the Labor-Market Status of Young Black Men in the 1980s." Jerome Levy Economics Institute at Bard College Working Paper 67. Annandale-on-Hudson, N.Y.: Bard College.

Koopmans, L. H. 1974. *The Spectral Analysis of Time Series*. New York: Academic Press.

Mason, Patrick L. 1995. "Race, Competition, and Differential Wages." *Cambridge Journal of Economics* 19: 545–67.

Mason, Patrick L., and Rhonda M. Williams. 1997 "The Janus-Face of Race: Reflections on Economic Theory." In *Race, Markets, and Social Outcomes*, edited by Patrick L. Mason and Rhonda M. Williams. Boston: Kluwer-Nijhoff.

Roediger, David. 1991 *The Wages of Whiteness*. New York: Verso.

Sargent, Thomas. 1979. *Macroeconomic Theory*. New York: Academic Press.

Shulman, Steven. 1990. "Racial Inequality and White Employment: An Interpretation and Test of the Bargaining-Power Hypothesis." *Review of Black Political Economy* 18(3): 5–20.

———. 1991. "Why Is the Black Unemployment Rate Always Twice as High as the White Unemployment Rate?" In *New Approaches to Economic and Social Analyses of Discrimination*, edited by Richard R. Cornwall and Phanindra V. Wunnava. New York: Praeger.

Struyk, Raymond, and Michael Fix. 1992. *Clear and Convincing Evidence: Measurement of Discrimination in America*. Washington, D.C.: Urban Institute Press.

Williams, Rhonda M. 1991a. "Competition, Discrimination, and Differential Wage Rates: On the Continued Relevance of Marxian Theory to the Analysis of Earnings and Employment Inequality." In *New Approaches to Economic and Social Analyses of Discrimination*, edited by Richard R. Cornwall and Phanindra V. Wunnava. New York: Praeger.

———. 1991b. "Living at the Crossroads: Explorations in Race, Nationality, Sexuality, and Gender." In *The House That Race Built: Black Americans, U.S. Terrain*, edited by Wahneema Lubiano. New York: Pantheon.

Williams, Rhonda M., and Robert E. Kenison. 1996. "The Way We Were? Discrimination, Competition, and Inter-Industry Wage Differentials in 1970." *Review of Radical Political Economics* 28: 1–32.

Wilson, Franklin D., Marta Tienda, and Lawrence Wu. 1991. "Racial Equality in the Labor Market: Still an Elusive Goal." Paper presented to the American Sociological Association, annual meeting. Cincinnati (August 23, 1991).

Commentary II

IN GOOD TIMES AND BAD: DISCRIMINATION AND UNEMPLOYMENT

CECILIA A. CONRAD

Racial discrimination in American labor markets is less overt today than it was forty years ago. Help-wanted signs no longer list the desired race of job applicants; there are no longer separate pay scales for black and white teachers or black and white social workers. A wage gap does persist, but, according to recent studies, up to 95 percent of that gap can be attributed to differences in human capital, occupation, and industry (O'Neill 1990). Some social scientists no longer regard racial discrimination as a "first order" problem in U.S. labor markets (Heckman 1998, 101).

Unfortunately, declarations that discrimination is ceasing to be much of an issue are probably premature. There are at least two reasons for such pessimism: First, as the papers in this volume document, racial inequalities in the workplace are sensitive to macroeconomic conditions. Most of the recent findings suggesting that discrimination is abating use data from a relatively short time period, 1991 through 1993, and it remains to be seen whether these results will be replicated at other points in a macroeconomic cycle. A second reason for pessimism is the persistent gap in unemployment rates and employment-to-population ratios. The ratio of black-to white-male unemployment rates has held steady at 2 to 1 since World War II (Vedder and Gallaway 1992; Spriggs and Williams, this volume), and the odds of a black man being not employed are 1.56 times higher than they are for a white man. A similar gap is emerging in the employment rates of young women as well.

Despite differences between the races in unemployment and employment rates, the economics literature has tended to define labor-market discrimination solely in terms of wages, not in terms of access. Gary Becker's (1971) classic work, for example, defines the market-discrimination coefficient as the difference between the ratio of two populations' wages measured with and without factoring in discrimination. Within the neoclassical framework, the wage in the absence of discrimination should reflect an individual's marginal productivity, and because marginal productivity depends on past investments in human capital, discrimination is defined as the existence of wage differences not attributable to differences in quantifiable stocks of human capital.

The econometric interpretation of Becker's market-discrimination coefficient is the Oaxaca-Blinder decomposition. This technique decomposes the wage differential between groups into two components: the "explained" component, or the wage differential attributable to differences in human-capital stocks, and the residual, or "unexplained," wage difference which is an estimate of the market-discrimination coefficient.

The essence of Becker's argument is that in a competitive market, individual employers' tastes for discrimination need not translate into a positive market-discrimination coefficient. In a competitive market, nondiscriminating firms will have lower costs of production and hence will tend to grow at the expense of discriminators. Thus, following this analysis, the market-discrimination coefficient in competitive markets will tend toward 0 (zero) even if individual firms prefer to hire white workers.

Becker's analysis coupled with the Oaxaca-Blinder methodology spawned a generation of empirical studies focused on estimating the market-discrimination coefficient. Through continued refinements in the measurement of human capital, these studies have progressively reduced the unexplained portion of the wage gap. For example, in the 1960s and 1970s, a typical wage regression might have included only age and years of schooling as explanatory variables. Today, the same wage regression might include variables such as age, work experience, job tenure, years of schooling, degrees earned, and, most recently, standardized-test scores. With the addition of standardized-test scores and controls for occupation and industry, some economists have been able to reduce the "unexplained" portion of the black-white wage difference to less than 5 percent (O'Neill 1990; England, Christopher, and Reid 1999; Neal and Johnson [1996] offer a more conservative estimate). The implication is that persisting racial inequality reflects premarket conditions, not contemporary discrimination in labor markets. Despite some employers continuing to discriminate, these empirical results suggest that the market-discrimination coefficient has gone to 0, just as Becker's model predicts.

The problem with this conclusion is that the market-discrimination coefficient may not capture discrimination in the employment process. In the neoclassical framework used by Becker, markets clear: those who are willing to work at the prevailing wage find employment, so the theory provides no explanation for involuntary unemployment and posits that employment rates vary across population groups for two reasons. One, if the market discrimination coefficient is 0, then racial differences in employment rates must reflect racial differences in reservation wages. There might be job segregation, but differences in employment rates could be explained only by differences in worker choices as reflected by reservation wages. Two, if the market discrimination coefficient is positive, then differences in employment rates may arise because blacks are unwilling to accept lower wage offers. The statistical theory of discrimination has similar implications.

The empirical literature recognizes that differences in employment rates will affect the estimation of the wage differential. If the black workers with the lowest wage offers drop out of the labor market, the estimated black-white wage gap will be smaller than the gap that would exist were all wage offers observed. Although several techniques have been introduced to correct for this selectivity bias, all implicitly assume that the worker has chosen not to work for the prevailing wage—not that the employer has chosen not to hire the worker.

In contrast to these neoclassical models, institutional theories of labor-market discrimination—such as the jobs-competition model cited by William Spriggs and Rhonda Williams (this volume)—pinpoint employment access as the principal mechanism of discrimination in labor markets. Again, while the focus of this literature is to explain the persistence of wage differences, it is also possible for employment discrimination to coexist with equal wage offers.

In the jobs-competition model, labor markets are characterized by persistent unemployment and queues from which employers choose for each job opening qualified workers whose reservation wages undercut the current wage offer. This model posits separate queues for black and white workers; employers prefer to hire from the white queue, but as they exhaust the pool of white workers, they turn to the black queue. Discrimination is costly because the firm could lower the wage offer and employ more blacks. But ending discrimination is also costly, because it might instigate unrest and resistance among white workers.

Wage differences emerge in the jobs-competition model because blacks will tend to occupy different, generally less desirable, jobs than whites. Where blacks and whites occupy the same jobs there can be wage parity, but the existence of longer queues of black workers testifies to the persistence of labor-market discrimination. In short, discrimination in employment may not be captured by an unexplained differential in wages.

What indicator best captures employment discrimination? Becker sought to determine just that by comparing wages in a world with discrimination to wages in a world without it. Spriggs and Williams (this volume) employ a similar approach. First, they calculate what the unemployment rate would have been for African American men if at each education level this cohort's unemployment rates mirrored those of white men. The researchers define a nondiscriminatory ratio as the ratio of this hypothetical unemployment rate to the actual unemployment rate of white men. According to Spriggs and Williams, findings show that in the absence of discrimination, the black-male unemployment rate would have been 1.2 times greater than the white unemployment rate for most of the years between 1974 and 1994. The actual black-male unemployment rate during most of that period was more than two times greater than that of white men.

The Spriggs and Williams method is a good start, but it has some limitations. Controlling for education, for instance, is not sufficient to capture premarket factors that affect employment status. Furthermore, as the Heather Boushey and Robert Cherry (this volume) analysis demonstrates, there are variations across regions.

The real question that must be addressed is whether there is one job queue or two in the present-day American labor market. In the absence of discrimination, there is one, and a worker's location in the queue is determined by his skills not his race. With discrimination, there are two queues, and the individual worker's place is determined not only by skill but by race as well: because workers are assigned to queues by race, a low-skilled white worker may be ahead of high-skilled black worker in the employer's hiring scheme. The problem is distinguishing cases in which there is only one queue with blacks disproportionately at the back of the line as a result of differences in average skill levels, from cases of separate queues formed on the basis of race. Differentials in aggregate unemployment rates can not tell the whole story, because if blacks are at the back of a single queue, their unemployment rates will be higher than those of whites.

Macroeconomic fluctuations provide an opportunity to investigate whether black and white workers occupy different queues. Economic expansion should shorten the length of the queue as well as the length of time spent there by a typical worker. However, in the absence of discrimination, there is little reason for labor-market tightness to change the relative location of a worker in a queue. Indicators of relative position in the queue, such as the black-white ratio of time spent in the queue, should not be sensitive to macroeconomic conditions.

Some of the findings reported in this volume, though not conclusive, indicate that such ratios are sensitive to macroeconomic conditions, and this suggests the existence of two queues. Even the good news that the current economic expansion has drawn in young African American workers must be tempered with the recognition that it has taken years to accomplish such a modest feat.

In an old edition of a principles textbook there is a cartoon with two panels. The first panel, labeled "recession," shows blacks and whites lined up at an unemployment window. The second, labeled "recovery," depicts the same window, this time with only blacks lined up before it. It is an old cartoon, but yet it is not completely out of date. The persistence of racial differences in unemployment rates, employment rates, and time spent in the job queue are clear indicators of discrimination in job access that wage ratios may not accurately measure.

REFERENCES

Becker, Gary S. 1971. *The Economics of Discrimination*. Chicago: University of Chicago Press.

England, Paula, Karen Christopher, and Lori L. Reid. 1999. "Gender, Race, Ethnicity, and Wages." In *Latinas and African American Women at Work: Race, Gender, and Economic Inequality,* edited by Irene Brown. New York: Russell Sage Foundation.

Heckman, James J. 1998 "Detecting Discrimination." *Journal of Economic Perspectives* 12(2): 101–16.

Neal, Derek A., and William R. Johnson. 1996. "The Role of Premarket Factors in Black-White Wage Differences." *Journal of Political Economy* 104: 869–95.

O'Neill, June. 1990. "The Role of Human Capital in Earnings Differences Between Black and White Men." *Journal of Economic Perspectives* 4 (4): 25–45.

Vedder, Richard K., and Lowell Gallaway. 1992. "Racial Differences in Unemployment in the United States." *Journal of Economic History* 52(3): 696–702.

PART III

Social Dimensions of the Boom

Chapter 7

LOOKING AT THE GLASS CEILING: DO WHITE MEN RECEIVE HIGHER RETURNS TO TENURE AND EXPERIENCE?

JOYCE P. JACOBSEN AND LAURENCE M. LEVIN

The last few years in the United States have been a period of general expansion and tighter labor markets. Despite that, however, earnings gains by women and minorities relative to white men have been unremarkable, and somewhat disappointing for women in particular, compared to progress made in the 1980s. Consider the Bureau of Labor Statistics data on median weekly earnings ratios for selected years in the 1980s and 1990s presented in table 7.1, contrasting specifically the rising relative earnings for women from 1984 to 1991 to the slowed gains of 1991 to 1998. White and black women alike record only one- to two-cent gains relative to white men over this latter seven-year period—as compared to four- to eight-cent gains during the preceding seven years—and Hispanic women actually record losses. Meanwhile, black men experience essentially no improvement in relative earnings, and Hispanic men display a relative earnings decline over the entire fourteen-year period.[1]

There are many possible reasons for these developments, including the winding-down of the sectoral restructuring period of the 1980s, which had seen a deceleration in earnings growth for white men, and the increased participation of younger, less-experienced women and minority-group members in the labor market. Still, there are some puzzling aspects to this pattern as well. For instance, in the 1990s, there is a larger number of women than ever with high levels of work experience and rising amounts of firm tenure, the lack of which has often been cited by economists as major causes of women's lower earnings. Yet why have improvements in these areas not paid off in terms of greater earnings parity with white men?

Table 7.1 Median Weekly Earnings Ratios, Relative to White Men,
For Full-Time Wage and Salary Workers, 1984, 1991, and
1998, by Demographic Group

	Men		Women		
	Black	Hispanic	White	Black	Hispanic
1984	0.75	0.71	0.66	0.60	0.56
1991	0.74	0.64	0.74	0.64	0.58
1998	0.76	0.63	0.76	0.65	0.55

Source: U.S. Department of Labor, Bureau of Labor Statistics, *Employment and Earnings*, various January issues.

In this chapter, we focus on the possible effects of one potential source of the drag on earnings: the existence of "glass-ceiling" effects that retard career advancement for women and minorities within firms and professions. We argue that glass-ceiling effects are real and measurable, and that in the near future, as other causes of reduced earnings for women and minorities—including overt discrimination, human-capital disparities, and differential occupational and industrial distributions—continue to recede, they will become increasingly relevant to explaining earnings differentials.

GLASS-CEILING EFFECTS

Interest in recent years has focused on the apparent existence of a "glass ceiling" in organizations and occupations (see, for example, Federal Glass Ceiling Commission 1995). Despite women's and minorities' paths to the top apparently being cleared by the passage and implementation of antidiscrimination laws and policies, both are still disproportionately underrepresented in the highest-paying and most-powerful positions. The term *glass ceiling* has come into widespread use to refer to this situation in which all obstacles to the top seem to have been cleared, but some invisible barrier prevents certain persons from advancing beyond certain levels.[2]

In looking for systematic differences by race and/or sex that appear to be unexplainable by human-capital characteristics or personal choice, studies of glass-ceiling effects have generally focused on either wage or promotion-rate differentials. For example, Harriet Orcutt Duleep and Seth Sanders (1992) show that highly educated

Asian men in the United States earn less than their white counterparts, and interpret this finding as suggestive of the existence of a glass ceiling for Asians. David R. Jones and Gerald H. Makepeace (1996) evaluated promotion possibilities within a United Kingdom firm and found that women had lower promotion probabilities and apparently had to pass higher hurdles at the lower levels of the firm than did men in order to advance to middle levels. Paul Gregg and Stephen Machin (1993), using data on top executives in the United Kingdom, also found lower promotion probabilities for women.

However, while it is likely that barriers to advancement would result in lower pay and lower proportions of women and minorities in top-paying positions, it is also true that there could be other causes of these phenomena. Part of the problem may be disagreement over the definition of *glass ceiling*. We take the term *glass ceiling* to refer to a situation in which discrimination is manifested not in unequal pay by race or sex in a particular job category, but rather in differing probabilities of advancement to the higher-paying job categories for persons who are equivalent in all productivity-related characteristics but of different race and/or sex.[3] If this situation occurs, glass-ceiling effects will be evident not only in lower promotion probabilities, but also in lower returns to tenure and experience.[4]

This definition distinguishes glass-ceiling effects on wages from other discriminatory effects that could also reduce wages for women and minorities. These could include differential pay by race or sex within a job category, or segregation within or among firms and occupations, whereby different jobs and/or promotion tracks exist for different race-sex groups.[5] It is important not to attribute these effects to the glass-ceiling phenomenon. Wage differential studies, therefore, are problematic in that they generally neither isolate the source of the wage differential, nor the contribution of various factors to the wage differential. However, it is possible to isolate the effects of differing returns to tenure and experience on wage differentials and thereby calculate the portion of the wage differential that is potentially attributable to glass-ceiling effects.

Using this definition, then, how might one detect the existence of a glass ceiling? One method is to use data for particular firms. While this has definite advantages, there also exist limitations on data availability (although such data often become available to researchers in the course of assisting on discrimination lawsuits). This method also potentially suffers from survivor bias, as persons not attaining promotion within a reasonable period of time might leave a firm rather than remain in its lower echelons and those with less-attractive outside options are more likely to stay. An alternative approach, which we explore in this paper, is to use data from a nationwide sample of workers. Although such information will not allow us to calculate promotion probabilities or control fully for each worker's job category, it does offer the opportunity to look at returns to tenure and experience for all workers and thereby identify potential glass-ceiling effects within the labor market as a whole as well as within firms. We contrast results for college graduates to results for those who did not attend college, to see whether glass-ceiling effects are more prevalent among the higher educated, as is implicitly assumed in much of the writing on the subject. Indeed, the difference in results between these two groups allows us to consider how much of differential returns to tenure and experience can be reasonably attributed to glass-ceiling effects.

It is important to consider returns to both tenure and experience in attempting to capture glass-ceiling effects. For while glass ceilings are often discussed in the context of an individual corporation, they can also arise from lack of opportunities in other firms within the same industry or in other industries. As few people spend their entire working lives with a single firm, it is important to recognize that glass-ceiling effects might also affect persons with short tenures at particular firms but high levels of total labor-market experience. In other words, the glass ceiling potentially affects not only one's position in a firm, but also one's position in the labor market in general.

DATA AND STATISTICAL METHODOLOGY

Few data sets pair the necessary level of detail regarding tenure and experience with sufficient sample size to allow for calculation of separate wage paths for different race and sex groupings. Fortunately, the Bureau of the Census's Surveys of Income and Program Participation (SIPP) does both. We use the combined 1984, 1985, 1987, 1988, and 1990 surveys to calculate returns to tenure and experience for a national random sample of workers.[6] The survey's topical modules on work history allow us to incorporate participants' tenure and work experience prior to entering the panel and to create a measure of actual work experience rather than forcing us to rely on the proxy of potential work experience.

The data cover the period from October 1983 to April 1992. Persons in each panel are divided into four rotation groups, with twenty-eight months of data available for each person. We include all persons from twenty-one to sixty-three years old at the start of the sample for whom there is earnings information in wave 7 and data from the earlier work-history topic module (usually collected in wave 2 or wave 3) available. For persons not reporting an hourly pay rate, we calculate the average hourly earnings on the basis of reported hours per week, number of weeks worked, and earnings for the relevant job, for use as the dependent variable in the wage regressions. Persons with calculated real average hourly earnings (1984 dollars) below one dollar or greater than one hundred dollars are excluded from the sample. Tenure and experience are calculated in monthly increments during the sample period and in six-month increments using the retrospective work history to yield accumulated tenure and experience for workers before they enter the panel time period. We calculate accumulated tenure using the answer to the work-history module question asking when the individual began his or her most recent job, and determine accumulated experience subtracting the sum of years of schooling, reported gaps in work, and six from age.[7] We calculate tenure and experience by hours, so, for example, a person working all year, but for less than thirty-five hours a week on average, receives a fraction of a year of credit towards both measures. Persons averaging thirty-five or more hours per week during the year receive a year's worth of credit.

Table 7.2 shows mean values for tenure, experience, mean hourly earnings, and geometric mean hourly earnings for the six demographic groups used in this analysis: white men, black men, Hispanic men, white women, black women, and Hispanic women.[8] Means for all variables denote their value at the end of wave 7. Among college graduates, our sample displays shorter tenure for white women and Hispanics than for white men, while women in general have fewer years of experience than men.[9] Among college nonattendees, white men have the most job tenure, and blacks of both sexes the most experience. Wages are expressed in 1984 dollars and are deflated using the overall average growth in nonmilitary wages as reported in the *Economic Report of the President*. These numbers are comparable to those found in other samples from this time period, such as the Current Population Survey, and show clear hourly-earnings shortfalls among all other demographic groups relative to white men.

Table 7.2 Tenure, Experience, Hourly-Earnings Means, Earnings Ratios, and Sample Sizes, by Demographic Group and College-Graduation Status

	College-Graduate Men			College-Graduate Women		
	White	Black	Hispanic	White	Black	Hispanic
Tenure (in years)	8.2	7.7	6.3	6.0	7.7	5.3
Experience (in years)	15.8	15.5	14.7	13.5	14.0	13.6
Hourly earnings (in $1984):						
arithmetic mean	$15.12	$12.15	$13.76	$10.80	$10.89	$10.86
percent of white men's earnings		80	91	71	72	72
geometric mean	$13.78	$10.97	$10.77	$10.42	$9.33	$9.73
percent of white men's earnings		80	78	76	68	71
Number of observations	12,293	599	1058	9,114	819	820

	College Nonattendee Men			College Nonattendee Women		
	White	Black	Hispanic	White	Black	Hispanic
Tenure (in years)	8.6	8.1	5.8	6.1	7.1	5.4
Experience (in years)	19.9	20.9	17.9	19.5	21.2	18.8
Hourly earnings (in $1984)						
arithmetic mean	$9.05	$7.19	$7.38	$6.35	$5.93	$5.89
percent of white men's earnings		79	82	70	66	65
geometric mean	$9.18	$7.24	$7.23	$6.16	$6.10	$5.83
percent of white men's earnings		79	79	67	66	64
Number of observations	22,511	2,592	3,377	19,711	2,999	2,551

Source: Authors' calculations using SIPP data.

We use ordinary least squares to estimate the returns to tenure and experience, as well as the combined returns, for the cross section of job-years.[10] Equations are run separately for each of the six groups (men and women separately crossed by white, black, or Hispanic) and separately for college graduates and college nonattendees. The dependent variable is the natural log of hourly earnings. Dummy variable controls are included in these equations for union status, geographic region (seven groupings, corresponding to Census divisions with two combined groups), occupation (one-digit Census classifications), industry (one-digit Census classifications), job class (six Census classifications, excluding unpaid family workers and self-employed workers), time since last gap in work experience, and, if any, length of gap. Additional dummy variables were age of youngest child (less than two years, two to five years, six to twelve years, or thirteen to eighteen years, excluded category is those with no children), number of children (two versus greater than two, excluded category is one or zero children), part-time work status, marital status (single or widowed versus divorced, excluded category is married), and educational attainment (for the college nonattendees, high school graduate versus non–high school graduate; for the college attendees, postgraduate training versus bachelor's degree only). We estimated equations for various polynomial specifications on experience and tenure, using up to a quartic in experience and a quartic in tenure. The equations using a quartic in tenure and a quadratic in experience fit the best across the various groups, so all results reported in the following section are based on these specifications. Regressions are comparable in fit to those found in comparable wage-regression studies, with adjusted R-squared ranging from 0.27 to 0.41, with a mean across the equations of 0.35. Coefficients follow usual sign patterns and relative sizes.[11]

RESULTS

In this section, we discuss two types of simulation results gained by using the regressions just discussed. First, we estimate wage-growth profiles, or paths, for the different demographic groups, and test to see if these paths are significantly different. Second, we decompose wage differentials between white men and the other demographic groups in order to evaluate how much of the differential is attributable to tenure and experience path differences.

We use the fitted equations to estimate tenure and experience paths, as well as paths showing the combined effects of tenure and experience, out through twenty years. The combined path considers the particular case of a person already with ten years of job experience entering a position at which they spend the next twenty years. Because this simulation choice needs some justification, we present four reasons for setting the initial level of experience at ten years when calculating the combined return to tenure and experience. First, Pamela Loprest (1992) found that turnover for young people is quite high and that the effects of turnover on wages are quite different for young men than for young women. We do not, however, consider this differential return to job switching by young individuals to be part of the glass-ceiling effect, so we do not want to include it in our estimates. Second, research by Kevin M. Murphy and Finis Welch (1990) revealed that for men, two-thirds of wage growth occurs in the first ten years of employment, and we do not want to include initial differences in wage-growth rates as part of the glass-ceiling effect we are estimating. Third, most women with ten years of market experience are likely to have had their children already and returned to the labor market. Since "gapping" (Jacobsen and Levin 1995) has a large effect on women's wages, excluding the first ten years of experience helps control for this effect, as does our use of time since gap and length of gap variables in the regressions. Fourth, setting the experience level upon entering a long-term job at ten years is a good approximation of many persons' actual career paths. On average, the initial experience at the beginning of long-term jobs (defined as lasting over ten years) is eight years. This number is almost certainly biased below the value of experience that an average person has before beginning a long-term job, as it excludes relatively young people who have not accumulated much job tenure in jobs that will eventually turn out to be long lasting. For individuals forty-five years old and older, the average initial level of experience for long-term jobs is twelve years. The results we report for the combined returns are not very sensitive to the choice of ten years as the initial level of experience; choosing a range of seven to fourteen years for initial experience produces similar results.

The results of these simulations are shown graphically in figures 7.1, 7.2, 7.3, and 7.4. In figures 7.1, 7.2, and 7.3, vertical axes show the percentage of starting earnings received for each subsequent year of

(*Text continues on page 229.*)

Figure 7.1 Tenure Paths of College Graduates and College Nonattendees, by Race and Gender

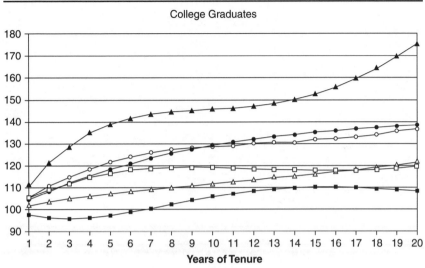

College Graduates

○ White Men   △ Black Men   ■ Hispanic Men   ● White Women   □ Black Women   ▲ Hispanic Women

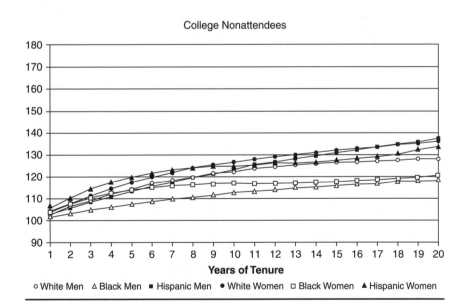

College Nonattendees

○ White Men   △ Black Men   ■ Hispanic Men   ● White Women   □ Black Women   ▲ Hispanic Women

Source: Authors' calculations using SIPP data.

Figure 7.2 Experience Paths of College Graduates and College Nonattendees, by Race and Gender

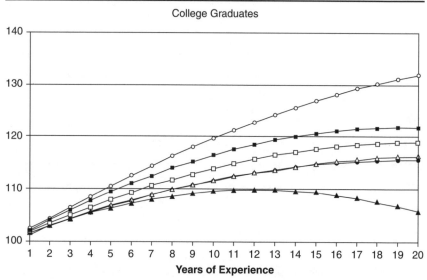

College Graduates

○ White Men △ Black Men ■ Hispanic Men ● White Women □ Black Women ▲ Hispanic Women

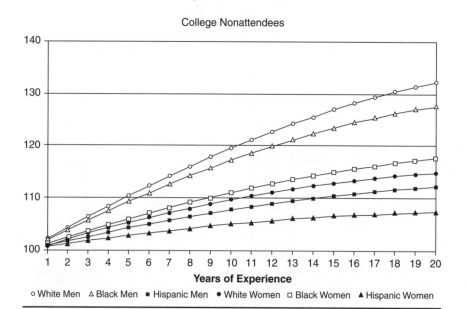

College Nonattendees

○ White Men △ Black Men ■ Hispanic Men ● White Women □ Black Women ▲ Hispanic Women

Source: Authors' calculations using SIPP data.

Figure 7.3 Combined Tenure and Experience Paths of College Graduates and College Nonattendees, by Race and Gender

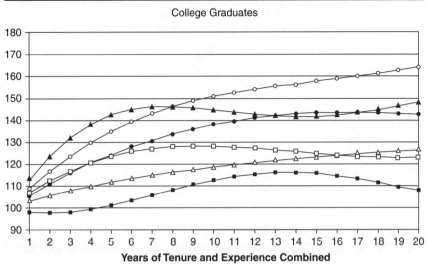

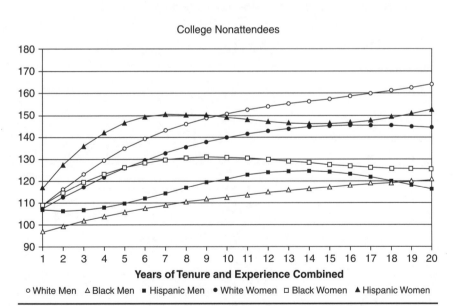

Source: Authors' calculations using SIPP data.

Figure 7.4 Combined Tenure and Experience Paths of College Graduates and College Nonattendees, Using White Men as a Base Case, by Race and Gender

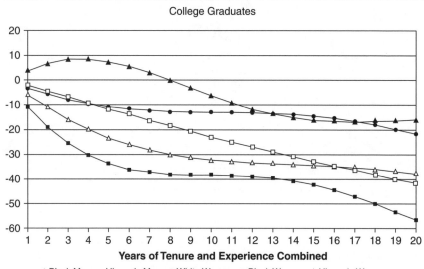

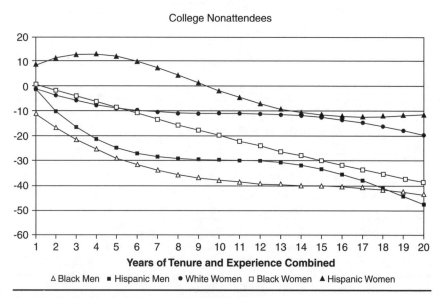

Source: Authors' calculations using SIPP data.

tenure and/or experience. All paths are therefore normalized to begin at 100 in year 0, and each chart begins the horizontal axis at year 1. Figure 7.1 shows tenure paths for the six demographic groups, depicting college graduates and college nonattendees separately. Figure 7.2 shows experience paths using the same format. Figure 7.3 presents the paths from the combined-path simulation previously described, showing for example, that after ten years of work with the same employer, white-male college graduates would be earning about 50 percent more than they did upon starting.

Both college-graduate and noncollege graduate white men have the highest returns to experience of any group, leading to greater combined returns for white men relative to all other groups. Among college graduates, Hispanic women reap the greatest returns for tenure, while the tenure paths are more closely bunched among college nonattendees. The paths in figures 7.1, 7.2, and 7.3 are generally rising over time for all groups, with notable exceptions being the experience path for Hispanic-female college graduates and the tenure and combined paths for Hispanic male college graduates, which show both early and later downturns. However, the greater error associated with the smaller sample sizes for Hispanics means that one cannot rule out level or even rising paths for these groups. The combined paths generally display more curvature and a greater dispersion of results across the groups.

Figure 7.4 shows the combined relative returns for tenure and experience for all groups, the benchmark, 0, representing white men. In this chart, the vertical axis shows in percentage terms how much less (or more) the group sees in wage growth for each subsequent year of tenure and experience relative to white men with the same number of years of tenure and experience. For example, after fourteen years of work with the same employer, black-male college nonattendees would be earning 40 percent less than their white-male peers. Here, the lower returns of the other groups are clearly shown in the generally downward-sloping relative paths. Even Hispanic females, who start out above the white-male path for both education groups, cross over at around the eight-to-ten-year mark. All other groups' paths are consistently below the line at zero, which indicates equality with white-male earnings growth.

While looking at the paths can help make sense of the data, these charts can also be misleading. In particular, it must be noted that given the relatively small size of some of the demographic groups, the paths are measured with error and should be thought of as having a confidence interval around them. This interval might in many cases contain the path of another group, and for that reason the paths cannot automatically be treated as significantly different. Therefore, we conduct formal statistical tests to see if the paths for white men are indeed statistically different from the other paths during each year for which we consider data. We construct the formal test of path equality by creating a standard error for every year on the three paths for the six groups. Then, we use the standard errors to calculate a T-statistic for the hypothesis that the value of a particular path year is equal for white men and for each of the other five groups. The T-statistic is created under the assumption that the variances of the two path-years were unequal.

Results of these tests are summarized in table 7.3. Paths are marked as significantly different if they pass a t-test at the 90 percent-significance level. We apply this weak standard of significance both to reduce discontinuities in the paths, given that each year must pass the test separately, and to underscore the cases in which the paths do not differ significantly.[12] The patterns are very different for college graduates and college nonattendees. Among college graduates, the combined tests show differences for all groups, save Hispanic

Table 7.3 Results of t-Tests for Whether White-Male Paths Are Significantly Different from Paths for Other Groups (Years of Difference)

	Black Men	Hispanic Men	White Women	Black Women	Hispanic Women
College graduates					
Tenure	none	all	none	17+	all
Experience	none	none	all	none	14+
Combined	13+	2+	5+	12+	none
College nonattendees					
Tenure	3+	18+	all	11+	1–3
Experience	none	all	all	all	all
Combined	6+	none	none	9+	11–19

Source: Authors' calculations using SIPP data.
Note: "All" denotes that for all twenty years the paths differed significantly; "none" denotes that for all twenty years the paths did not differ significantly; numeric ranges show the years for which the paths did differ significantly.

women, relative to white men. However, the paths separate at different points, with Hispanic men and white women diverging sooner than black men and women. All of the tenure paths diverge at some point from the white male path, but white women only diverge in the first two years; Hispanics do throughout. The experience paths are not significantly different for the three groups of men and black women, but white women receive lower returns throughout.

For college nonattendees, experience paths differ from the white-male path for all groups save black men. Tenure paths all diverge at some point, although Hispanic women only diverge in the first five years. On the combined paths, blacks show greatest divergence, with no significant differences for Hispanic men and white women.

To sum up the evidence for glass-ceiling effects from these estimated paths, it appears that among college graduates, all groups except for Hispanic women diverge significantly from the white-male combined experience-tenure path. This divergence appears to be due mainly to differences in the return to tenure, although white women also receive significantly lower returns to experience. The result is that by year ten, white men outstrip all other groups on the combined path.

It might be helpful at this point to put our results in the context of prior literature on differential returns to tenure by gender. Elizabeth Becker and Cotton M. Lindsay (1994) find that the return to tenure is larger for white women than it is for white men. They credit this result to the relatively higher turnover of women; this higher quit rate makes firms less willing to invest in women's firm-specific human capital, forcing women to bear more of the cost of that capital (perhaps through a lower initial wage). But because women bear more of the cost of firm-specific human capital, their wages will include a return on the extra investment. Therefore, women should have a higher return to tenure than men.[13]

More recently, Anne Beeson Royalty (1998) has shown that for less-educated individuals, the turnover rate is higher among women than men. However, Royalty also finds that among the better educated, the turnover rates by gender are approximately the same. Interestingly, our results integrate the findings of Royalty with those of Becker and Lindsay: we find that the return to tenure is higher for women than for men among college nonattendees, but not for the women who are college graduates (after the first two years of tenure).

Thus, the group of women with the higher turnover rate receives a higher return to tenure, but the group that has the same turnover rate as men does not.

Next, we consider how much of the measured wage differentials among demographic groups, in particular between white men and the other groups, can be attributed to glass-ceiling effects. Table 7.4 shows the results of a geometric-mean hourly-earnings differential decomposition that focuses on the portion of the decomposition attributable to tenure and experience.[14] The top part of each table section displays a conventional wage decomposition wherein the wage resulting from entering each group's means into the equation for white men is contrasted with the actual geometric-mean wage for the group. The remaining difference is then attributable to differences in means rather than differences in coefficients. The part of the earnings gap attributable to differences in means is shown, as is the part of the earnings gap remaining unaccounted for by differences in means (and therefore attributable to differences in coefficients). The "unexplained" part is then further decomposed into those parts accounted for by differences in tenure coefficients, differences in experience coefficients, and differences in the regression control-variable coefficients.

By way of example, consider the table data for college-graduate white women. Their actual geometric-mean hourly earnings are $10.37, while college-graduate white men make $14.41 (row 1). This difference, $4.04 (row 2), is 38.94 percent of white women's earnings (row 3). The predicted hourly earnings for white women if their means are multiplied by the white men's coefficients, are $12.29 (row 4). Therefore, the portion explained by differences in means is ($14.41 − $12.29) = $2.12 (row 5), or ($2.12/$10.37) = 20.43 percent of white women's actual earnings (row 6). The portion explained by differences in coefficients is ($12.29 − $10.37) = $1.92 (row 7), which when divided by $10.37 gives the remaining 18.5 percent of the difference between white women and men (row 8). This can be decomposed into the portions due to differences in returns to control variables, to differences in returns to the first ten years of experience and to subsequent years of experience (these differ due to the nonlinear estimation of experience effects), and to differences in returns to tenure (rows 8a through 8d). Note also that the percentage of the earnings gap explained by differences in coefficients is ($12.29 − $10.37)/$4.04 = $1.92/$4.04, for 47.53 percent of

Table 7.4 Wage-Differential Decompositions at Group Means

	White Men	Black Men	Hispanic Men	College Graduates			Source
				White Women	Black Women	Hispanic Women	
(1) actual wage	$14.41	$11.31	$12.23	$10.37	$10.52	$10.93	
(2) difference from white men		$3.10	$2.18	$4.04	$3.89	$3.47	$14.41–(1)
(3) difference as percentage of actual		27.37	17.79	38.94	36.96	31.79	(2)/(1)
(4) predicted wage		$13.55	$14.31	$12.29	$12.49	$12.54	
(5) difference explained by means		$0.85	$0.09	$2.12	$1.92	$1.86	$14.41–(4)
(6) percentage difference explained		7.52	0.78	20.43	18.23	17.05	(5)/(1)
(7) unexplained (predicted –actual)		$2.24	$2.08	$1.92	$1.97	$1.61	(4)–(1)
(8) percentage difference unexplained		19.85	17.01	18.50	18.74	14.73	(7)/(1)
(a) from control variables		-7.28	-12.73	5.77	4.15	14.74	Effect/(2)
(b) from first ten years of experience		4.48	-2.32	3.93	1.14	3.58	Effect/(2)
(c) from subsequent years of experience		6.87	7.64	6.16	6.57	10.67	Effect/(2)
(d) from tenure		15.77	24.42	2.64	6.87	-14.25	Effect/(2)
(9) percentage unexplained wage gap attributable to late experience and tenure		114.10	188.48	47.53	71.76	-24.32	([8c]+[8d])/(8)
(10) percentage total wage gap attributable to late experience and tenure		82.74	180.26	22.59	36.37	-11.27	([8c]+[8d])/(3)

(*Table continues on page 234.*)

Table 7.4 *Continued*

				College Nonattendees				
	White Men	Black Men	Hispanic Men	White Women	Black Women	Hispanic Women	Source
(1) actual wage	$9.12	$7.01	$6.97	$6.24	$5.79	$5.77	
(2) difference from white men		$2.10	$2.14	$2.87	$3.33	$3.35	$9.12–(1)
(3) difference as percentage of actual		30.01	30.70	46.06	57.52	57.97	(2)/(1)
(4) predicted wage		$8.24	$8.18	$8.19	$7.83	$7.93	
(5) difference explained by means		$0.87	$0.94	$0.92	$1.28	$1.19	$9.12–(4)
(6) percentage difference explained		12.46	13.49	14.78	22.18	20.58	(5)/(1)
(7) unexplained (predicted – actual)		$1.23	$1.20	$1.95	$2.05	$2.16	(4)–(1)
(8) percentage difference unexplained		17.56	17.21	31.28	35.34	37.39	(7)/(1)
(a) from control variables		4.84	–0.44	18.42	18.90	18.83	Effect/(2)
(b) from first ten years of experience		–1.39	9.65	7.61	6.16	13.94	Effect/(2)
(c) from subsequent years of experience		5.41	7.29	8.53	7.91	9.99	Effect/(2)
(d) from tenure		8.70	0.71	–3.28	2.37	–5.37	Effect/(2)
(9) percentage unexplained wage gap attributable to late experience and tenure		80.34	46.49	16.77	29.07	12.36	([8c]+[8d])/(8)
(10) percentage total wage gap attributable to late experience and tenure		47.00	26.06	11.39	17.86	7.97	([8c]+[8d])/(3)

Source: Authors' calculations using SIPP data.

the gap (row 9). This leaves 52 percent unexplained by differences in coefficients—that is, attributable to differences in the means. Finally, in rows 9 and 10 of the table, we highlight the percentages of the unexplained portions of the wage gap and total wage gap attributable to later years of work experience (time after the first ten years in the labor force) and firm tenure, which in the case of white women is 47.53 percent of the unexplained wage gap and 22.59 percent of the total wage gap.

Our basic decomposition results are comparable to those found in work by other researchers, finding generally that between one-half to two-thirds of the wage differential remains unexplained after accounting for differences in means (this can be calculated as row 8 divided by row 3). Among college graduates, a much larger proportion of the earnings differential is explained by the differences in coefficients for men than for women. Also, among college graduates, more of the difference between women's wages and white men's wages is explained by differences in means than among college nonattendees. Among college nonattendees, differences in means explain a similar proportion of the earnings gap for women and minority men.

It is also clear from these results that differential returns to tenure and experience across demographic groups account for a significant proportion of the wage differentials across these groups. For example, as shown in table 7.4, among college-graduate white women, (2.64 percent/18.50 percent), or 14.3 percent of the unexplained percentage difference (rows 8d and 8), is attributable to differential returns to tenure, while ([3.93 percent + 6.16 percent)]/18.50 percent), or 54.5 percent of the unexplained percentage difference (rows 8b, 8c, and 8), is attributable to differential returns to experience. The differential returns to control variables, including graduate school attendance and family-type variables, comprise the remaining 31 percent. Therefore, differential returns to tenure and experience together account for about 70 percent of college-graduate white women's unexplained difference and 33 percent of the total earnings difference from white men.[15]

These effects are of similar magnitude relative to the control variables for the other groups as well, showing the importance of tenure- and experience-return differences in determining wage differentials. Notably, for college-graduate minority men, differences in returns to the control variables (row 8a) actually reduce earnings differences, but their effects are negated by the strong differences in returns to tenure and experience in contrast to those of white men.

Among college graduates, differential returns for tenure are more important than differential returns to experience in explaining the earnings gap among minority men, while for women, returns to experience are more important—for Hispanic women they go so far as to offset the equalizing effect of that group's higher returns to tenure. Among college nonattendees, a similar pattern holds for women, with their tenure returns partially offsetting the large experience-returns differential for white and Hispanic women. For Hispanic men, differential returns to experience are also more important, while for black men, tenure is more important.

Note that comparison of the results for college graduates to those for college nonattendees allows us to evaluate the degree to which the differential returns to tenure and experience are due to movement along different job paths rather than setbacks along the same path. If we assume that college nonattendees are ineligible for many of the same advancement opportunities that college graduates are eligible for, then differences in their returns to tenure and experience are more likely to reflect systematic differences in job placement throughout their working lives; that is, occupational and firm segregation, both by worker's choice and due to discrimination both prelabor market and labor market. Therefore, any additional differential that college graduates experience above what the college nonattendees experience is likely to be caused by glass-ceiling effects rather than job-segregation effects.

For example, among white women, the combined-tenure-and-late-experience effect comprises 47.5 percent of the unexplained difference among college graduates, but only 16.8 percent of that among college nonattendees. However, these effects comprise 22.6 percent of the total earnings difference from white men for college graduates and 11.4 percent for the college nonattendees, relatively more similar amounts. These latter numbers imply that the proportion of differential returns to tenure and late experience that can be considered glass-ceiling effects is relatively small for this group. In addition, white-female college nonattendees face a wider proportional gap relative to white men, implying a larger absolute effect of these differential returns (driven in the women's case mainly by the differential returns to experience).

Black women generate similar comparisons, with the combined tenure-and-late-experience effect composing 71.8 percent of the unexplained difference among college graduates, but only 29.1 percent of the unexplained difference among college nonattendees. However, these effects constitute 36.4 percent of black-female college graduates' total earnings difference from white men and 17.9 percent of the same for black-female college nonattendees, a larger differential than for white women (although, again, there is more difference to be explained for the college nonattendees). Among Hispanic women, the combined effect explains nothing for college graduates, due to the offsetting tenure and experience effects.

Turning to men, the combination of tenure and late-experience effects explain essentially the entire wage gap between white and minority-male college graduates, and about a quarter to a half of the wage gap for college nonattendees. This can be taken to imply that even though discrimination might be more important in a general sense for women than for men, glass-ceiling effects are actually more important as an explanation of lower wages for minority men than for women.[16]

That said, there is still an alternative way to consider the more-educated versus less-educated differential. If job segregation is lower for the more-educated worker, then part of the tenure and experience differentials attributed to job segregation are actually attributable to glass-ceiling effects. This would say that even as differentials are equalized as increasingly educated women and minorities move into the same job planes as white men, new differentials occur through these glass-ceiling effects. By this perspective, the large existing tenure- and experience-return differentials among the college graduates provide strong evidence of the potent effect of the glass ceiling on wages. Indeed, there is reason to believe that job segregation is lower among the college educated, at least by gender. Gender segregation indexes as reported in Jacobsen (1998), using 1990 Census data, show lower levels of segregation among college graduates and persons with postgraduate training than among those with lower levels of education.

Our results regarding the importance of glass-ceiling effects are consistent with those found in other studies using European data (for example, the Jones and Makepeace [1996] and Gregg and Machin [1993] studies use data from the United Kingdom; Hannan, Schömann, and Blossfeld [1990] use German data), indicating that this is by no means a purely American phenomenon. Further evidence is provided by J. Zweimüller and R. Winter-Ebner (1994), who, using Austrian data, perform a similar wage decomposition and show that, in both the private and public sectors, a substantial portion of the unexplained gender-wage differential is attributable to divergent promotion rates.

CONCLUSION

Glass-ceiling effects exist and have a measurable effect on wage differentials among demographic groups; they are manifested in a divergence in tenure and experience profiles across demographic groups. We have demonstrated that differential returns to tenure and experience can account for much of the wage gap between white men and women and minorities. However, these effects might well also be attributable to job segregation, as is implied by the similar results derived from analyses of educational category's role in the overall effect of these returns (although returns to tenure and experience follow different paths by educational level).[17] The use of national data divided finely by job type would allow us to separate out these effects, but the data requirements for such an analysis are greater than can be met by extant data sources.

Another lesson to be gained from these data is that race (or ethnicity) and sex interact to cause different ethnic-sex groups to have very different labor-market experiences with regard to returns to tenure and experience. The experience of black women, for instance, is different from to those of white women and black men. In the glass-ceiling context, this corresponds with recent anecdotal evidence indicating that minority women experience very different dynamics regarding promotion possibilities than do minority men (see Gaiter 1994). While these different dynamics make it more difficult to tell a unified story about wage differentials, attempting to model them can lead to a fuller understanding of the myriad of ways in which labor markets lead to different outcomes for their participants.

Clearly, there is much more to be done in terms of testing the robustness of our results, including their applicability to other time periods and different cohorts. In particular, in the next few years sufficient data will be available from subsequent panels of the SIPP so that these preexpansion results could be compared to results for the mid-1990s. In the interim, we view this paper as exploratory research that considers how glass-ceiling effects might be more carefully defined and measured.

Comments by Paul Carlin, Shoshana Grossbard-Shechtman, Sanders Korenman, and Joanne Spetz, and research assistance by Rachel Mandal, are gratefully acknowledged. The data used in this paper were made available by the Inter-university Consortium for Political and Social Research. The data for Survey of Income and Program Participation (1984, 1985, 1987, 1988, and 1990 panels) were originally collected by the United States Department of Commerce, Bureau of the Census. Neither the collectors of the original data nor the Consortium bears any responsibility for the analyses or interpretations presented in this paper.

NOTES

1. The results for the 1990s vary greatly with the beginning and ending points chosen, as, for example, the data generally show an increase in earnings for all groups from 1990 to 1991, and an increase from 1996 to 1998 for all groups save Hispanic women. Still, there is little evidence of substantial increase in earnings ratios over the 1990s so far. This flattening of earnings ratios compared to their growth in the 1980s is found in U.S. Department of Commerce data series taken from the Current Population Survey's Annual Demographic Survey (published in the *Current Population Reports Series P-60*) as well.

2. The first use we have found of *glass ceiling* was in the March 24, 1986, edition of *The Wall Street Journal*, in a special-report section called "The Corporate Woman." An article entitled "The Glass Ceiling: Why Women Can't Seem to Break the Invisible Barrier That Blocks Them from the Top Jobs" ran on the first page of the section. The *Readers' Guide to Periodicals* began to use *glass ceiling* as a subject heading in 1991, at which time there were six articles listed under it.

3. Note that it is also generally assumed that these different probabilities are caused by demand-side actions, not supply-side differences. In other words, persons are not assumed to have different probabilities of refusing an offered promotion once observable personal characteristics other than race, ethnicity, and sex are held constant. Nevertheless, the possibility of uncontrolled-for personal characteristics that are correlated with race and/or sex and that affect the probability of taking an offered promotion is always an issue. But, as we discuss in note 10, fixed-effects estimates are not significantly different from OLS, (ordinary

least squares), implying that unobservable time-invariant personal characteristics do not affect the results.

4. Our definition of a glass-ceiling effect is very different, for instance, from that used by sociologists Erik Olin Wright and Janeen Baxter (1995), who define it as a circumstance in which "barriers to upward promotions for women in authority hierarchies are greater than the barriers they face in getting into hierarchies in the first place" (407). Wright and Baxter do not find support for this hypothesis in their seven-country study. We posit no hypothesis regarding the relative size of these types of barriers, but also narrow our focus to wage effects in studying glass-ceiling effects.

5. Wim Groot and Henriëtte Maaseen van den Brink (1996), for instance, using United Kingdom data, found that women are less likely than men to be in jobs that offer promotion possibilities, but that if they are in jobs that offer promotion possibilities, they are not less likely than men to be promoted within the firm. They also find that occupational segregation in their sample appears to be due to differences in treatment rather than differences in characteristics.

6. The 1986 panel was not usable for this study because a retrospective work history was not collected from its participants. There is no 1989 panel.

7. Comparing the results from using this definition of experience with results from using experience determined by respondents' answers to a question asking for the year in which they first started to work, we found that the answer to this latter question yielded a larger number for years of experience, as respondents generally cited their first part-time job taken during their teenage years. The equation fits were notably weaker using this alternative definition.

8. Hispanics can be of any race; however, for the purposes of this study, the black and white categories exclude persons identifying themselves as Hispanic. And while it would have been interesting to study Asian men and women as well, sample sizes for these groups proved to be prohibitively small even when we pooled multiple panels from the SIPP.

9. A substantial fraction of the sample has large amounts of work experience. In the noncollege attendee sample, between two-thirds and four-fifths of the various subgroups have ten or more years of experience, and 40 to 50 percent have twenty years or more. The college sample, being somewhat younger, has a slightly lower proportion at ten or more years (between 60 and 70 percent by subsample) and 23 to 31 percent at twenty or more years. For both college and noncollege attendee

samples, between 18 and 33 percent have ten or more years of tenure, and between 3 and 15 percent have twenty or more years of tenure. White men are more likely to be in these distribution tails than the other groups. Nonetheless, there is a significant number of persons of all groups in the higher ranges of tenure and experience, which means that our estimation results are by no means based on extrapolation from a sample of predominantly low values for tenure and experience.

10. Note that there is a possibility that the error term is correlated with the regressors. In other words, the error term might contain a component attributable to the quality of the match between worker and firm, another component attributable to person-specific characteristics (for example, ability), and a stochastic component. If the quality of the job match is positively correlated with job duration, then the error term will be positively correlated with both experience and tenure in a cross section of workers. Robert Topel (1991) has suggested a two-step estimation technique that he claims will give a lower bound for the return to tenure. However, in other research (Jacobsen and Levin 1998), we have found that implementing this two-stage fixed-effects technique does not significantly change the qualitative findings. In addition, construction of a Hausman test statistic (see Amemiya 1985, 145–46) that compares the two-step fixed-effects technique to OLS does not reject the OLS technique.

11. Full results from the regressions are available from the authors upon request.

12. Note the possibility that significance-test results can be very different for the separate tenure and experience paths as compared with the combined path. This is the case for black-male college graduates as well as for white-female college nonattendees. This can occur because the estimated coefficients for the tenure and experience paths can be significantly correlated (either positively or negatively).

13. For the complete sample (not stratified by educational category and including persons with some college), our statistical results are very similar to those found by Elizabeth Becker and Cotton M. Lindsay (1994). We find that the return to tenure is larger for white women than it is for white men and that the difference is statistically significant after five years.

14. To create the decompositions, we compared each group's wage rate using their mean level of tenure and experience for the first- and higher-order terms (otherwise, we would be constructing a decomposition that uses different tenure and experience values for those higher-order terms). For example, when calculating the experience effect, the

second-order term is the square of mean experience, not the larger mean of squared experience. Because the means of these higher-order terms are different from the values we use, the simulated earnings that we calculate are different from the geometric mean.

15. Returning to the issue raised in note 3, one might wonder if we have simply identified a difference in aspirations for promotion—in other words, the existence of a self-selected "mommy track." While we are controlling in our specifications for factors, including time off from work, marital status, and children, we also split the samples of white women into those with and without children and reestimated the regressions. Among both the college educated and the college nonattendees, women with children actually experienced a higher tenure path and therefore a higher combined path than women without children.

16. These patterns persist if we decompose wage differentials using above-mean values for tenure and experience. For example, if we consider a decomposition ascribing persons with twenty years of job tenure (and thirty years of job experience), the proportion of the unexplained and total wage gaps attributable to late experience and tenure for college nonattendees changes only slightly, but for college attendees, the proportion of earnings differences attributable to returns on later years of experience rises substantially.

17. Reuben Gronau (1988), using Panel Survey of Income Dynamics data from the late 1970s, finds little difference in returns to tenure and experience by sex when differences in job-skill requirements between those jobs held by men and women are accounted for.

REFERENCES

Amemiya, Takeshi. 1985. *Advanced Econometrics*. Cambridge, Mass.: Harvard University Press.

Becker, Elizabeth, and Cotton M. Lindsay. 1994. "Sex Differences in Tenure Profiles: Effects of Shared Firm-Specific Investment." *Journal of Labor Economics* 12(1): 98–118.

Duleep, Harriet Orcutt, and Seth Sanders. 1992. "Discrimination at the Top: American-Born Asian and White Men." *Industrial Relations* 31(3): 416–32.

Economic Report of the President. 1999. Washington: U.S. Government Printing Office.

Federal Glass Ceiling Commission. 1995. *Good for Business: Making Full Use of the Nation's Human Capital: The Environmental Scan: A Fact-Finding*

Report of the Federal Glass Ceiling Commission. Washington: United States Department of Labor.

Gaiter, Dorothy J. 1994. "Black Women's Gains in Corporate America Outstrip Black Men's." *The Wall Street Journal*, March 5, 1994, pp. A1, A4.

Gregg, Paul, and Stephen Machin. 1993. "Is the Glass Ceiling Cracking?: Gender Compensation Differentials and Access to Promotion Among U.K. Executives." Working paper. London: National Institute of Economic and Social Research and Centre for Economic Performance, London School of Economics

Gronau, Reuben. 1988. "Sex-Related Wage Differentials and Women's Interrupted Labor Careers: The Chicken or the Egg." *Journal of Labor Economics* 6(3): 277–301.

Groot, Wim, and Henriëtte Maassen van den Brink. 1996. "Glass Ceilings or Dead Ends: Job Promotion of Men and Women Compared." *Economics Letters* 53(2): 221–26.

Hannan, Michael T., Klaus Schömann, and Hans-Peter Blossfeld. 1990. "Sex and Sector Differences in the Dynamics of Wage Growth in the Federal Republic of Germany." *American Sociological Review* 55 (October): 694–713.

Jacobsen, Joyce P. 1998. *The Economics of Gender*, 2nd ed. Cambridge, Mass.: Blackwell.

———. 1995. "Effects of Intermittent Labor Force Attachment on Women's Earnings." *Monthly Labor Review* 118(9): 14–19.

Jacobsen, Joyce P., and Laurence M. Levin. 1998. "Tenure and Experience: Relative Returns by Race and Sex." Working paper. Middletown, Conn.: Wesleyan University.

Jones, David R., and Gerald H. Makepeace. 1996. "Equal Worth, Equal Opportunities: Pay and Promotion in an Internal Labour Market." *Economic Journal* 106(March): 401–9.

Loprest, Pamela. 1992. "Gender Differences in Wage Growth and Job Mobility." *American Economic Review* 82(2): 526–32.

Murphy, Kevin M., and Finis Welch. 1990. "Empirical Age-Earnings Profiles." *Journal of Labor Economics* 8(2): 202–29.

Royalty, Anne Beeson. 1998. "Job-to-Job and Job-to-Nonemployment Turnover by Gender and Education Level." *Journal of Labor Economics* 16(2): 392–443.

Topel, Robert. 1991. "Specific Capital Mobility, and Wages: Wages Rise with Job Seniority." *Journal of Political Economy* 99(1): 145–76.

U.S. Department of Commerce, Bureau of the Census. Various years. *Current Population Reports Series P-60*. Washington: U.S. Government Printing Office.

U.S. Department of Labor, Bureau of Labor Statistics. Various years. *Employment and Earnings*. Washington: U.S. Government Printing Office.

Wright, Erik Olin, and Janeen Baxter. 1995. "The Gender Gap in Workplace Authority: A Cross-National Study." *American Sociological Review* 60 (June): 407–35.

Zweimüller, J., and R. Winter-Ebner. 1994. "Gender Wage Differentials in Private and Public Sector Jobs." *Journal of Population Economics* 7(3): 271–85.

Chapter 8

BARRIERS TO THE EMPLOYMENT OF WELFARE RECIPIENTS

SANDRA DANZIGER, MARY CORCORAN, SHELDON DANZIGER, COLLEEN HEFLIN,
ARIEL KALIL, JUDITH LEVINE, DANIEL ROSEN, KRISTIN SEEFELDT,
KRISTINE SIEFERT, AND RICHARD TOLMAN

The Personal Responsibility and Work Opportunity Reconciliation Act (PRWORA) of 1996 ended the federal guarantee of cash
assistance and replaced the Aid to Families with Dependent Children Program with the Temporary Assistance for Needy Families
(TANF) Program. Receipt of TANF funds is limited to five years or
less, at state option.[1] Such changes at the federal level reflect, in part,
state-level experiments that had been conducted over the past two
decades. Prior to 1996, more than half of the states had instituted
work requirements for some portion of their welfare caseloads (under
the Job Opportunity and Basic Skills Program of the Family Support
Act of 1988), and thirty-one states had received waivers from the
federal government to test time-limited welfare receipt (United States
Department of Health and Human Services, Administration for Children and Families, 1996). These state-level reforms, coupled with a
strong economy, contributed to pre-PRWORA declines in the welfare
caseload: between fiscal years 1994 and 1996, the average monthly
AFDC caseload dropped almost 14 percent (United States Department of Health and Human Services 1996a).

With the implementation of TANF and the continuing, robust
economic recovery, caseloads have continued to decline into the late
1990s, falling an additional 35 percent between August 1996 and
September 1998 (United States Department of Health and Human
Services, Administration for Children and Families, 1998; Ziliak,
Figlio, Davis, and Connolly 1997). The caseload decline for Michigan
from the start of TANF, February 1996 to February 1997 (the month
in which this study sample was drawn), was 15 percent. From

August 1996 to September 1998, Michigan's number of recipients fell by 39 percent, slightly above the rate for the United States as a whole. At the same time, the employment opportunities for low-income women were no doubt expanding with the tight labor market. Michigan's unemployment rate was at 5.1 percent in February 1997, fell to 3.7 percent in September 1997, and stood at 3.4 percent by September 1998.

The dramatic caseload reductions over this early period of welfare reform have led policy-makers, researchers, and advocates to analyze the employability of recipients remaining on the rolls and to evaluate what services might be required to foster their transition from welfare to work. Some have hypothesized that many personal problems—for example, poor physical or mental health, lack of transportation, and/or low skills—diminish the labor-market prospects of current recipients and might interfere with their ability to comply with expanded work requirements. Recipients with a complex set of such barriers, who are neither exempt nor provided specific help to resolve their problems, are especially vulnerable to losing assistance for failure to meet these requirements, even if they have no alternative means of support.

Analysis of potential barriers to employment, especially during a tight labor market, can reveal the extent to which current welfare recipients have problems that either singly or in combination interfere with participating in training programs, complying with new rules, and, ultimately, securing jobs, keeping jobs, and increasing wages. The robustness of the economy allows us to assume fewer demand-side employment constraints and perhaps arrive at a more-accurate measure of supply-side constraints. To what degree these potential impediments to work put women and children in jeopardy depends on what service programs, training programs, and employers do in response to the problems and whether such problems are addressed prior to the removal of the families from public assistance rolls.

Currently, most state programs emphasize job-search-assistance services that are designed to move as many recipients as possible quickly into jobs. Typically, the states do not systematically assess whether undiagnosed barriers to employment, such as lack of basic work skills and experience, inadequate knowledge of workplace norms, transportation problems, health and mental-health problems, substance abuse, and domestic violence, limit recipients' capability to work regularly (Seefeldt, Sandfort, and Danziger 1998). As we suggest in this chapter, such a "work-first" strategy might be appropriate for many welfare recipients who were on the caseload when PRWORA was passed. However, given the large decline in caseloads since its passage, recipients who have not yet entered the workforce are likely to have more of these problems than pre-1996 recipients no longer receiving assistance.

In this chapter, we use a new survey of a representative sample of single mothers who were welfare recipients in an urban Michigan county to explore how such employment barriers, often ignored by previous welfare researchers and by policy-makers, constrain their employability. We answer four questions about these barriers:

- How prevalent among women who were welfare recipients is each of a large number of barriers to employment?

- What percentage of these women face multiple barriers?

- Is the number of barriers faced associated with welfare mothers' employment?

- How much does employment decrease as the number of barriers increases?

- Which individual barriers matter for employment and how much more do we learn when we examine a comprehensive set of barriers than when we predict employment as a function of their schooling, work experience, and past welfare status?

We begin with a review of the literature relevant to welfare mothers' employment in order to identify a comprehensive set of potential barriers to the transition to work. Then we describe our data, sample, measures, and methodology. We next present our results, which show that welfare recipients in the sample have unusually high levels of some barriers to work, such as self-reported physical- and mental-health problems, domestic violence, and lack of transportation, but relatively low levels of other barriers, such as drug or alcohol dependence and lack of understanding of work norms; most recipients have multiple barriers; and the number of barriers is strongly and negatively associated with employment status. In addition, we find that an expanded regression model that includes these barriers is a significantly better predictor of employment than is a model that includes only variables traditionally measured, such as education, work experience, and welfare history. We conclude with a discussion of the implications of these results for understanding the employment and post-welfare experiences of single mothers and for reforming welfare-to-work policies.

LITERATURE REVIEW

Most welfare-to-work programs now being operated by the states seek to move recipients into the workforce quickly. Typically, the states do not conduct assessments for or provide services to address a wide array of potential employment barriers, even though previous studies indicate that a number of personal factors impede employment (for a review, see Kalil et al. 1998).

Many studies indicate that a sizable minority of recipients are unable to keep jobs and cycle between work and welfare (Harris 1993, 1996; Pavetti 1993; Spalter-Roth, Burr, Hartmann, and Shaw 1995). Some recipients are unable to find jobs, while others secure jobs, only to lose them on account of inadequate job skills (Bane and Ellwood 1994; Harris 1996; Wagner, Herr, Chang, and Brooks 1998). Harry J. Holzer (1996) surveyed 3,200 employers about entry-level jobs available to workers without a college degree and reported that most jobs required credentials (high school diploma, work experience, references) that many welfare recipients do not have. For example, about half of all welfare recipients are high school dropouts, and about 40 percent had no work experience prior to their first welfare spell (Harris 1996).

Holzer (1996) also reported that most entry-level jobs required workers to perform one or more of the following tasks on a daily basis: reading and writing paragraphs, dealing with customers, doing arithmetic, and using computers. The average welfare recipient reads on a sixth- to eighth-grade level and might not be able to perform many of these basic tasks (Barton and Jenkins 1995).

Another possibility is that recipients are not "work ready"—that is, they do not understand or follow workplace norms or behaviors. Evaluations of the Project Match and New Chance Demonstrations report that many recipients lost their jobs because they failed to understand the importance of punctuality, the seriousness of absenteeism, and resented or misunderstood the lines of authority and responsibility in the workplace (Berg, Olson, and Conrad 1991; Hershey and Pavetti 1997).

Employer discrimination might also inhibit employment prospects. Employer audit studies demonstrate that African Americans and Hispanics are less likely to receive job offers than are whites with comparable credentials (Turner, Fix, and Struyk 1991), and qualitative data suggest that employers negatively stereotype African Americans (Kirschenman and Neckerman 1991). Almost half of African-American women in a Los Angeles survey report having experienced job-related discrimination (Bobo 1995).

Mental-health problems may further limit welfare recipients' employability. High levels of depressive symptoms among recipients have been documented (Steffick 1996; Olson and Pavetti 1996). In addition, many welfare mothers experience traumas—rape, domestic violence, and sexual molestation, for instance—that put them at high risk for post-traumatic stress syndrome (PTSD). Among participants in a welfare-to-work program in New Jersey, 22 percent reported having been raped; 55 percent, having experienced domestic abuse; and 20 percent, having been sexually molested as a child (Curcio 1996). Previous studies document the negative consequences of mental-health problems on men's employment and work hours, but as yet little information is available on the nature of the relationship between such problems and work for welfare mothers (Jayakody, Danziger, and Pollack 2000; Kessler and Frank 1997).

Substance abuse also might negatively affect employment. Estimates of prevalence of substance abuse among welfare recipients range widely from 6.6 to 37.0 percent, depending in large part on the measure used (Olson and Pavetti 1996). The 1992 National Household Survey of Drug Abuse reported that 15.5 percent of public-assistance recipients were impaired by drugs or alcohol—twice the rate of nonrecipients.

Olson and Pavetti (1996) hypothesize that mothers' and children's physical-health problems could reduce employment. Rates of physical-health problems are higher among welfare mothers and their children than among women and children in the general population (Loprest and Acs 1995; Olson and Pavetti 1996), and there is a positive association between women's own employment and health (Kessler, Turner, and House 1987; Bird and Fremont 1991). Wolfe and Hill (1995) found that a single mother's health affects her work effort through her potential wage rate and estimated value of public and private insurance. They further found that her child's health affects a single mother's hours worked, but not her probability of employment. Several evaluation studies of welfare programs suggest that health problems caused recipients to lose jobs (Hershey and Pavetti 1997).

Involvement in violent personal relationships is another potential barrier to work. Domestic violence is present in the lives of a high percentage of women on welfare (see Raphael and Tolman 1997 for a review). Bassuk, Browne, and Buckner (1996), Bassuk, Weinreb, Buckner, Browne, Salomon, and Bassuk (1996), and Lloyd and Taluc (1999) found lifetime prevalence rates of domestic violence among welfare recipients ranging from 48 to 63 percent, and current rates of domestic violence ranging from 10 to 31 percent. Violent partners potentially sabotage mothers' attempts to enter the workforce.

This review suggests the need to evaluate whether a variety of these factors reduce welfare recipients' employability. Olson and Pavetti (1996) note that the presence of any single problem is not necessarily an insurmountable barrier to work, but the presence of multiple problems might reduce employment. Using data from the 1991 National Longitudinal Study of Youth, they estimate that 30 percent of welfare recipients faced more than one of the following: mother's and child's poor health, alcohol and drug problems, depression, and low basic skills. However, expanding the definition of barriers to include milder forms of skill deficits and additional barriers, such as the exposure to domestic violence, could substantially increase the percentage of the welfare population with multiple barriers (Olson and Pavetti 1996, 27). In sum, many potential barriers to work, their prevalence and co-occurrence, and their effects on work have been ignored in past studies of welfare recipients and in policy discussions on how to move recipients from welfare to work. This study seeks to remedy these omissions.

DATA, SAMPLE, AND MEASURES

Data and Sample

In late 1997, the Women's Employment Study (WES) first surveyed a random sample of 753 single mothers who were on the welfare rolls in an urban Michigan county in February 1997. The sample was systematically selected with equal probability from an ordered list of the universe of active single-mother cases of the Michigan Family Independence Agency. To be eligible for the sample, the women had to be between the ages of eighteen and fifty-four, white or African American,[2] and U.S. citizens.

The completed in-person interviews lasted about one hour; the response rate was 86 percent. The interviews were conducted between September 1997 and December 1997, seven to ten months after the sample was drawn. Respondents were interviewed a second time in late 1998 and were interviewed for a third time in late 1999 or early 2000.

In designing this study, we cast a wide interdisciplinary net over the potential problems possibly prevalent among welfare mothers and impeding their move from the welfare rolls into the workforce. We included measures of traditional human-capital variables, such as failure to complete high school and low work experience, but also extended our measures to focus on mental- and physical-health problems, and other psychosocial and familial disadvantages.

Demographic Measures

In late 1997, at the time of the survey, 72 percent of the respondents were receiving cash welfare benefits. Of these welfare recipients, about half were fulfilling the state's requirement of working at least twenty hours per week. About 60 percent of all nonworking welfare recipients had participated in the mandated job-search-training program within the past year. Among the 28 percent of the respondents who were no longer receiving welfare, about three-quarters were working at least twenty hours a week, and about half were working at least thirty-five hours a week.

Table 8.1 describes the employment status and demographic characteristics of the sample as a whole. Fifty-eight percent of all respondents were working at least twenty hours per week, as required by Michigan as a condition for assistance.[3] Another 4 percent worked less than half-time. Most of the jobs that these women filled were in the service sector, and few provided benefits.[4] Of those women who were employed at the time of the survey (62 percent), almost half (30 percent) were working thirty-five hours a week or more.

Fifty-six percent of respondents were African American and 44 percent were white. About 28 percent of the sample was between eighteen and twenty-four years old; 46 percent was between twenty-

Table 8.1 Sample Characteristics

Characteristic	Percentage of Respondents
Current welfare recipients	72
Employment status	
Currently employed	62
Working less than twenty hours per week	4
Working twenty to thirty-four hours per week	28
Working thirty-five or more hours	30
Race	
African American	56
White	44
Age	
Eighteen to twenty-four years	28
Twenty-five to thirty-four years	46
Thirty-five years or more	26
Residence	
Urban census tract	86
Rural census tract	14
Marital status	
Living with spouse or partner at time of interview	24
Other	76
Presence of young children	
Any children, infant to two years	43
Mean number of children, infant to two years	.49
Any children, three to five years	42
Mean number of children, three to five years	.51
Welfare history	
Mean number of years since age eighteen in which received AFDC/FIP	7.3

Source: Authors' calculations.
Note: The sample includes 753 women who received cash welfare in February 1997 and who were interviewed between September and December 1997. Because the respondents represent a random sample of all single-parent recipients in the county, no sample weights are utilized.

five and thirty-four years old, and 26 percent between thirty-five and fifty-four years old. Almost 90 percent of the women lived in urban census tracts in the county. While all of the respondents were receiving welfare as single mothers in February 1997, 24 percent were living with a spouse or partner at the time of the survey; we do not know how many were cohabiting in February. About two-fifths were the primary care giver for at least one child younger than two years, and about an equal percentage did the same for a child between the ages of three and five. The average number of years of welfare receipt since turning age eighteen was 7.3, ranging from 1 to 30 years.

Employment Barrier Measures

Table 8.2 lists our measures of fourteen barriers to employment.[5] These measures were defined with the cutoff point for a potential barrier as follows.

Table 8.2 Measures of Employment Barriers

Education, Work Experience, Job Skills, and Workplace Norms

1. Less than a high school education
2. Low work experience (worked in fewer than 20 percent of years since age eighteen)
3. Fewer than four job skills (out of a possible nine) on a previous job
4. Knows five or fewer work norms (out of a possible nine)

Perceived Discrimination

5. Reports four or more instances of prior discrimination on the basis of race, gender, or welfare status (out of a possible sixteen)

Transportation Problem

6. Does not have access to a car and/or does not have a driver's license

Psychiatric Disorders and Substance Dependence Within Past Year

7. Major depressive disorder
8. Post-traumatic stress disorder (PTSD)
9. Generalized anxiety disorder
10. Alcohol dependence
11. Drug dependence

Physical Health Problems

12. Mother's health problem (self-reported fair or poor health and age-specific physical limitation)
13. Child-health problem (has a health, learning, or emotional problem)

Domestic Violence

14. Severe abuse from a partner within past year

Source: Authors' compilation.

Education, Work Experience, Job Skills, and Workplace Norms
A respondent is considered to have an education barrier if she neither graduated from high school nor received a general education diploma (GED).[6] A respondent was considered to have low work experience if she worked in less than 20 percent of the years since she turned age eighteen. Respondents were asked about having performed nine tasks on a daily, weekly, or monthly basis in previous jobs: worked with a computer; written letters or memos; watched gauges; spoken with customers face-to-face; spoken with customers on the telephone; read instructions; filled out forms; done arithmetic; worked with electronic machines. If a respondent had performed fewer than four of these tasks, she was classified as having a work-experience barrier. These skill questions were adapted from Holzer (1996).

Respondents were also asked about the appropriateness of nine behavioral workplace norms. They answered "yes" or "no" to whether it would be a problem at work if they missed work without calling in; did not correct a problem pointed out by a supervisor; came to work late; made personal calls on the job; argued with customers; left work early without prior approval; took a longer break than scheduled; refused tasks not in the job description; or did not get along with a supervisor. Those who replied that five or more of these behaviors would "*not* be a serious problem" were classified as having this barrier. These questions were based on Berg, Olson, and Conrad (1991).

Perceived Discrimination
Respondents were asked sixteen questions about discrimination, including whether they thought that they had ever been refused a job, fired, or not promoted because of their race, sex, or welfare status (Turner, Fix, and Struyk 1991; Bobo 1995; Kirschenman and Neckerman 1991).[7] The women were asked if their current or most-recent supervisor made racial slurs, insulting remarks about women, or insulting remarks about welfare recipients. They were asked about whether they thought that they had experienced discrimination on the basis of race, gender, or welfare status on their current or most-recent job, including whether they had been sexually harassed at work. Women who reported four or more instances of any combination these experiences were classified as having this barrier. These

questions were adapted from Bobo's Los Angeles household survey (1995).

Transportation
We considered a respondent to have a transportation problem if she lacked access to a car and/or did not have a driver's license.

Mental Health and Substance Dependence
Mental health and substance dependence were assessed with using diagnostic screening batteries for the twelve-month prevalence of five psychiatric disorders as defined in the *Diagnostic and Statistical Manual of Mental Disorders,* revised third edition (DSM-III-R): major depression, post-traumatic stress disorder (PTSD), generalized anxiety disorder, alcohol dependence, and drug dependence. Questions come from the Composite International Diagnostic Interview (CIDI) used in the National Comorbidity Survey (NCS), the first nationally representative survey to administer a structured psychiatric interview (Kessler et al. 1994). The items in each of the five indices are scored for clinical caseness, and all respondents who meet the scale criteria for a disorder are defined as having the mental-health or substance-abuse barrier.

Physical Health
Sample members were asked about physical limitations and to rate their general health using the health questions taken from the SF-36 Health Survey (Ware, Snow, Kosinski, and Gandek 1993). Respondents who rated their general health as poor or fair *and* who scored in the lowest age-specific quartile (based on national norms) of the multiple-item physical-functioning scale were defined as having a health problem. Respondents who reported at least one child having a physical, learning, or emotional problem that limited the child's activity were defined as having a child with a health problem.

Domestic Violence
Domestic violence is measured by the Conflict Tactics Scale (CTS), a widely used measure of family violence (Straus and Gelles 1986, 1990). We defined the barrier from the items indicating current recent (past twelve months) severe physical abuse. This subscale indicates whether the respondent has been hit with a fist or object, beaten,

choked, threatened with a weapon, or forced into sexual activity against her will.

METHODOLOGY

The analysis sample includes the 728 respondents who had no missing data on employment status, selected demographic characteristics, or on any of the fourteen barrier measures. We begin by estimating the prevalence of individual and multiple barriers in the sample, because this tells us how many recipients face obstacles in these domains.

Next, we examine whether the number of barriers a recipient has affects her employment status by estimating equation (8.1), which expresses employment status as a function of the number of barriers, prior welfare receipt, and a series of demographic controls:

$$\text{EMP} = \alpha_0 + \sum_{i=1}^{7} \alpha_i N_i + \beta W + \sum_{j=1}^{n} \theta_j X_j + \mu_1 \tag{8.1}$$

where:

EMP = 1 if working 20 or more hours/week; 0 otherwise
N_i = 1 if the number of barriers = i; 0 otherwise; i = 1 . . . 6
N_7 = 1 if the number of barriers is 7 or more; 0 otherwise
W = number of years of prior welfare receipt
X_j = set of demographic controls (marital status, race, age, number and ages of children, urban or rural residence)
μ = random error term

We estimate equation 8.1 using logistic regression.

As a last step, we investigate how each of the individual barrier indicators affects a recipient's employment status by estimating equation 8.2, which expresses employment status as a function of each of the fourteen individual barrier measures, prior welfare receipt, and demographic controls:

$$\text{EMP} = \beta_0 + \sum_{k=1}^{14} \beta_k \text{ Bar}_k + \gamma W + \sum_{j=1}^{n} \theta_j X_j + \mu_2 \tag{8.2}$$

where Bar_k = a set of fourteen dummy variables representing each of the barrier measures.

For comparison purposes, we also estimate a model that expresses employment status as a function of education, work experience, prior welfare receipt, and demographic controls—the model typically used in past analyses of welfare to work transitions. This comparison provides an estimate of how much an expanded set of barriers improves our ability to predict the employment of welfare recipients.

RESULTS

Prevalence of Specific Barriers

Table 8.3 reports in column A the prevalence among respondents of each of the fourteen barriers, and, in column B (where possible), their prevalence in national samples of adult women. Welfare recipients are much less likely to have graduated from high school and much more likely to have experienced transportation problems, to meet screening criteria for health problems, and to report mental-, physical-, and child-health problems, and severe physical abuse than women in the general population. On the positive side, recipients were no more likely to meet the screening criteria for drug or alcohol dependence than were adult women in the general population.

Thirty-five percent of respondents met the criteria for at least one of the five DSM-III-R diagnoses. A quarter reported symptoms of a major depression within the past year; 15 percent met criteria for post-traumatic stress disorder; and 7 percent showed characteristics of generalized anxiety disorder. These rates are considerably higher than those for fifteen- to fifty-four-year-old women in the National Comorbidity Study, where the rate of major depression was 13 percent and that of generalized anxiety disorder 4 percent. There are no national estimates for twelve-month prevalence of PTSD, but 29 percent of our sample meet the criteria for a lifetime experience of PTSD, compared to less than 10 percent of women in the NCS. It should be noted, however, that the NCS used the full diagnostic batteries for each disorder.

Self-reported substance dependence was low in this sample and comparable to prevalence rates in the NCS. Despite the popular view that many women on welfare abuse alcohol and drugs, only 3.3 percent of sample met the DSM-III-R diagnostic screening criteria for drug dependence, and only 2.7 percent fit the standard for alcohol dependence. It is possible that respondents (as well as the national sample of women) underreported their alcohol and drug dependence, because dependence involves a stricter definition of impairment than does use or abuse.[8] In addition, as noted, we used the screening version of the NCS measures. These substance-dependence rates are

Table 8.3 Prevalence of Employment Barriers

Barriers	(1) Percentage in Sample with Barrier	(2) Percentage Women Nationally with Barrier	Percentage in Sample Working Twenty or More Hours/Week	
			(3) With Barriers	(4) Without Barriers
Less than high school education	31.4	12.7[a]	38.7*	66.3
Low work experience	15.4		33.3*	62.3
Fewer than four job skills	21.1		34.2*	64.0
Knows five or fewer work norms	9.1		56.7	57.8
Perceived discrimination	13.9		46.7*	59.5
Transportation problem	47.1	7.6[b]	44.8*	69.2
Major depressive disorder	25.4	12.9[c]	47.9*	61.0
Post-traumatic stress disorder	14.6		55.0	58.1
Generalized anxiety disorder	7.3	4.3[c]	54.5	57.9
Alcohol dependence	2.7	3.7[c]	70.0	57.3
Drug dependence	3.3	1.9[c]	40.0**	58.3
Mother's health problem	19.4		39.0*	62.2
Child-health problem	22.1	15.7[d]	48.5*	60.6
Domestic violence	14.9	3.2–3.4[e]	55.4	58.1

Source: Authors' calculations.

* Difference between columns 3 and 4 is significant at the .05 level.

** Difference between columns 3 and 4 is significant at the .10 level.

[a] Percentage of all women ages eighteen to fifty-four who do not have a high school diploma or equivalent (Current Population Survey [1998]).

[b] Percentage of all women ages eighteen to fifty-four who live in households with no vehicles available (1990 Census).

[c] 1994 National Co-morbidity Survey: Percentage of all women ages fifteen to fifty-four who meet criteria for clinical caseness on each of these disorders (Kessler et al. 1994).

[d] Percentage of all mothers ages twenty-nine to thirty-seven with children who have one of six limitations, according to National Longitudinal Survey of Youth (1994).

[e] 1993 Commonwealth Fund Survey and 1985 National Family Violence Survey: Percentage of all women ages eighteen and over who report current severe physical abuse.

somewhat lower than those reported among welfare recipients in national samples (Jayakody, Danziger, and Pollack, 2000).

About one in five mothers reported a health problem, and a similar fraction reported that at least one of their children had a health, learning, or emotional problem. Our composite measure of maternal health is not directly comparable to measures used in national surveys (thus not reported in table 8.3), but we can compare mothers' scores on its two components to findings from national surveys. Respondents were twice as likely as the general population of adult women to report physical limitations and three to five times as likely to report their general health as poor or fair as are nonelderly women nationally (McDowell and Newell 1996). The prevalence of having a child with an activity-limiting physical, emotional, or learning condition was higher in our sample than in an NLSY sample of young mothers. However, the measure used in the national sample is slightly more complex, and its mothers' age range is narrower than that in our sample. About 15 percent of the women in our sample reported being severely physically abused by a husband or partner in the last year. This rate is four to five times higher than the rates found in national surveys (Straus and Gelles 1986; 1990; Plichta 1996), but similar to rates reported in other studies of welfare recipients (Raphael 1995).

We hypothesized that each of these fourteen characteristics listed in table 8.3 is a potential barrier to work, and bivariate analysis documents a strong relationship between many of these variables and work. The last two columns in the table show the proportion of women in our sample who work at least twenty hours per week, first for women with and then for those without each barrier. For nine of the fourteen barriers (less than a high school education or GED; little work experience; previous use of fewer than four of nine job skills; four or more prior perceived experiences of job discrimination; lack of access to a car and/or no driver's license; recent major depressive disorder; drug dependence; poor health; and a child with health, learning, or emotional problems), women who have the barrier are significantly less likely to work than those without it. For example, 34.2 percent of women with few job skills worked at least twenty hours per week, compared to 64.0 percent of those with more previous job skills.

There were few differences between whites and African Americans in the prevalence of individual barriers. Only three of the fourteen individual barriers—lacking a car and/or a driver's license, having previously used less than four job skills, and meeting the screening criteria for a major depressive disorder within the past twelve months—differ significantly between African American and white respondents. African American welfare recipients are more likely to have the transportation and skills barriers, while white recipients are more likely to meet the criteria for major depression. The distribution of the number of barriers does not differ significantly by race.

Prevalence of Multiple Barriers

The majority of the women in our sample met the criteria for several barriers, thus potentially compounding their disadvantages in the labor market. One or two barriers might have little effect on employment, but multiple barriers could seriously impede employment. For example, mental-health and physical-health problems might require frequent doctor visits, leading to absences from work. One of these problems alone might not interfere with work, but the combination of either, or both, with low education and few job skills could create obstacles on the job or in a job search. Lack of a high school diploma by itself does not constitute a rigid barrier to employment, but an employer might be less willing to hire a high school dropout who also has few work skills, transportation problems, and is visibly depressed.

Figure 8.1 displays the distribution of the number of barriers among respondents. Almost all welfare recipients in our sample, 85 percent had at least one barrier to employment. In contrast to Olson and Pavetti's (1996) 1991 NLSY data, in which most recipients had only one barrier, only 21 percent of our respondents currently have just one of the fourteen barriers. Multiple barriers were common: 37 percent had two or three barriers; 24 percent, four to six barriers; and 3 percent, seven or more barriers. Given the high prevalence of the co-occurrence of barriers across this wide range of domains, we next examine how the number of barriers is related to employment.

Barriers and Employment Outcomes

We explored the association between the number of barriers and the respondent's employment status at the time of the interview by estimating equation 8.1. The dependent variable in equation 8.1 indi-

Figure 8.1 Number of Barriers Experienced

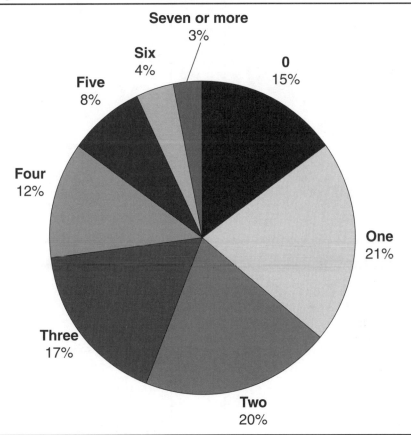

Source: Authors' calculations.

cates whether a woman was working at least twenty hours per week at the time of the survey. Independent variables include seven dummies for the number of barriers, number of years received welfare since the age of eighteen, and demographic control variables (marital status, race, residence in an urban census tract, age, and whether she cares for children and, if so, how many). Column A of table 8.4 reports the results.

The probability that a woman worked at least twenty hours (as required for a recipient to be in compliance with Michigan's welfare rules) decreases as her number of potential barriers to work increases. All of the coefficients on the number of barriers are negative and significant. The sizes of the coefficients cluster into five groups: zero bar-

Table 8.4 Effects of Multiple Barriers on Whether Woman Works Twenty or More Hours per Week

	Column A			Column B		
Number of Barriers	Coefficient	Standard Error	Odds Ratio	Coefficient	Standard Error	Odds Ratio
One	−0.604*	0.297	0.547			
Two	−0.925*	0.294	0.396			
Three	−1.129*	0.305	0.323			
Four	−1.901*	0.331	0.149			
Five	−1.828*	0.367	0.161			
Six	−2.218*	0.461	0.109			
Seven or more	−4.403*	1.055	0.012			
Grouped barriers						
One				−0.604*	0.297	0.547
Two to three				−1.016*	0.270	0.362
Four to six				−1.929*	0.290	0.145
Seven or more				−4.397*	1.055	0.012

	Coefficient	Standard error	Odds ratio	Coefficient	Standard error	Odds ratio
Demographics						
Married or cohabitates	−0.261	0.201	0.770	−0.253	0.201	0.776
African American	−0.132	0.182	0.876	−0.122	0.181	0.886
Urban census tract	0.469**	0.251	1.598	0.467**	0.251	1.595
Age						
Twenty-five to thirty-four	0.539*	0.223	1.714	0.549*	0.222	1.731
Thirty-five and over	0.710*	0.312	2.034	0.725*	0.310	2.065
Number of children						
Infant to two years old	−0.260**	0.149	0.771	−0.238	0.148	0.788
Three to five years old	−0.055	0.126	0.947	−0.049	0.126	0.952
Years on welfare	−0.037**	0.020	0.964	−0.038**	0.020	0.963
Constant	1.154	0.367		1.131	0.366	
−2 log likelihood	880.4			881.8		
Number of observations	728			728		

Source: Authors' calculations.
* Significant at the .05 level
** Significant at the .10 level

riers, one barrier, two or three barriers, four to six barriers, and seven or more barriers. We next estimated an equation that replaces the seven dummy variables in column A with four dummy variables representing these five clusters. Column B of table 8.4 reports the results. Again, employment decreases sharply as the number of concurrent barriers increases, and all four of the coefficients are significant. Of the demographic characteristics, living in an urban census tract, respondent's age, and the number of years of prior welfare receipt were all significantly associated with women's employment; however, neither marital status nor race were significant predictors of work.

Table 8.5 converts the estimated regression coefficients reported in column B of table 8.4 into predicted probabilities. The values represent the probabilities that a single, twenty-five- to thirty-four-year-old African American mother who lived in an urban census tract, had one child under two years of age, no children between the ages of three and five, and had received welfare for seven years would work at least twenty hours per week if she had zero barriers, one barrier, two or three barriers, four to six barriers, or seven or more barriers. The results are striking: the greater the number of barriers, the less likely the woman is to work. Even women with only one barrier had a significantly lower probability of working compared to women with no barriers (71.5 versus 82.1 percent), and after that, employment drops sharply and significantly as the number of barriers rises. A woman has three in five chances of working if she has two or three barriers; two in five chances of working if she has four, five, or six barriers; and only a one in twenty chance of working if she has seven or more barriers to work.[9]

The coefficient on race in table 8.4 is small and not significant, so the employment probabilities for whites, holding other characteristics constant, are similar to those shown in table 8.5 for an African American single mother. The probabilities for a white single mother with these characteristics with zero, one, two or three, four to six, or seven or more barriers are, successively, 83.8, 73.9, 65.2, 42.9, and 6.0 percent.

Human-Capital Versus Expanded-Barrier Model

The analyses thus far show that multiple barriers are associated with the diminished employment among welfare recipients. However, the analyses do not identify which of the individual barriers

Table 8.5 Employment Probabilities by Number of Barriers

Number of Barriers	Probability of Working Twenty or More Hours per Week
Zero	82.1
One	71.5
Two to three	62.4
Four to six	40.0
Seven or more	5.3

Note: Given that respondent is single, black, lives in an urban census tract, is twenty-five to thirty-four years old, has one child between infancy and two years old, has no children age three to six, and has received welfare for seven years. Predicted probabilities are based on the coefficients in column B of table 8.4.

Employment Probability by Number of Barriers

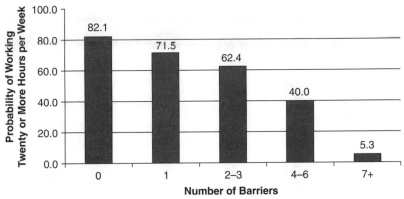

Source: Authors' calculations.

have the most significant effects, and do not show how well the expanded set of indicators improves our understanding over previous studies that typically predict employment on the basis of recipients' education, work experience, welfare experience, and demographic characteristics.

Table 8.6 presents this analysis by estimating two versions of equation 8.2. Column A reports results when employment status is regressed on schooling, work experience, years of welfare receipt, and demographic controls—the human-capital model used in prior research based on measures typically available in data sets. The results are consistent with these earlier studies. The presence and number of very young children and lower levels of schooling and work experience are negatively associated with employment.

Table 8.6 Effects of Individual Barriers on Whether Woman Works Twenty or More Hours per Week

	Column A			Column B		
	Coefficient	Standard Error	Odds Ratio	Coefficient	Standard Error	Odds Ratio
Demographics						
Married or cohabitates	−0.206	0.196	0.814	−0.138	0.210	0.871
African American	−0.189	0.179	0.828	−0.075	0.194	0.928
Urban census tract	0.396	0.247	1.485	0.540*	0.262	1.715
Age twenty-five to thirty-four	0.346	0.219	1.414	0.386	0.235	1.471
Age thirty-five and over	0.421	0.306	1.523	0.631**	0.333	1.879
Number of children, infant to two	−0.245**	0.144	0.782	−0.290**	0.154	0.748
Number of children, three to five	−0.026	0.123	0.975	−0.040	0.131	0.961
Years on welfare	−0.026	0.020	0.974	−0.022	0.021	0.978
Barriers						
Less than high school education	−0.946*	0.177	0.388	−0.685*	0.196	0.504
Low work experience	−0.912*	0.234	0.402	−0.640*	0.262	0.528

	Coefficient (1)	S.E. (1)	Coefficient (2)	S.E. (2)	Odds ratio
Other barriers from WES					
Fewer than four job skills			−0.717*	0.228	0.488
Knows five or fewer work norms			−0.003	0.301	0.997
Perceived discrimination			−0.915*	0.246	0.400
Transportation problem			−0.685*	0.186	0.504
Major depressive disorder			−0.493*	0.215	0.611
Post-traumatic stress disorder (Twelve months)			0.215	0.259	1.240
General anxiety disorder			0.282	0.342	1.326
Alcohol dependence			0.855	0.604	2.352
Drug dependence			−1.035*	0.524	0.355
Mother's health problem			−0.666*	0.223	0.514
Child-health problem			−0.232	0.210	0.793
Domestic violence			0.155	0.257	1.168
Constant	0.653	0.298	1.107	0.325	
−2 log likelihood	913.5		841.9		
Cox and Snell R-squared	0.099		0.183		
Chi-square (df)	75.9 (10)		147.4 (22)		
Number of observations	728		728		

Source: Authors' calculations.
* Significant at the .05 level
** Significant at the .10 level

The column B of table 8.6 reports results when employment status is regressed on work experience, schooling, years received welfare, our additional twelve barrier measures, and the demographic controls.[10] This expanded model is a better overall predictor of employment, and most of the barrier measures that had exhibited significant bivariate associations with employment (shown in table 8.3) remain significant in the full model. In addition to low education and lack of work experience, six other barriers are negatively and significantly associated with working at least twenty hours per week: having few work skills, perceiving four or more experiences of workplace discrimination, lack of access to transportation, and meeting the screening criteria for depression, drug dependence, or poor health. In addition to these barriers, being younger, having very young children, and not living in an urban census tract also reduce employment. Factors such as race, marital status, lack of knowledge of workplace norms, and recent domestic abuse are not significantly associated with employment.

Table 8.7 converts the eight significant estimated regression coefficients reported in column B of table 8.6 into probabilities and presents the difference in the likelihood of working with and without each of the seven barriers. Column A shows the prevalence of each barrier in the sample (as reported previously in table 8.3) for comparative purposes. Column B, row 1, reports the employment probability of a typical woman in the sample (single, African American, lives in an urban census tract, has one child two years of age or under but no children age three and five, and has received welfare for seven years) who reports none of these barriers. Rows 2 through 8 of column B report the probability that a typical woman with only the barrier listed in that row was working twenty or more hours per week. The numbers in the third column report the difference between the probability of working for women with no barriers and that of working with only the single barrier in that row. For example, almost half of the women in the sample have transportation problems, and there is a 12.4 percentage-point difference in the probabilities of working between those with and without access to a car, or in possession of or not in possession of a driver's license. The largest individual barrier effects are for perceived discrimination, few work skills, and drug dependence—about 17, 13 and 20 percentage points respectively. But about 14 percent of the sample felt that they had been discriminated against in the workplace, and one-fifth lack work

Table 8.7 Relative Effects of Individual Barriers on Whether Woman Works Twenty or More Hours per Week

Barriers	Prevalence (Percentage)	Predicted Probability of Working Twenty or More Hours[a]	Difference in Probability With and Without Barrier
None	15.4	81.9	—
Less than high school education	31.4	69.6	12.4
Low work experience	15.4	70.5	11.4
Fewer than four job skills	21.1	68.9	13.0
Perceived discrimination	13.9	64.5	17.4
Transportation problem	47.1	69.6	12.4
Major depressive disorder	25.4	73.5	8.5
Drug dependence	3.3	61.7	20.2
Mother's health problem	19.4	70.0	12.0

Source: Authors' calculations.
[a] Given that respondent is single, black, lives in an urban census tract, is twenty-five to thirty-four years old, has one child infant to two years old, no children age three to five, and has received welfare for seven years. Predicted probabilities are based on the coefficients in Column B of table 8.6.

skills, while only 3.3 percent of the women meet the criteria for drug dependence.

SUMMARY

We began this paper with four questions:

- How prevalent among women who were welfare recipients is each of a large number of potential barriers to employment, such as physical- or mental-health problems, few job skills, and inadequate knowledge of workplace norms?

- What percent of these women face multiple barriers?

- Is the number of barriers associated with welfare mothers' employment?

- How much does employment decrease as the number of barriers increases?

- Which individual barriers matter for employment, and how much do we gain by adding this comprehensive set of factors to a model of employment?

Barriers to work are quite prevalent. Only 15 percent of our study's respondents had none of the fourteen barriers analyzed. The women in the WES sample, all of whom received welfare in February 1997, reported much higher rates of personal-health problems, health problems among their children, mental-health problems, and domestic-violence experiences than did women in contemporary national samples. In addition, substantial percentages of respondents had not completed high school, possessed few job skills, reported multiple instances of perceived workplace discrimination, and lacked access to a car and/or a driver's license. There are some positive findings with regard to these barriers: most recipients knew most workplace norms, most had at least some past work experience, and recipients were no more likely to meet criteria for drug or alcohol dependence than were women in the general population.

Given the high prevalence of many of the individual barriers, it is not surprising that multiple barriers were common. Almost two-thirds of the women had two or more potential barriers to work, and over one-quarter had four or more. These barriers were strongly associated with women's employment in late 1997: the more barriers a woman had, the less likely she was to be working. For example, only two-fifths of women with four to six barriers and one in twenty with seven or more barriers worked at least twenty hours per week. We expect that the women in this cohort who remain on welfare over the next few years will, like current long-term recipients, have even greater numbers of barriers and hence, an even more difficult time securing employment.

Finally, the individual barriers that were significantly associated with working at least twenty hours a week, controlling for a variety of other factors, include low education, few work skills, lack of work experience, poor access to transportation, health problems, drug dependence, major depression, and experiences of perceived workplace discrimination.

POLICY IMPLICATIONS

The continuing strong economic recovery has contributed to the recent welfare caseload declines and the increased employment of welfare recipients (see also Ziliak, Figlio, Davis, and Connolly 1997). The fact that over half of our sample was fulfilling the work requirement of at least twenty hours per week suggests that when the county unemployment rate is about 5.7 percent, many recipients can meet policy expectations. However, most of these women were working in low-wage, service-sector jobs that provide few benefits (data not shown).

For the groups with few or no barriers to employment, the low wages and lack of health insurance in many of these jobs suggests a continuing need for policies that make work pay. Refundable child-care credits at the federal level, a state earned-income tax credit, and further promotion of newly available child-health coverage might be the kinds of reforms that will promote well-being among those who can succeed in moving into the labor market. And, when the economy turns down, there will be a need for transitional jobs or special unemployment-insurance provisions for those who are able to work but cannot find an employer to hire them (Holzer 1998).

Even with the current extent of job availability, however, the heterogeneity of the welfare caseload means that different strategies will be needed to move mothers from welfare to work. For example, Project Match reports documented a variety of pathways that characterize the routes women take from welfare to work (Wagner, Herr, Chang, and Brooks 1998). These trajectories could well be a result of both the risk profiles of the women and their access to services focused on ameliorating their particular problems.

For the sizable minority of women in our sample who had none or only one barrier (most of whom were already working at least twenty hours per week), the emphasis on "work first" and job-search assistance common to many state programs might meet their needs in today's robust economy.

Yet for the recipients who have more of these barriers, welfare-to-work programs and services might need to be more finely targeted. Several policy and program-design questions raised by these findings include whether exemptions from work or temporary exemptions should be expanded. Should the states be required to deliver needed services to help these families and to facilitate the transition from assistance? And how will professional-service delivery in the communities adapt to supply the needed services to welfare recipients and the working poor?

Our results on the association between specific barriers and work suggest that each of the following steps could accomplish much to maximize the chances of large numbers of recipients moving into the labor force:

- improving access to transportation
- increasing specific types of job skills
- improving the women's health status or accommodating disability
- treating major depression

Lack of a high school degree and perceptions of workplace discrimination are also significantly associated with the probability of becoming employed, but current state programs are not designed to address these issues. Furthermore, reductions in drug dependence would also likely promote employment; but only a small proportion of the caseload meets these diagnostic screening criteria.

For the sizable minority of recipients who reported two or three barriers, about 60 percent were predicted to work twenty or more hours per week. Reducing the number of barriers they face by one or two could potentially increase their employment at relatively modest costs. However, the costs of risk reduction depend on the particular combination of barriers the women have and the availability and effectiveness of the services provided.

Another sizable group of recipients had four to six barriers, and only 40 percent of them were predicted to be employed. Here, more intensive interventions are probably required. Some recipients might need to be temporarily exempted from work while receiving counseling, schooling, or physical- or mental-health services.

Finally, a very small percentage of recipients (3 percent) reported seven or more of the fourteen barriers that we examined. Virtually none of these women were predicted to be employed, and their multiple barriers make it unlikely that an employer will hire them or that they will be able to hold a job over the long run. Enhanced and possibly long-term services, ranging from literacy and skills training to screening and treatment for depression, substance abuse, and domestic violence, may be required for them. In addition, many of these welfare recipients might need to work in sheltered workshops or community-service jobs before they can handle the demands of the workplace. We doubt that the states are adequately prepared to serve this very disadvantaged group of recipients, who might become an increasing share of the caseload in coming years, given current trends. At this point, they appear to be candidates for the 20 percent of the caseload that can be exempted from TANF's federal time limit.

Our findings of a high prevalence of physical-health problems, mental-health problems, and domestic abuse in today's welfare population have implications for service-delivery programs and employment. More, better, and/or more-accessible physical- and mental-health counseling, and social-service programs, along with transportation services and skills-enhancing opportunities, could potentially improve the quality of life for welfare families, as well as facilitate their transition from welfare to work.

Many people provided helpful comments on a previous draft of this paper. They include Lawrence Aber, Robert Cherry, Harry Holzer, Rukmalie Jayakody, Sanders Korenman, James Kunz, Rebecca Maynard, Kara Mikulich, Robert Moffitt, Harold Pollack, Lauren Rich, William Rodgers III, Robert Schoeni, Alan Werner, Barbara Wolfe, Alan Yaffe, and James Ziliak. Nathaniel Anderson, Heidi Goldberg, and Yunju Nam provided valuable research assistance; Barbara Ramsey typed the manuscript. Special thanks are due to survey manager Bruce Medbery and the interviewing staff from the Institute for Social Research Survey Research Center and to the Michigan Family Independence Agency, especially Charles Overbey, Steve Smucker, and Robert Syers. Any opinions expressed are those of the authors. This research was supported in part by grants from the Charles Stewart Mott and Joyce Foundations; the National Institute of Mental Health (R-24M551363) to the Social Work Research Development Center on Poverty, Risk, and Mental Health; and the Office of the Vice-President for Research at the University of Michigan to the Program on Poverty and Social Welfare Policy.

NOTES

1. To date, twenty states have adopted shorter time limits (National Governor's Association, 1997). However, most of these states allow extensions and exemptions to the shorter limit.

2. Given the demographic composition of this urban county, we excluded about 3 percent of the cases in which the single parent was not a citizen and/or was self-reported as Hispanic. In the 1990 census, only 2.1 percent of the population was Hispanic. For further information on the sample, see the sample description and survey procedures, contact the authors.

3. The work requirement for remaining in compliance with welfare rules increased to twenty-five hours per week in 1998.

4. The average weekly earnings for workers in the sample was $212; 39 percent of the sample worked in the service sector and 41 percent worked in wholesale or retail trade. About 21 percent of those who were working and no longer receiving cash assistance had no health insurance.

5. Other measures included in the survey, such as child-care arrangements, were not utilized in this analysis of the first-wave data. We also collected information on child-behavior concerns and parenting stresses, child-care use and problems, access to social support, exposure to stressful life events and material hardship, perceived personal efficacy or mastery, residential mobility, and the like. Future project papers will analyze these data.

   Child care was an important barrier to employment in this sample, but our measure is confounded with the probability of working. More than two-fifths of the respondents report that in the last year, they either lost or quit a job or were unable to take a job because of problems with child care or care of other family members. Those who reported this barrier were significantly less likely to be working twenty hours or more per week at the time of the interview than those who did not have this child-care problem. However, we asked the questions in such a way that only those who participated in work or training in the first place could report that child care impeded their work prospects. Thus, we do not include this barrier in the set of barriers reported in this paper. The second wave of the survey includes a less endogenous measure of child-care difficulties.

6. Seven percent of the sample had a GED. We treated them as high school graduates because they are quite similar to the high school graduates in our sample in terms of work experience, job skills, and extent of work.

7. These questions were adapted from surveys conducted in Los Angeles by Professor Lawrence Bobo of Howard University (Bobo 1995) and by Professors James Jackson and David Williams of the University of Michigan, in a Detroit Area Study.

8. Drug *use* is more common than dependence. About one-fifth of the sample reported using an illegal substance at least once during the year prior to the survey. Most who used any drug used marijuana. For example, 16.2 percent reported the use of marijuana or hashish in the past year, whereas only 2.5 percent used cocaine or crack.

9. The number of barriers is also correlated with continuing receipt of welfare (data not shown). Michigan's income disregard ($200 per month plus 20 percent of additional earnings) allows many women who work part-time to continue to receive cash assistance. As a result, many of those working part-time still receive cash welfare. For example, of those with no barriers, 65 percent were still welfare recipients, compared to 83 percent of those with six or more barriers.

10. The correlation matrix for the fourteen barriers reveals no correlation above .33 and very few above .20.

REFERENCES

Bane, Mary Jo, and David T. Ellwood. 1994. *Welfare Realities: From Rhetoric to Reform.* Cambridge, Mass.: Harvard University Press.

Barton, Paul, and Lynn Jenkins. 1995. "Literacy and Dependency: The Literacy Skills of Welfare Recipients in the United States." Report. Princeton, N.J.: Educational Testing Service Research.

Bassuk, Ellen L., Angela Browne, and John C. Buckner. 1996. "Single Mothers and Welfare." *Scientific American* 275(4): 60–67.

Bassuk, Ellen L., Linda F. Weinreb, John C. Buckner, Angela Browne, Amy Salomon, and Shari S. Bassuk. 1996. "The Characteristics and Needs of Sheltered Homeless and Low-Income Housed Mothers." *Journal of the American Medical Association* 276(8): 640–46.

Berg, Linnea, Lynn Olson, and Aimee Conrad. 1991. "Causes and Implications of Rapid Job Loss Among Participants in a Welfare-to-Work Program." Paper presented to the Association for Public Policy and Management, annual research conference. Bethesda, Md. (October 24–26, 1991).

Bird, Chloe E., and Allen M. Fremont. 1991. "Gender, Time Use, and Health." *Journal of Health and Social Behavior* 32(2): 114–29.

Bobo, Lawrence. 1995. "Surveying Racial Discrimination: Analyses from a Multiethnic Labor Market." Russell Sage Foundation Working paper 75. New York: Russell Sage Foundation

Curcio, William. 1996. "The Passaic County Study of AFDC Recipients in a Welfare-to-Work Program: A Preliminary Analysis." Paterson, N.J.: Passaic County Board of Social Services.

Harris, Kathleen M. 1993. "Work and Welfare Among Single Mothers in Poverty." *American Journal of Sociology* 99(2): 317–52.

————. 1996. "Life After Welfare: Women, Work, and Repeat Dependency." *American Sociological Review* 61(3): 407–26.

Hershey, Alan M., and LaDonna Pavetti. 1997. "Turning Job Finders into Job Keepers: The Challenge of Sustaining Employment." *The Future of Children* 7(1): 74–86.

Holzer, Harry. 1996. *What Employers Want: Job Prospects for Less-Educated Workers.* New York: Russell Sage Foundation.

————. 1998. "Will Employers Hire Welfare Recipients? Recent Survey Evidence from Michigan." Working paper. Lansing: Michigan State University

Jayakody, Rukmalie, Sheldon Danziger, and Harold Pollack. 2000. "Welfare Reform, Substance Use and Mental Health." Michigan Program on Poverty and Social Welfare Policy Working Paper. Ann Arbor: University of Michigan School of Social Work. *Journal of Health Politics, Policy, and Law* (August).

Kalil, Ariel, Mary Corcoran, Sandra Danziger, Richard Tolman, Kristin Seefeldt, Daniel Rosen, and Yunju Nam. 1998. "Getting Jobs , Keeping Jobs, and Earning a Living Wage: Can Welfare Reform Work?"

Kessler, Ronald C., and Richard G. Frank, R. 1997. "The Impact of Psychiatric Disorders on Work-Loss Days." *Psychological Medicine* 27: 861–73.

Kessler, Ronald. C., Katherine McGonagle, Shenyang Zhao, Christopher Nelson, Michael Hughes, Suzann Eshleman, Hans-Ulrich Wittchen, and Kenneth Kendler. 1994. "Lifetime and 12-Month Prevalence of DSM-III-R Psychiatric Disorders in the United States: Results from the National Comorbidity Survey." *Archives of General Psychiatry* 51(1): 8–19.

Kessler, Ronald C., Blake J. Turner, and James S. House. 1987. "Intervening Processes in the Relationship Between Unemployment and Health." *Psychological Medicine* 17: 949–61.

Kirschenman, Joleen, and Kathryn Neckerman. 1991. "'We'd Love to Hire Them But . . .': The Meaning of Race for Employers." In *The Urban Underclass,* edited by Christopher Jencks and P. Peterson. Washington, D.C.: Brookings Institution.

Lloyd, Susan, and Nina Taluc. 1999. "The Effects of Violence on Women's Employment." *Violence Against Women* 5: 370–92.

Loprest, Pamela, and Greg Acs. 1995. "Profile of Disability Among Families on AFDC." Working paper. Washington, D.C.: Urban Institute.

McDowell, Ian, and Claire Newell. 1996. *Measuring Health: A Guide to Rating Scales and Questionnaires.* Oxford.: Oxford University Press.

National Governors' Association. Center for Best Practices. 1997. "Summary of Selected Elements of State Plans for TANF." Washington, D.C.: National Governors' Association.

Olson, Krista, and LaDonna Pavetti. 1996. "Personal and Family Challenges to the Successful Transition from Welfare to Work." Working paper. Washington, D.C.: The Urban Institute.

Pavetti, LaDonna. 1993. "The Dynamics of Welfare and Work: Exploring the Process by Which Women Work Their Way off Welfare." Ph.D. diss., Harvard University.

Plichta, Stacey B. 1996. "Violence and Abuse: Implications for Women's Health." In *Women's Health: The Commonwealth Fund Survey*, edited by Marilyn M. Falik. Baltimore: Johns Hopkins University Press.

Raphael, Jody. 1995. *Domestic Violence: Telling the Untold Welfare-to-Work Story*. Chicago: Taylor Institute.

Raphael, Jody, and Richard Tolman. 1997. "Trapped by Poverty, Trapped by Abuse: New Evidence Documenting the Relationship Between Domestic Violence and Welfare." Chicago/Ann Arbor : Taylor Institute/University of Michigan.

Seefeldt, Kristin, Jodi Sandfort, and Sandra K. Danziger. 1998. "Moving Toward a Vision of Family Independence: Local Managers' Views of Michigan's Welfare Reforms." Michigan Program on Poverty and Social Welfare Policy Working paper. Ann Arbor: University of Michigan School of Social Work. Retrieved from the world wide web: http://www.ssw.umich.edu/poverty/pubs.html.

Spalter-Roth, Roberta, Beverly Burr, Heidi Hartmann, and Lois Shaw. 1995. *Welfare That Works: The Working Lives of AFDC Recipients*. Washington, D.C.: Institute for Women's Policy Research.

Steffick, Diane. 1996. "NLSY: Self-Esteem, Depression, and Wages." Draft paper. Ann Arbor: University of Michigan

———. 1986. Societal Change and Change in Family Violence from 1975 to 1985 as Revealed by Two National Surveys. *Journal of Marriage and the Family* 48: 465–79.

Straus, Murray A., and Richard Gelles, eds. 1990. *Physical Violence in American Families: Risk Factors and Adaptations to Violence in 8,145 Families.* New Brunswick, N.J.: Transaction Books.

Turner, Margery A., Michael Fix, and Raymond Struyk. 1991. "Opportunities Denied, Opportunities Diminished: Racial Discrimination in Hiring." Working paper. Washington, D.C.: Urban Institute.

United States Department of Health and Human Services. Administration for Children and Families. 1996a. *Decline in AFDC Caseloads Since FY1994*. Washington: United States Department of Health and Human Services.

————. 1996b. *State Welfare Demonstrations*. Washington: United States Department of Health and Human Services.

————. Office of Public Affairs. 1998. *Change in Welfare Caseloads Since Enactment of the New Welfare Law*. Washington: United States Department of Health and Human Services.

Wagner, Suzanne, Toby Herr, Charles Chang, and Diana Brooks. 1998. "Five Years of Welfare: Too Long? Too Short? Lessons from Project Match's Longitudinal Tracking Data." Project Match working paper. Chicago: Erikson Institute.

Ware, John E., Kristin K. Snow, Mark Kosinski, and Barbara Gandek. 1993. *SF-36 Health Survey: Manual and Interpretation Guide*. Boston: The Health Institute, New England Medical Enter.

Wolfe, Barbara, and Steven C. Hill. 1995. "The Effect of Health on the Work Effort of Single Mothers." *Journal of Human Resources* 30(1): 42–62.

Ziliak, James P., David N. Figlio, Elizabeth E. Davis, and Laura Connolly. 1997. "Accounting for the Decline in AFDC Caseloads: Welfare Reform or Economic Growth?" Institute for Research on Poverty discussion paper 1151–97. Madison: University of Wisconsin, Madison.

Chapter 9

THE IMPACT OF LABOR MARKET PROSPECTS ON INCARCERATION RATES

WILLIAM DARITY JR. AND SAMUEL L. MYERS JR.

There is a long-standing theoretical proposition stating that prisons serve as labor-market equilibriating devices (Rusche and Kirchheimer 1939). When there is superfluous labor, imprisonment rates rise to drain off unwanted workers. When labor shortages exist, imprisonment rates adapt to release needed workers into the labor market. If this proposition is correct, then during the most recent period of substantially tightening of labor markets, should there have been a reduction in imprisonment? Should the least-wanted workers, young black males, have experienced declines in their incarceration rates? In other words, if the proposition is correct, tighter labor-market conditions should be accompanied by less-restrictive patterns of punishment.

Conventional economic models posit another link between incarceration and unemployment. Lower incarceration rates and reduced crime should flow from improved labor-market prospects in conventional economic models (Myers 1998; Myers and Simms 1988; Witte 1980; Phillips, Votey, and Maxwell 1972). There might be no relationship at all between arrests, incarceration, and crime and the business cycle: the operable connection is the connection between *crime* and *unemployment*. This alternative perspective, frequently presented by economists, asserts a passive role for the government in the determination of imprisonment. However, the Georg Rusche and Otto Kirchheimer proposition posits an active role of the government much in the same way that Piven and Cloward (1971) see an active role of the state in the operation of welfare rules regulating the poor.

In this chapter, we show that there has indeed been a long-term pattern of higher incarceration rates accompanying higher unemployment rates, consistent with the Rusche and Kirchheimer thesis. However, data from the United States in more recent years reveals a marked departure from this pattern. A more-detailed analysis of recent patterns of black imprisonment across states suggests that tightness of labor markets not only fails to dampen the impact of unemployment on incarceration rates, it can even worsen those impacts. Indeed, in the 1990s black incarceration rates across the fifty states have increased measurably over rates observed in the 1970s. Moreover, we conclude that changing labor-market conditions cannot be the only source of the surge in imprisonment. Policy changes during the 1980s exercise a considerable influence on black imprisonment in the 1990s.

Theoretical Context

Conventional wisdom holds that conditions of high unemployment are, at least in part, linked to increased participation in crime (Freeman 1988; Myers 1983). Among blacks, particularly black males, unemployment also has been viewed as a causal force contributing to widening racial disparities in arrests and incarceration (Darity, Myers, Sabol, and Carson 1994).

Recent reports of dramatic reductions in crime in many urban areas during a period of low unemployment seem to support the relationship between joblessness and criminality. However, the connection between joblessness and a widening racial gap in incarceration rates requires a more fundamental macroeconomic understanding of the social function of imprisonment. Prisons might serve as repositories for those segments of the population deemed superfluous or as a "surplus" (see Darity 1983, 1995)—a surplus whose numbers swell even more during business cycle downturns (see Myers and Sabol 1987a, 1987b).

The recent observation that racial disparities in arrests and incarceration persist and, in many metropolitan areas, widen raises core questions about the asymmetrical nature of improved employment opportunities. It also suggests that the so-called surplus population is increasingly identified and contained according to criteria that are now largely independent from employment conditions and employability.

One of the earliest statements to hypothesize a systematic relationship between imprisonment and surplus populations is found in Rusche and Kirchheimer's (1939) classic study, *Punishment and Social Structure*. In their study, the authors trace the prison system's evolution from the mercantilist period through industrialization and modern capitalism in Europe. They argue that changes in punishment and imprisonment were dictated by fluctuations in the economy. For example, Rusche and Kirchheimer (citing L. O. Pike [1876]) observe:

> The year 1815, when the troops returned home and began to compete with other laborers, saw a marked increase in convictions, as did 1825, the year of the great commercial depression. In 1835, on the other hand, a sharp drop in the price of corn, continuing the price fall of the three previous years, was accompanied by a considerable decrease in the number of prison commitments. (97)

Furthermore, Rusche and Kirchheimer contend that the *form* of punishment responds to the demands of the economic system. In early medieval Europe, where there was little need for state punishment in a feudal economic system, fines and penance dominated. Variations in the harshness of punishment resulted from class distinctions among wrongdoers (9). In the later Middle Ages, as the inability of the lowest classes to pay monetary fines increased, punishment shifted to corporal and capital. By the seventeenth century, with the ascent of mercantilism, imprisonment as a form of punishment emerged as a preferred labor-market equilibrating device:

> The possibility of exploiting labor of prisoners now received increasing attention. Galley slavery, deportation, and penal servitude at hard labor were introduced, the first two only for a time, the third as the hesitant precursor of an institution which has lasted into the present. Sometimes they appeared together with the traditional system of fines and capital and corporal punishment; at other times they tended to displace the latter. These changes were not the result of humanitarian considerations, but of certain economic developments which revealed the potential value of a mass of human material completely at the disposal of the administration. (24)

Correspondingly, the central hypothesis advanced in Rusche (1978) and Rusche and Kirchheimer (1939) is that the punishment of the lowest classes responds to the tightness of labor markets:

[T]he criminal law and the daily work of the criminal courts are directed almost exclusively against those people whose class background, poverty, neglected education, or demoralization drove them to crime. . . . If penal sanctions are supposed to deter these strata from crime in an effective manner, they must appear worse than the strata's present living conditions. One can also formulate this proposition as follows: all efforts to reform punishment of criminals are invariably limited by the situation of the lowest socially significant proletarian cells which society wants to deter from criminal acts. . . . Unemployed masses, who tend to commit crimes of desperation because of hunger and deprivation, will only be stopped from doing so through cruel penalties. . . . In a society in which workers are scarce, penal sanctions have a completely different function. They do not have to stop hungry masses from satisfying elementary needs. If everybody who wants to work can find work, if the lowest social class consists of unskilled workers and not of wretched unemployed workers, then punishment is required to make the unwilling work, and to teach other criminals that they have to content themselves with the income of an honest worker. (Rusche 1978, 3–4)

Empirical tests of the Rusche and Kirchheimer hypothesis yield conflicting results. Some reviews show an association between changes in the labor market and incarceration rates (D'Alessio and Stolzenberg 1995, 351; Chiricos and DeLone 1992). Others contend that these findings only relate to aggregate data sets (Chiricos and Bales 1991; Sabol 1989) or analyses relating unemployment rates and incarceration rates for young black males exclusively (Chiricos and Bales 1991).

One criticism of tests that do show support for the Rusche and Kirchheimer hypothesis is that those tests rely too heavily on incarceration data. Even when using disaggregated data, Stewart J. D'Alessio and Lisa Stolzenberg (1995) assert, preincarceration data should be used, arguing that it is the actions of courts that bring into operation the Rusche and Kirchheimer mechanisms. Using such data, D'Alessio and Stolzenberg find no statistically significant impact of unemployment rates on incarceration rates.

But is the use of unemployment data appropriate for a test of the Rusche and Kirchheimer idea? The intellectual tradition that has prompted a resurgence of the proposition seems far less concerned with "unemployment" per se than it is concerned with joblessness and the marginalization of the lowest social classes (Jankovic 1978;

Chambliss 1969; Chambliss and Seidman 1971). Therefore, tests that limit investigation to unemployment alone potentially provide inadequate assessments of the Rusche and Kirchheimer model. Nonparticipation in the labor force, joblessness, and duration of unemployment or nonemployment are all plausible surrogates for the phenomenon of marginalization that the Rusche and Kirchheimer articulated more than a half century ago.

Post–World War II Trends

Figure 9.1 plots prison incarceration rates in the United States for the period spanning 1948 to 1995 against overall unemployment. There is a distinct, though slightly positive, trend evidenced in the figure. Generally speaking, when unemployment is high, incarceration rates are high also.

However, there are substantial deviations from the trend in the post-1980s era, and figure 9.1 shows that these outliers rise far above the fitted line. The departures from the long-term proportional rela-

Figure 9.1 Unemployment Versus Incarceration

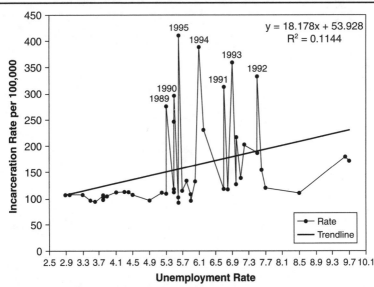

Source: Unemployment rates—United States Bureau of the Census, Historical Statistics of the United States, Colonial Times to 1970, and Economic Report of the President, Feb. 1998. Incarceration rates and crime index rates—Bureau of Justice Statistics Bulletin and Prisoners in 1993.

tionship between unemployment and imprisonment share one thing in common: they all occur during the 1990s. The substantial rise in incarceration rates in America dates to the late 1980s, a period that coincided with increases in overall unemployment, particularly among black males. But the rise in imprisonment continued long after black (and overall) unemployment began to ebb. The departures observed in figure 9.1 contradict the hypothesis that imprisonment serves as a straightforward vehicle for disciplining and containing the surpluses that arise from high unemployment. When one plots in figure 9.2 the relationship between unemployment and incarceration in the period since 1980, a reversal is apparent; there is an unexpected inverse relationship between unemployment rates and incarceration rates. At least since 1980, higher unemployment rates are associated with lower incarceration rates. This derives principally from the coincidence of soaring incarceration and tight labor markets in recent years.

If the Rushe and Kirchheimer model speaks to superfluous labor, then one should observe a relationship between black unemploy-

Figure 9.2 Unemployment Versus Incarceration, Post 1980

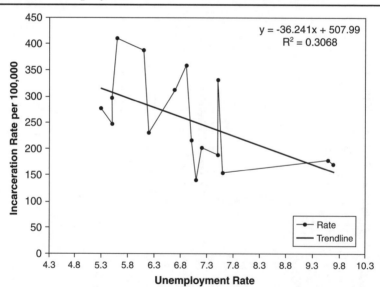

Source: Unemployment rates—United States Bureau of the Census, Historical Statistics of the United States, Colonial Times to 1970, and Economic Report of the President, Feb. 1998. Incarceration rates and crime index rates—Bureau of Justice Statistics Bulletin and Prisoners in 1993.

ment and black incarceration. It is not possible, however, to explore such a relationship using published data for any sustained period: from 1948 until the 1990s, for example, there are many gaps in the racial coverage of incarceration rates.

Nevertheless, we report in table 9.1 alternative specifications of the relationship between black-male unemployment nationally and overall imprisonment rates between 1948 and 1995. The apparent correlation between unemployment and incarceration observed in figure 9.1 could be wholly spurious. It is true that in 1970 there were less than 200,000 persons incarcerated in America, and it is also true that black unemployment rates were lower in the late 1960s than they were throughout most of the following decades. Still, it is hard to conclude that the rise of imprisonment during the 1990s—reaching previously unattained levels of more than 1.5 million persons incarcerated in state and federal prisons—can be blamed solely on black-male unemployment, for that conclusion would have required black-male unemployment rates to continue to explode during the 1990s while incarceration rates also were growing at unprecedented rates. But black-male unemployment rates did not continue to rise in the 1990s.

Therefore, results reported in table 9.1 take appropriate account of the possibility that the correlation between black unemployment and national incarceration rates is spurious. Generalized least-squares estimates that correct for first-order autocorrelation are compared with ordinary least-squares estimates with and without control for lagged crime-index rates. (Note that the sample of states with complete time series on the crime index is only thirty-seven.) We also consider specifications that include the ratio of black unemployment to white unemployment. The conclusion is inescapable: when correction is made for first-order autocorrelation, the apparent impact of black unemployment on incarceration rates disappears altogether. Table 9.1 presents results detailing this conclusion. Definitions of all variables are provided in table 9.2.

We list the impacts of increases in the black-male unemployment on incarceration rates obtained from OLS (ordinary least squares) estimates in first and second columns of table 9.1. Increases in the black-male unemployment rate increase incarceration. The marginal impact drops, however, when control is made for lagged crime

(*Text continues on page 291.*)

Table 9.1 OLS and GLS Estimates of Effects of Unemployment Rate on Incarceration Rate from 1948 to 1995 Time Series Data (*t*-Statistics in Parentheses)

| | Dependent Variables: Incarceration Rate | | | | | | | |
| | (1) (N = 48) | | (2) (N = 37) | | (3) (N = 48) | | (4) (N = 37) | |
Independent Variables	OLS	GLS[a]	OLS	GLS[a]	OLS	GLS[a]	OLS	GLS[a]
Unemployment rate for black males	10.249 (9.097)	0.304 (0.394)	4.270 (1.572)	−0.091 (−0.072)				
Post-1980	118.044 (5.178)	15.383 (1.321)	100.256 (3.498)	14.776 (1.064)	165.475 (9.222)	15.357 (1.281)	179.564 (6.194)	13.101 (0.855)
Ratio of unemployment rates for black males/white males					47.726 (8.216)	6.667 (0.522)	52.295 (4.889)	15.833 (0.857)
Low gap of unemployment rate between white males and black males					36.800 (3.050)	−0.257 (−0.054)	57.975 (2.474)	1.343 (0.206)

High unemployment rate for black males				-71.383 (-3.121)	-2.337 (-0.381)	-68.057 (-2.597)	-3.051 (-0.411)
Low unemployment rate for black males				-20.238 (-1.356)	-4.143 (-0.775)	-38.985 (-1.678)	-5.890 (-0.529)
Lag of crime index rate		18.566 (2.219)	3.934 (0.501)			-5.908 (-0.75)	5.217 (0.624)
Auto-correlation	0.998		0.997		0.998		
Adjusted R^2	0.465	0.511	0.997	0.765	0.998	0.741	0.996
F	41.87	19.84		39.19		21.56	

Source: Unemployment rates—United States Bureau of the Census, Historical Statistics of the United States, Colonial Times to 1970, and Economic Report of the President, Feb. 1998. Incarceration rates and crime index rates—Bureau of Justice Statistics Bulletin and Prisoners in 1993.

[a] The GLS models correct for first-order autocorrelation.

Table 9.2 Definitions of the Variables Used

	1948 Through 1995 Time-Series Data Analysis	
Variables	Mean	Description
IR	158.677	Number of incarcerations per 100,000 residents[a]
Log IR	4.961	Log of incarceration rate
Unemployment for white totals	5.098	Unemployment rate for total whites (percentage)[b]
Unemployment for white males	5.006	Unemployment rate for white males (percentage)[b]
Unemployment for minorities	10.917	Unemployment rate for total nonwhites (percentage)[b]
Unemployment for black males	10.712	Unemployment rate for black males (percentage)[b]
Ratio of unemployment, minorities/whites	2.127	The ratio of unemployment rates for total nonwhites to total whites
Ratio of unemployment, blacks/whites	2.138	The ratio of unemployment rates for black males to white males
Offense	9.209	Crime index total[a]
Offense Rate	3.989	Crime index rate[a]
Lag of offense rate	3.954	Lag of crime-index rate
Low gap of unemployment rate	.563	A dummy variable indicating low gap of unemployment rate between white males and black males :If RU_BMWM<2.2, then 1. Elsewhere 0.
High unemployment rate for black males	.104	A dummy variable indicating high unemployment rate for black males :If U_BM>=15, then 1. Elsewhere 0.
Low unemployment rate for black males	.417	A dummy variable indicating low unemployment rate for black males :If U_BM<10, then 1. Elsewhere 0.
Post-1980	.313	A dummy variable indicating post- or prior to 1980

Pooled Cross Sectional-Time Series State Level Data Analysis

Variables	Mean		Descriptions
	Blacks	Whites	
incarceration rate	1241.03	137.77	The number of incarcerations per 100,000 residents[c]
unemployment rate	.169	.068	The proportion of males unemployed last week
weeks unemployed	2.677	.917	The number of weeks looking for job up to the survey week
weeks not working	10.803	7.102	(Fifty-two—the number of weeks working last year)
labor-force nonparticipation rate for age group twenty-four and under	.501	.361	The proportion of males not in the labor force last week for age group twenty-four and under
labor-force nonparticipation rate for age group twenty-five to thirty-four	.125	.052	The proportion of males not in the labor force last week for age group twenty-five to thirty-four
labor-force nonparticipation rate for age group thirty-five and over	.358	.286	The proportion of males not in the labor force last week for age group thirty-five and over
weeks not in the labor force for age group twenty-four and under	12.608	9.901	Weeks not in the labor force last year for age group twenty-four and under: (fifty-two weeks working –weeks looking for job)
weeks not in the labor force for age group twenty-five to thirty-four	12.113	6.025	Weeks not in the labor force last year for age group twenty-five to thirty-four: (fifty-two weeks working–weeks looking for job)
weeks not in the labor force for age group thirty-five and over	20.970	16.143	Weeks not in the labor force last year for age group thirty-five and over: (fifty-two weeks working –weeks looking for job)
top quartile of unemployment rate	.299	.284	A dummy variable indicating high unemployment rate: if unemployment rate is in the top quartile of unemployment rates from 1979 to 1995 within a state, then 1; elsewhere 0.

(Table continues on page 290.)

Table 9.2 *Continued*

Pooled Cross Sectional-Time Series State Level Data Analysis

Variables	Mean		Descriptions
	Blacks	Whites	
bottom quartile of unemployment rate	.172	.228	A dummy variable indicating low unemployment rate: if unemployment rate is in the bottom quartile of unemployment rates from 1979 to 1995 within a state, then 1; elsewhere 0.
p_centcity	.516	.229	The proportion of residents in central cities
p_manufact	.089	.092	The proportion of workers employed in manufacturing
kid6	.447	.356	Average number of children under six
kid618	.905	.757	Average number of children six to eighteen
p_poor	.307	.111	The proportion of family on the poverty level
income	$7,530.	$11,974.	Average income (continuous)
age	28.212	34.589	Average age (continuous)
education	9.019	10.308	Average education level (continuous)
p_college	.133	.213	The proportion of people over twenty-five who are college graduates
neast	.173	.176	A dummy variable for northeast region
mwest	.238	.235	A dummy variable for Midwest
west	.251	.255	A dummy variable for West
POST91		.235	A dummy variable for periods post-1991

Source: United States Bureau of the Census, Current Population Survey (CPS).

[a] United States Department of Justice, Bureau of Justice Statistics, *Bulletin and Prisoners in 1993.*

[b] United States Bureau of the Census, *Historical Statistics of the United States, Colonial Times to 1970* and *Economic Report of the President* (1998).

[c] United States Department of Justice, *Sourcebook of Criminal Justice Statistics.*

rates. Increases in the black-white ratio of male unemployment also lead to reductions in incarceration rates, as seen in third and fourth columns for the OLS estimations. The estimated effect of a one-unit increase in the black-white ratio increases the numbers of persons incarcerated per 100,000 population from 48 to 52 in the OLS model. The effect is statistically significant. When lagged crime rates are controlled for in this specification, the effect of crime is statistically insignificant.

These results, which appear to support the Rushe and Kirchheimer results, vanish when one takes account of autocorrelation. The Generalized Least Squares (GLS) model reveals substantially smaller impacts—ranging from 7 to 16 prisoners per 100,000 population—of relative black-male unemployment on incarceration rates. These diminished impacts are not statistically different from zero.

The effects of lagged crime rates are uniformly statistically insignificant in the GLS models. That is, upon correction for autocorrelation, crime has no apparent impact on incarceration. While conventional economic models of crime suggest a reverse of this relationship by positing a causal impact of punishment on crime, such endogeniety of crime cannot arise in our specification because we use lagged crime rates as an independent variable.

In short, support for the Rushe-Kirchheimer model is not consistent. The long-term pattern shown in figure 9.1 is not robust with respect to alternative specifications and estimation techniques. It is questionable, given the evidence from table 9.1, precisely how imprisonment works as a reservoir for the unwanted, superfluous labor in our society. The evidence presented in table 9.1 also leads to doubts over whether incarceration works as such a reservoir at all.

In summary, using simple descriptive measures, we reach these initial conclusions:

- There is a visual association between unemployment and incarceration between 1948 and 1995.

- The association between unemployment and incarceration is not robust with respect to various model specifications and estimation methods.

- There are significant outliers in the long-term incarceration and unemployment patterns that arise in the post-1990 time frame.

One can inquire, therefore, what if any impact tightness of labor markets has on incarceration rates: Does the relationship between employment prospects and imprisonment depend on how one evaluates disengagement from work? Does it depend on the age or racial group? We address these issues next.

EFFECTS OF UNEMPLOYMENT AND LABOR-FORCE PARTICIPATION ON BLACK VERSUS WHITE INCARCERATION RATES

Two immediate objections can be made to our findings above. First, if there is any relationship at all between black unemployment and incarceration, it arguably would be between black unemployment and *black* incarceration. Such a comparison, though, would be extremely difficult to make for the 1948 to 1995 period, because data on black incarceration rates is unavailable in a long, uninterrupted time series. Furthermore, comparisons of black imprisonment across years using the National Prisoner Statistics data can be misleading: prior to the 1980s, not all states provided full reporting on race and imprisonment.

A second objection is that unemployment rates imprecisely state the degree to which black males are marginalized in the labor market. High rates of joblessness are accompanied by low levels of labor-force attachment and long periods of absence from legitimate labor-market activities. Those persons out of the labor force do not enter into the numbers of the officially measured unemployed, but they could be construed as swelling the ranks of the surplus population.

To account for these two objections, we have compiled data on black and white incarceration rates and on various measures of black and white unemployment and labor-force participation between 1979 and 1995 by state. By creating a pooled cross section and time series, we overcome the immediate limitation posed by the short time series. As an added benefit, this particular period covers the puzzling epoch when incarceration rates rose continuously even though there were wide swings in black and white unemployment rates.

To create the pooled cross-section time-series data set, we compiled unemployment rates by state and race from the Unicon-Current Population Survey-March Supplement Tapes for 1967 through 1996. The actual series of state unemployment rates by race is for 1979 through 1995, in order to match the criminal-justice statistics. The *Sourcebook on Criminal Statistics* (United States Department of Justice, Bureau of Justice Statistics, 1996) was used to obtain state incarceration rates by race (thirty-seven states for blacks) for 1979 through 1995. Other variables include income, age, education, manufacturing employment, poverty, number of children, central city residence, and region were computed from the Current Population Survey data.[1]

It must be noted that using state level incarceration rates introduces another problem. Just as incarceration rates differ substantially from state to state, racial differences in incarceration rates also vary quite dramatically across states. For example, Minnesota, with a relatively low black population, has one of the nation's highest racial disparities in incarceration rates, a fact owing principally to the relatively low white incarceration rates in that state. Moreover, drug policies, "three strikes and you're out" legislation, and sentencing reforms leading to longer prison sentences all have different impacts on state-level incarceration rates. Finally, differing prison construction policies and alternatives-to-prison strategies have resulted in widely varied implications for changes in imprisonment across states. Accordingly, a model that ignores the possibility of state-specific effects is likely to misstate the relationship between black unemployment and labor-force participation and black incarceration.

We hypothesize, then, that the incarceration rate in time t for state i for the kth racial group, ir_{it}^k, is a function of the unemployment rate (or nonparticipation in the labor force) in time t for state i for the kth racial group, un_{it}^k, and a vector of characteristics of states given by x_{it}^k. Or,

$$ir_{it}^k = \mu^k + \beta^k x_{it}^k + \gamma^k un_{it}^k + u_{it}^k$$

more formally (Hsaio 1986, 11–47; Greene 1993, 444–80):

where:

ir_{it}^k = prison incarceration rate for the ith state in time t for the kth racial group;

a_i^k = a fixed or random effect of the ith state for the kth racial group;

μ^k = a fixed or random common intercept across all states;

β^k = a vector of (constant) coefficients estimated separately for each racial group;

x_{it}^k = a vector of independent variables observed for each race for each state in each year;

γ^k = a coefficient measuring the effect of unemployment (or labor force participation) on incarceration rates, estimated for each racial group;

un_{it}^k = unemployment (or nonparticipation in the labor force) for each racial group for each state in each year; and

u_{it}^k = an error term randomly distributed with a zero mean and a common variance.

As established by Cheng Hsaio (1986) and William H. Greene (1993), OLS estimates of this model will be biased. Two alternative estimators, fixed effects and random effects, are considered in table 9.3, for five different models. To capture annual labor-market outcomes for each race in each state, the first uses unemployment rates, the second weeks unemployed, and the third weeks not working.

The fourth model uses annual labor-force nonparticipation rates for each race in each state and each year, computed separately for three different age groups. The fifth and final model uses weeks not in the labor force for each race in each state and each year, computed separately for three different age groups: persons under twenty-four years of age, persons twenty-five to thirty-four, and persons over thirty-five. Note that inclusion of the means for these three age groups within a state for each year for each race does not introduce an inappropriate collinearity, as would be the case if these were dummy variables representing age groups in a model estimated using individual-level data. Instead, we have age-specific measures of labor-force nonparticipation aggregated at the state level.[2]

Our findings, reported in table 9.3, lead us to the following conclusions:

- Higher unemployment either does not lead to increased incarceration rates, or the OLS estimates overstate (in absolute value) the effects of unemployment on incarceration.[3]

- When labor-market outcomes are measured by weeks not working or not participating in the labor force, there are consistent proportional effects of these measures on incarceration rates. These impacts—when they are statistically significant—are considerably larger for blacks than for whites. These effects for blacks remain evident under alternative estimates of the effects on incarceration of weeks not working.

Table 9.3 Effects of Unemployment and Labor Force Nonparticipation on Incarceration from State-Level Longitudinal Data from 1979 to 1995 (*t*-Statistics in Parentheses)

	Independent Variable(s)	Blacks (N = 551 for Models 1 to 3, N = 285 for Models 4 to 5)	Whites (N = 699)
		Dependent Variable: Incarceration Rate per 100,000 Residents	
Model 1			
OLS	Unemployment rate	−404.617 (−1.419)	−237.383 (−3.362)
Random Effect		−60.658 (−0.261)	−47.250 (−0.891)
Fixed Effect		−13.637 (−0.049)	−53.683 (−1.045)
Model 2			
OLS	Weeks unemployed	−12.338 (−1.179)	−11.650 (−3.625)
Random Effect		1.401 (0.162)	−3.423 (−1.428)
Fixed Effect		3.933 (0.390)	−3.831 (−1.699)
Model 3			
OLS	Weeks not working	10.692 (1.418)	−2.294 (−1.280)
Random Effect		10.246 (1.696)	−.751 (−0.613)
Fixed Effect		10.294 (1.452)	−.858 (−0.680)
Model 4			
OLS	Labor-Force Nonparticipation rate		
	for age group twenty-four and under	21.584 (0.109)	−40.287 (−1.307)
	for age group twenty-five to thirty-four	644.932 (2.575)	115.663 (1.461)
	for age group thirty-five and over	180.022 (0.630)	18.476 (0.289)
Random Effect[a]	Labor-Force Nonparticipation rate		
	for age group twenty-four and under	—	20.133 (0.945)
	for age group twenty-five to thirty-four	—	66.382 (1.281)
	for age group thirty-five and over	—	109.239 (2.200)

(*Table continues on page 296.*)

Table 9.3 *Continued*

	Dependent Variable: Incarceration Rate per 100,000 Residents	
Independent Variable(s)	Blacks (N = 551 for Models 1 to 3, N = 285 for Models 4 to 5)	Whites (N = 699)
Fixed Effect		
Labor-Force Nonparticipation rate		
for age group twenty-four and under	−53.198 (−0.291)	21.659 (1.050)
for age group twenty-five to thirty-four	519.100 (2.311)	67.967 (1.361)
for age group thirty-five and over	381.295 (1.324)	112.345 (2.298)
Model 5 OLS		
Weeks not in the labor force		
for age group twenty-four and under	−10.316 (−1.271)	−3.159 (−2.440)
for age group twenty-five to thirty-four	7.368 (1.647)	−1.259 (−0.996)
for age group thirty-five and over	8.482 (1.456)	.662 (−0.547)
Random Effect[a]		
Weeks not in the labor force		
for age group twenty-four and under	—	−.608 (−0.738)
for age group twenty-five to thirty-four	—	.220 (0.273)
for age group thirty-five and over	—	1.261 (1.400)
Fixed Effect		
Weeks not in the labor force		
for age group twenty-four and under	−14.466 (−1.953)	−.403 (−0.472)
for age group twenty-five to thirty-four	4.148 (1.062)	.215 (0.257)
for age group thirty-five and over	6.938 (1.192)	1.210 (1.271)

Source: U.S. Bureau of the Census, Current Population Survey (CPS) and *Sourcebook of Criminal Justice Statistics.*
The OLS models and the random-effect models control for the proportion of residents in central cities, the proportion of workers employed in manufacturing, the number of children under six and six to eighteen, the proportion of family on poverty level, income, age, education level, the proportion of college graduates, regional variables, and the fixed-effect models control for all the same variables except for the regional variables.
[a] These random-effect models for blacks cannot be estimated due to negative variances of individual effect.

- When labor-force nonparticipation rates are computed separately by age group, the positive effect of labor-market detachment on black incarceration rates is larger for twenty-five- to thirty-four-year-olds than it is for other age groups.[4]

The estimates provided in the table come from equations that control for the proportion of residents residing in central-city areas, the proportion of workers employed in manufacturing, the average number of children under six years of age, the average number of children between six and eighteen years of age, the proportion of families with incomes below the poverty level, average income, average age, mean education completion, proportion of residents with college degrees, and, in the OLS and random-effects models, regional dummies.

Effects of Labor-Market Tightness on Incarceration Rates

Tables 9.4 and 9.5 examine more closely the specification of the effect of non-labor-force participation on incarceration by focusing on weeks not in the labor force and the non-labor-force participation rate. Doing so permits an assessment how tight labor markets influence incarceration rates.

We measure tightness of labor markets in the following manner: On a state-by-state basis, we compiled unemployment rates from 1979 to 1995 for each race. Ranking those rates from highest to lowest, we created a dummy variable indicating whether the unemployment rate for a given group is in the top quartile or lowest quartile of rates during the period. Operationally, a state in a given year was identified as having a "tight" labor market when its unemployment rate fell into the bottom quartile and a "loose" labor market when its unemployment rate was in the upper quartile.

Fixed-effects and random-effects estimates of the influence of top- and bottom-quartile years on incarceration rates are presented in table 9.4. The impact of bottom-quartile years is consistently larger than that of top-quartile years. And while both impacts are statistically insignificant among whites, bottom-quartile impacts are uniformly significant among blacks. Controlling for nonparticipation in the labor force or weeks not working within each age group reveals that tightness of labor markets raises black incarceration rates by 57 to 67 persons per 100,000 black residents.

Table 9.4 Effects of Labor-Market Tightness and Labor-Force Nonparticipation on Incarceration from State-Level Longitudinal Data from 1979 to 1995 (*t*-Statistics in Parentheses)

Dependent Variable: Incarceration Rate per 100,000 Residents

Independent Variables	Blacks (N = 285)				Whites (N = 699)			
	Random Effect		Fixed Effect		Random Effect		Fixed Effect	
Top quartile of unemployment rate	28.005 (1.821)	32.463 (1.292)	24.753 (0.744)	23.157 (0.680)	−1.246 (−0.463)	−1.574 (−0.607)	−1.500 (−0.585)	−1.911 (−0.714)
Bottom quartile of unemployment rate	56.876 (3.512)	65.496 (2.465)	57.200 (1.646)	66.650 (1.892)	1.518 (0.550)	1.724 (0.670)	1.627 (0.619)	1.807 (0.680)
Labor-force nonparticipation rate								
for age group twenty-four and under	−46.766 (−0.550)		−38.531 (−0.210)		22.551 (1.039)		24.434 (1.172)	
for age group twenty-five to thirty-four	536.399 (5.126)		539.179 (2.398)		64.208 (1.225)		65.772 (1.314)	
for age group thirty-five and over	353.919 (2.656)		364.160 (1.265)		108.188 (2.156)		111.119 (2.266)	
Weeks not in the labor force								
for age group twenty-four and under		−14.985 (−2.701)		−15.178 (−2.044)		−0.507 (−0.610)		−0.283 (−0.328)
for age group twenty-five to thirty-four		4.985 (1.648)		5.008 (1.242)		0.453 (0.537)		0.486 (0.555)
for age group thirty-five and over		8.073 (1.854)		7.758 (1.312)		1.361 (1.502)		1.328 (1.386)

Source: U.S. Bureau of the Census, Current Population Survey and *Sourcebook of Criminal Justice Statistics.*

The random-effect models control for the proportion of residents in central cities, the proportion of workers employed in manufacturing, the number of children under six and six to eighteen, the proportion of family on poverty level, income, age, education level, the proportion of college graduates, regional variables, and the fixed-effect models control for all the same variables except for the regional variables.

In table 9.5 we present reestimates of the models described in table 9.4, but we include only the labor-force nonparticipation rates and weeks in the labor force for twenty-five- to thirty-four-year-olds. Table 9.5 also displays estimates that control only for bottom-quartile unemployment rates and exclude the dummy variable for top-quartile years. The estimated coefficients on the labor-market-tightness variable remain remarkably stable. When a state's black-unemployment rates are low relative to the state's rate over the 1979 to 1995 period, black incarceration rates are consistently higher by around 55 persons per 100,000.

The conclusion we reach from the information displayed in these two tables is that the degree of a labor market's tightness does exacerbate incarceration rates of blacks, but regardless of whether labor markets are "loose" or "tight," black males experience rates of imprisonment higher than others. No such effect is observed for white males.

The Post-1990 Era

The conclusion that the degree of labor-market tightness contributes to heightened black incarceration rates must be balanced against the fact that low unemployment characterized a number of the outliers shown in figure 9.1. These outlying dates occurred during the 1990s. Could the observed effects of unemployment or labor-force participation be the result of failure to account for the more-recent general surge in black-male incarceration rates? Do the estimated labor-market effects survive a final respecification of the model that replaces controls for tightness of labor markets with measures of the post-1990 phenomenon of rapidly rising black incarceration rates?

Table 9.6 provides data to address these questions. We estimate equations separately for black and white incarceration rates, controlling for unemployment rates, weeks unemployed, weeks not working, age-specific labor-force nonparticipation rates, and age-specific weeks not in the labor force. In each equation we also control for the post-1990 era. Across a wide variety of fixed as well as random effects specifications—using various measures of unemployment and labor-force nonparticipation—the post-1990 effects are quite robust.

In the post-1990 decade, black incarceration rates rose by around 500 to 600 prisoners per 100,000 population. White incarceration rates systematically fell by approximately 50 per 100,000. These highly

Table 9.5 Effects of Labor-Market Tightness on Incarceration from State-Level Longitudinal Data from 1979 to 1995 (*t*-Statistics in Parentheses)

	Dependent Variable: Incarceration Rate per 100,000 residents							
	Blacks (N = 285)							
Independent Variables	Random Effect				Fixed Effect			
Top quartile of unemployment rate	—ᵃ	—ᵃ	30.946 (1.17)		27.798 (0.842)		22.131 (0.654)	
Bottom quartile of unemployment rate	—ᵃ	—ᵃ	57.669 (2.05)	50.857 (1.78)	58.347 (1.68)	51.902 (1.53)	59.237 (1.68)	54.875 (1.59)
Labor-Force Nonparticipation rate for age group twenty-five to thirty-four	—ᵃ	—ᵃ			521.14 (2.32)	524.83 (2.34)		
Weeks not in the labor force for age group twenty-five to thirty-four			4.880 (1.52)	5.538 (1.68)			4.729 (1.16)	5.213 (1.31)

Source: U.S. Bureau of the Census, Current Population Survey and *Sourcebook of Criminal Justice Statistics.*

Note: The random-effect models control for the proportion of residents in central cities, the proportion of workers employed in manufacturing, the number of children under six and six to eighteen, the proportion of family on poverty level, income, age, education

significant and consistent findings remain even after accounting for variations in the social and demographic characteristics of the black and white populations in each state.

Our findings are robust with respect to differing assumptions about the way in which the assumption of homogeneous intercepts is violated. The substantial stability of the estimated coefficients on the post-1990 dummy variable suggests that far more important than tightness of labor markets in the 1990s is a simultaneous process that appears to be driving black incarceration rates upward while producing slightly lower white incarceration rates.

There are several plausible explanations for the most-recent surge in black incarceration rates. One is changing state policies regarding the organization and management of prison systems; privatization is a particular example. State policies encouraging privatization break

Whites (N = 699)							
Random Effect				Fixed Effect			
−1.334		−1.572		−1.584		−1.864	
(−0.537)		(−0.595)		(−0.620)		(−0.702)	
1.147	1.512	1.431	1.783	1.187	1.609	1.483	5.690
(0.447)	(0.628)	(0.544)	(0.697)	(0.451)	(0.633)	(0.561)	(1.19)
61.387	60.934			62.246	61.673		
(1.27)	(1.29)			(1.25)	(1.24)		
		0.374	0.237			0.418	0.322
		(0.434)	(0.287)			(0.479)	(0.248)

level, the proportion of college graduates, regional variables, and the fixed-effect models control for all the same variables except for the regional variables.
[a] These random-effect models cannot be estimated due to negative variances of individual effect.

the conventional tie between incarceration and the business cycle: even when unemployment rates are low, private prisons seek to keep empty beds at a minimum.

A second plausible explanation is that drug-enforcement policies of the 1980s have created long prison sentences for the crimes—such as possession of crack cocaine—that are associated with high black-arrest rates. This explanation suggests that the dummy variable for the post-1990s is capturing an accumulation of black prisoners who received longer sentences during the late 1980s "war on drugs."

A third possible reason is that the war on drugs of the 1980s and "three strikes and you're out" legislation of the 1990s sought to reduce crime via increased incarceration. To achieve that result, states increased prison capacity continuously, even after the growth in violent crime rates slowed. To keep prison space fully utilized, the state

Table 9.6 Post-1990 Impact on Labor-Market Model of Incarceration from State-Level Longitudinal Data from 1979 Through 1995 (*t*-Statistics in Parentheses)

	Independent Variables	Dependent Variable: Incarceration Rate per 100,000 Residents	
		Blacks (N = 551 for Models 1 to 3, N = 285 for Models 4 to 5)	Whites (N = 699)
Model 1 Random Effect	Unemployment rate	-44.924 (-0.194)	-35.571 (-0.687)
	Post-1990	546.574 (3.077)	-43.554 (-2.219)
Fixed Effect	Unemployment rate	-1.012 (-0.004)	-41.048 (-0.799)
	Post-1990	555.734 (2.646)	-51.959 (-2.620)
Model 2 Random Effect	Weeks unemployed	-.255 (-0.029)	-2.895 (-1.231)
	Post-1990	547.174 (3.014)	-41.842 (-2.071)
Fixed Effect	Weeks unemployed	2.071 (0.206)	-3.236 (-1.434)
	Post-1990	552.684 (2.625)	-50.508 (-2.547)
Model 3 Random Effect	Weeks not working	9.809 (1.664)	-.395 (-0.330)
	Post-1990	540.902 (1.924)	-45.011 (-2.440)
Fixed Effect	Weeks not working	9.850 (1.397)	-.450 (-0.355)
	Post-1990	548.710 (2.617)	-52.586 (-2.642)
Model 4 Random Effect[a]	Labor-Force Nonparticipation rate		
	for age group twenty-four and under	—	21.648 (1.039)
	for age group twenty-five to thirty-four	—	62.700 (1.237)
	for age group thirty-five and over	—	113.780 (2.341)
	Post-1990	—	-46.633 (-2.392)

Fixed Effect		
Labor-force nonparticipation rate		
for age group twenty-four and under	-60.142 (-0.334)	23.347 (1.137)
for age group twenty-five to thirty-four	500.269 (2.257)	64.243 (1.293)
for age group thirty-five and over	297.090 (1.040)	115.352 (2.372)
Post-1990	613.772 (2.830)	-54.596 (-2.775)
Model 5 **Random Effect**		
Weeks not in the labor force		
for age group twenty-four and under	-9.086 (-2.473)	-.841 (-1.063)
for age group twenty-five to thirty-four	3.810 (2.055)	.365 (0.473)
for age group thirty-five and over	6.327 (2.301)	1.493 (1.726)
Post-1990	511.237 (4.687)	-51.419 (-2.840)
Fixed Effect		
Weeks not in the labor force		
for age group twenty-four and under	-8.838 (-1.146)	-.681 (-.798)
for age group twenty-five to thirty-four	3.688 (0.951)	.384 (0.461)
for age group thirty-five and over	6.051 (1.047)	1.443 (1.520)
Post-1990	543.043 (2.376)	-58.186 (-2.914)

Source: U.S. Bureau of the Census, Current Population Survey and *Sourcebook of Criminal Justice Statistics.*
The OLS models and the random effect models control for the proportion of residents in central cities, the proportion of workers employed in manufacturing, the number of children under six and six to eighteen, the proportion of family on poverty level, income, age, education level, the proportion of college graduates, regional variables, and the fixed-effect models control for all the same variables except for the regional variables.
[a] The random-effect model for blacks cannot be estimated due to a negative variance of individual effect.

increased the use of imprisonment for less and less serious offenses, largely targeting young black males who were out of the labor force.

A final explanation, one that embraces parts of the previous three, is that there is an asymmetry in impacts of policies designed to curb or contain superfluous classes. During earlier periods of regular shifts between high and low unemployment rates, prison capacity remained largely stable. Adjustments in incarceration rates could accommodate both increases and reductions in unemployment or joblessness. In more recent years, however, after sustained increases in incarceration via increased use of imprisonment for less-serious crimes, it is no longer possible to reverse the process of incarceration when joblessness declines. Too much excess prison capacity would result.

These explanations converge in the view that labor-force nonparticipation and not unemployment is the operable measure of superfluity in the Rusche and Kirchheimer (1939) proposition when it is applied to the late twentieth century. We consistently find differential impacts of labor-force detachment on black versus white incarceration rates. This labor-force detachment, however, is imperfectly measured by unemployment rates in the current era, for which unemployment rates do not capture the notion of a superfluous pool of workers. That is why even when there are tight labor markets—unemployment rates registering in the lowest quartile over time within a state—black nonparticipation in the labor force continues to exert a large and persistent influence on black incarceration.

SUMMARY OF RESULTS

The foregoing discussion leads to the following conclusion: There is a visible pattern relating rising black unemployment or heightened gaps in black and white unemployment to overall incarceration rates. This visible pattern may be a case of spurious correlation and is not robust with respect to alternative model specifications. After 1990, significant outliers appear in long-term patterns of incarceration and unemployment. When alternative measures of labor-market detachment are investigated, we find that black labor-force nonparticipation—particularly among twenty-five- to thirty-four-year-olds—is indeed a significant determinant of rising black incarceration rates. Tightness of labor markets explains some of the rise in black incarceration rates in recent years. However, it seems to explain less of the rise than it does for the past. Labor-market tightness has no apparent effect on white incarceration rates. The most consistent and persistent factor explaining black and white incarceration rates is timing, particularly the unique dynamics of the post-1990 era. The impacts differ between blacks and whites. Controlling for social and demographic features of different states, we discover remarkably robust estimates of increased black incarceration—on the order of magnitude of 500 to 600 prisoners per 100,000 persons—and of reduced white incarceration rates equalling about 50 prisoners per 100,000.

We conclude that while labor-market tightness as well as labor-market detachment play large roles in the phenomenon of black incarceration rates in the 1990s, the larger puzzle of how and why the black incarceration rates soared in the 1990s remains. We speculate that the answer must lie in the intersection between privatization of prisons and the hardening of the social status of black males as a permanent surplus population. We also conclude that policy shifts in the 1990s, particularly those designed to punish less-serious crimes via incarceration, are far more important in understanding the rise in black imprisonment than are changes in the business cycle.

An earlier version of this paper was presented for the Russell Sage Conference on Labor Market Tightness and Black Employment, October 4, 1998. Helpful comments were received from Sanders Korenman and other participants of the seminar. Valuable research assistance was rendered by Yongjin Nho and Kevin Monroe. The time-series data set was created by Kevin Monroe while he was a McNair Fellow at the Roy Wilkins Center for Human Relations and Social Justice. Support from the McNair program is gratefully acknowledged.

NOTES

1. In earlier versions of this model, we also used lagged index crime rates by state. The sample size was further reduced by including crime rates. The substantive conclusions discussed in the paper, however, do not change when controls for lagged crime rates are added.

2. This aggregation was performed using the Unicon-Current Population Survey data set for 1962 through 1995. When merged with state imprisonment data for 1979 through 1995—the years for which a consistent race series is available—the result is a sample of less than all fifty states. The excluded states include those with insufficient data on blacks in the

CPS data or nonreporting of race in the National Population Survey data on imprisonment.

3. Table 9.3 does not display this information, but we have computed tests for the appropriateness of the OLS model. We reject the hypothesis that for each measure of unemployment the intercepts are homogeneous across states.

4. The conventional wisdom that low labor-force attachment among young black males leads to higher incarceration is not testable using these specifications, as the data are not broken down by gender. Also, nonparticipation in the labor force incorporates two opposing aspects of labor force withdrawal: persons not at work, not looking for work, and not in school, as well as persons not looking for work but in school.

REFERENCES

Chambliss, William J. 1969. *Crime and the Legal Process.* New York: McGraw-Hill.

Chambliss, William J., and Robert B. Seidman. 1971. *Law, Order, and Power.* Reading, Mass.: Addison-Wesley.

Chiricos, Theodore G., and William D. Bales. 1991. "Unemployment and Punishment: An Empirical Assessment." *Criminology* 29(4): 701–24.

Chiricos, Theodore G., and Miriam A. DeLone. 1992. "Labor Surplus and Punishment: A Review and Assessment of Theory and Evidence." *Social Problems* 39: 421–46.

D'Alessio, Stewart J., and Lisa Stolzenberg. 1995. "Unemployment and the Incarceration of Pretrial Defendants." *American Sociological Review* 60(3): 350–59.

Darity, William A., Jr. 1983. "The Managerial Class and Surplus Population." *Society* 21(1): 54–62.

———. 1995. "The Undesirables, America's Underclass in the Managerial Age: Beyond the Myrdal Theory of Racial Inequality." *Daedalus* 124(1): 145–66.

Darity, William A., Jr., Samuel L. Myers Jr., William Sabol, and Emmett Carson. 1994. *The Black Underclass: Critical Essays on Race and Unwantedness.* New York: Garland Press.

Freeman, Richard B. 1988. "Relation of Criminal Activity to Black Youth Employment." *Review of Black Political Economy* 16(1/2): 99–107

Greene, William H. 1993. *Econometric Analysis.* 2nd ed. London: MacMillan.

Hsiao, Cheng. 1986. *Analysis of Panel Data.* Cambridge, Eng.: Cambridge University Press.

Jankovic, Ivan. 1978. "Social Class and Criminal Sentencing." *Crime and Social Justice* (Fall/Winter): 9–16.

Myers, Samuel L., Jr. 1983. "Estimating the Economic Model of Crime: Employment vs. Punishment Effects." *Quarterly Journal of Economics* 98(1): 157–67.

———. 1986 "Black Unemployment and Its Link to Crime." *Urban League Review* 10(1): 98–105.

Myers, Samuel L., Jr. and William J. Sabol. 1987a. "Business Cycles and Racial Disparities in Punishment." *Contemporary Policy Issues* 5(October): 46–58.

———. 1987b. "Unemployment and Racial Differences in Imprisonment." *Review of Black Political Economy* 16(1/2): 189–209.

Myers, Samuel L., Jr., and Margaret Simms (eds.) 1988. *Economics of Race and Crime.* New Brunswick, N.J.: Transaction Books.

Phillips, Llad, Harold L. Votey Jr., and Darold Maxwell. 1972. "Crime, Youth, and the Labor Market." *Journal of Political Economy* 80(3, part 1): 491–504.

Pike, Luke O. 1876. *History of Crime in England: Illustrating the Changes of the Laws in the Progress of Civilization.* London: Smith, Elder and Co.

Piven, Frances Fox, and Richard Cloward. 1971. *Regulating the Poor: The Functions of Public Welfare.* New York: Pantheon Books.

Rusche, Georg. 1978. "Labor Market and Penal Sanction: Thoughts on the Sociology of Criminal Justice." *Crime and Social Justice* (Fall/Winter): 2–8.

Rusche, Georg, and Otto Kirchheimer. 1939. *Punishment and Social Structure.* New York: Columbia University Press.

Sabol, William J. 1989. "The Dynamics of Unemployment and Imprisonment in England and Wales, 1946–85." *Journal of Quantitative Criminology* 5(2): 147–68.

Witte, Anne D. 1980. "Estimating the Economic Model of Crime with Individual Data." *Quarterly Journal of Economics* 94(1): 57–83.

United States Department of Justice. Bureau of Justice Statistics. 1996. *Sourcebook of Criminal Justice Statistics.* Washington: United States Government Printing Office.

Commentary III

GLASS CEILINGS, IRON BARS, INCOME FLOORS

SANDERS KORENMAN

Differences and changes in economic status across demographic groups have been well documented. The occupation of policy-oriented scholars has been to interpret these differences and to propose remedies. A central point of disagreement and focus of investigation has been whether low economic status results from individual failures of one sort or another, or from forces that lie largely outside individuals' control. These papers, although far ranging, all touch upon this common theme.

Chapters by Joyce P. Jacobsen and Laurence M. Levin, and William Darity Jr. and Samuel L. Myers Jr. fall into the "outside forces" camp. Jacobsen and Levin focus on gender and racial inequality in the labor market, carefully documenting that women and blacks have lower returns than do white men to job tenure and later labor-market experience (experience beyond the first ten years). The evidence is consistent with the existence of a glass ceiling: discriminatory barriers that make it more difficult for certain groups, in this case women and minorities, to rise to positions of high pay and prestige. Skeptics, however, may remain unconvinced that the authors give adequate consideration to competing hypotheses. For example, an alternative interpretation of the lower return to experience or tenure for women emphasizes family responsibilities (see, for example, the articles collected in Blau and Ehrenberg 1997), which could affect human-capital investment decisions and career trajectories well beyond the tenth year of labor-market experience. Moreover, recent evidence has given more weight to the role of family responsibilities, revealing, for instance, that although gaps in pay between men and women persist, by the early 1990s, thirty-year-old childless women had reached pay parity with men, virtually eliminating a wage gap that stood near 30 percent in 1980 (Waldfogel 1998).

Continued research on the source of the gender differential is critical for formulating effective policy. If discriminatory treatment in promotion is to blame for gender (or race) differences in the returns to experience and tenure, stronger enforcement of civil rights laws is called for. If conflict between careers and family responsibilities is to blame, then expansion of family-leave benefits or child-care subsidies should be considered.

Darity and Myers ask whether economic conditions can account for the surge in incarceration of young black men in the 1980s and 1990s, and they conclude that incarceration has risen far beyond what can be explained by labor-market forces. To blame for this growth, they assert, is a new enforcement regime, possibly fueled by the privatization of prison management. This interesting hypothesis could be explored with state-level data. One must be careful not to confuse cause and effect in such analyses, however: states might be attracted to privatization to contain the costs of a growing prison population. Regardless of the cause, incarceration may have endangered the long-term economic prospects of a generation of black men (Freeman 1996; Freeman and Rodgers, this volume). More research is needed to guide policy to help integrate men released from prison into the labor market. State-level analyses such as those in the Darity and Myers paper could prove particularly useful in this regard.

Sandra Danziger and her team's description of barriers to work among Michigan welfare recipients suggests that both individual attributes and outside forces influence economic success. Their research provides data on the success of the landmark 1996 welfare reform legislation, the Personal Responsibility and Work Opportunity Reconciliation Act (PRWORA), to which I devote the remainder of my comments. The Danziger study and others like it are putting us in a better position to answer long-standing questions about the nature of poverty and the effects of welfare reform, and, perhaps, to pose new questions about the future direction of social-welfare policy.

- Can the typical welfare recipient or those at high risk of welfare receipt be expected to work?

Here, the answer is a clear yes. Danziger and her colleagues find that, despite multiple barriers to work, 62 percent of the sample of Michigan single mothers on welfare in February 1997 were employed ten months later; 57 percent worked over twenty hours per week and 28 percent worked over thirty-five hours per week. This result is consistent with the findings of other research that employment among single mothers has risen sharply. According to the *Economic Report of the President* (Economic Council of Advisers 1999), over 80 percent of single mothers participate in the labor force. Between the second quarter of 1996 and the second quarter of 1997 alone (roughly the year following the passage of PRWORA), the employment-to-population ratio of single mothers with children under age six—those most likely to be affected by welfare reform—jumped a whopping nine percentage points. Studies of persons leaving welfare in the post-reform era typically find that over half are employed (see, for example, Parrott 1998), a higher rate than found among those leaving pre-reform AFDC (see Bane and Ellwood 1994).

- Are those who work better off financially?

The answer to this question is a qualified yes. Take the case of Michigan, where the maximum monthly welfare benefit for a single mother with two children and no other income is $459. According to Danziger and colleagues, the (conditional) average weekly earnings for the Michigan sample was $208 (n. 4). At this rate, average monthly earnings would be $832, nearly twice the maximum welfare benefit. (Of course, the availability of subsidized child care is critical in all these comparisons; see chapter 8, appendix 8B.) Earnings could also be boosted by up to 40 percent by the federal earned-income tax credit (EITC), bringing monthly income to over $1,100, about two and one-half times the maximum welfare benefit.

We could also ask how much work it takes to be as well-off financially working as one would be on welfare. The answer depends on the state of residence, child-care costs, and whether the recipient has undisclosed sources of income, among other factors. A recipient can replace the $459 welfare benefit in Michigan with eighty-nine monthly hours of work at the federal minimum wage of $5.15, or about twenty-two hours per week. With the EITC, only fifteen hours per week are needed to pull above a welfare-level income. In a low-benefit state such as Mississippi, just five hours of work per week at the minimum wage (plus the EITC) brings a single mother of two children a higher income than welfare.

But what if there are insufficient employment opportunities in the areas in which welfare recipients live? Would we then seek to repeal work-oriented welfare reform? I expect this question to be at the core of future debates over welfare policy. If we oppose the present direction of welfare reform, do we prefer a system that sustains families in deep poverty in locations that cannot generate—in the extreme example of Mississippi—even one half-shift (five hours) of minimum-wage work per week, despite one of the strongest economies on record? At some point, it makes more sense to encourage relocation of families and absorption into labor markets with better long-term economic opportunities.

The Danziger chapter also reminds us that Michigan, like many states, has expanded the earnings disregard for welfare recipients; that is, Michigan has decreased the effective "tax rate" on recipients' earnings. This policy can help raise the incomes of welfare mothers and increase incentives to work while on welfare. But it can also increase incentives among working recipients to remain on welfare. Further research could help resolve whether generous earnings disregards are effective and prudent, especially with a five-year lifetime limit on eligibility for federal TANF (temporary assistance to needy families) assistance.

- Is there a residual group of recipients who are very unlikely to be able to work?

The answer is clearly yes, but this group appears far smaller than earlier analyses suggested (see Olson and Pavetti 1996). The Danziger et al. data are particularly informative on this point. The Michigan sample reports many barriers to employment; the median is two. Nonetheless, 62 percent of the mothers in the sample worked. Even among those who reported four to six barriers, more than 40 percent worked over twenty hours per week. The extent of work is doubly impressive because this sample is by no means the "cream" of the Michigan caseload. At the time of the baseline interview, the Michigan caseload had dropped by one-third from the 1993 peak, leaving long-term recipients; on average, they had received benefits for over seven years since age eighteen. Yet only 3 percent fell into the category with a very low employment rate (seven or more barriers, with an employment rate of 6 percent). Danziger and colleagues appropriately conclude that recipients in this small group "are candidates for the 20 percent of the caseload that can be exempted from TANF's federal time limit." I would add only that consideration should be given to amending the federal legislation so that the 20 percent exemption is based on historic rather than current caseloads, in order to treat fairly recipients with many barriers to work who live in states where the welfare caseload has fallen dramatically.

The unusually strong economy has been important—perhaps key—to the success of welfare reform to date. When the next recession hits, those who have recently left the welfare rolls will be vulnerable to job loss. It would be far better for potential welfare recipients to draw unemployment benefits, rather than deplete or exhaust eligibility for federal welfare benefits. The unemployment insurance system might require reform to ease eligibility for former welfare recipients who lose jobs, perhaps by the development of a separate system for part-time employees (see, for example, Nicholson 1997).

REFERENCES

Bane, Mary Jo, and David T. Ellwood. 1994. *Welfare Realities: From Rhetoric to Reform.* Cambridge, Mass.: Harvard University Press.

Blau, Francine, and Ronald G. Ehrenberg, eds. 1997. *Gender and Family Issues in the Workplace.* New York: Russell Sage Foundation.

Council of Economic Advisers. 1999. *Economic Report of the President.* Washington: U.S. Government Printing Office.

Freeman, Richard B. 1996. "Why Do So Many Young American Men Commit Crimes and What Might We Do About It?" *Journal of Economic Perspectives* 10(1): 25–42.

Nicholson, Walter. 1997. "Initial Eligibility for Unemployment Compensation." In *Unemployment Insurance in the United States: Analysis of Policy Issues,* edited by Christopher J. O'Leary and Stephen A. Wandner. Kalamazoo, Mich.: W. E. Upjohn Institute.

Olson, Krista, and LaDonna Pavetti. 1996. *Personal and Family Challenges to the Successful Transition from Welfare to Work.* Washington, D.C.: Urban Institute.

Parrott, Sharon. 1998. "Welfare Recipients Who Find Jobs: What Do We Know About Their Employment and Earnings?" Report. Washington, D.C.: Center on Budget and Policy Priorities.

Waldfogel, Jane. 1998. "Understanding the 'Family Gap' for Women with Children." *Journal of Economic Perspectives* 12(1): 137–56.

INDEX

Numbers in **boldface** refer to tables and figures.